The In

"One of the best and sharpest books for beginners that I've ever come across."
—Mark Lerner, for *Welcome to Planet Earth*

"Clearly written. *The Inner Sky* is a top-class introduction to the zodiac."
—Debbi Kempton-Smith, author of *Secrets from a Stargazer's Notebook*

"No astrology book has impressed me as much as *The Inner Sky*.
—Velma Austin-Chatham, Professional Astrologers Incorporated, for *The Delineator*

"A new student to astrology cannot do better than start out with Steven Forrest. In fact...learning from Forrest could guarantee becoming a good astrologer!"
—*The Astrotherapy Newsletter*

"Beautifully written in simple language, yet amplified with stunning verbal imagery throughout, the book is a reading experience worth savoring. Throw in the fact that it is undoubtedly one of the clearest, simplest astrology primers ever written and you begin to glimpse the miracle Steven Forrest has wrought." —Richard Nolle, for *Dell Horoscope*

"[*The Inner Sky]* is written by an expert communicator... Even if you feel that you're well past the beginner's stage, *The Inner Sky* can give you insights into the basics of astrology that you never dreamed possible."
—American Astrology

"Excellent introduction to astrology. I wish I had this book when I was first learning astrology years ago! Steven does an excellent job explaining the mechanics and interactions of basic astrology. His illustrations are accurate and taken from everyday life. A great book for someone wanting to get a handle on the subject."
—A reader from Scottsdale, Arizona

The Inner Sky

How to Make Wise Choices
For a More Fulfilling Life

Steven Forrest

Seven Paws Press
Borrego Springs, CA

Published in 2012 by Seven Paws Press, Inc.
PO Box 82
Borrego Springs, CA 92004
www.sevenpawspress.com

ISBN-13: 978-0-9790677-1-6
LCCN: 2010909907

Eleventh Printing August 2012

Cover design: Tony Howard - ravendreamspdx.com
Book design and production by:
Raven Dreams Productions, LLC

Printed in the United States of America

Also by Steven Forrest

The Changing Sky

The Night Speaks

Measuring the Night (with Jeffrey Wolf Green)

Measuring the Night Vol. 2 (with Jeffrey Wolf Green)

Stalking Anubis

Skymates (with Jodie Forrest)

Skymates II (with Jodie Forrest)

Yesterday's Sky

The Book of the Moon

Dedication

One world, one people –
if you can feel it,
then this book is dedicated to you.

Contents

Now the fundamental madness or abnormality of men lies in the divergence between essence and personality. The more nearly a man knows himself for what he is, the nearer he approaches wisdom. The more his imagination about himself diverges from what he actually is, the madder he becomes.

–Rodney Collin

ACKNOWLEDGMENTS

I would like to express my gratitude to the following people. Each one made the experience of writing this book a little richer and little more possible.

Peter Guzzardi, Melanie Jackson, Barry Denenberg, Gene Stone, Michele Anders, Marc Penfield, Jennie Knoop, Dick and Bunny Forrest, Phyllis Hophan, and Sahni Hamilton of the Bodyworks Clinic.

I would also like to thank the many thousands of people who have shared their birthcharts with me over the years. Without you, there would have been nothing to write.

And finally, a special thanks to my good friend, Laurel Goldman, my teacher, Marian Starnes, and to Jodie Forrest.

PREFACE

Back in the fifties, when I was a little boy, I once put a quarter in a vending machine inscribed with paintings of various improbable creatures. Out came a packet containing a description of the traits associated with my sun sign, Capricorn. In essence, the message was that I was shy and uptight, but that while no one would ever be very excited about me, I could console myself with the knowledge that I was practical and industrious and would probably get rich.

Thinking back, I suppose it retarded my development by six months.

Shy and uptight. No argument there. The machine was right on target. Shyness was a painful, inescapable part of my daily reality. But the mechanical astrologer went further. It told me that since I was born on the sixth day of January, I was doomed to be shy and uptight for the rest of my life. The word doomed was not used, but I sure read it between the lines.

How many people have been misled in the same way? Somewhere astrology got off the track. In its healthy form it is one of humanity's most precious allies, the oldest form of psychotherapy. Gradually, though, the aim of helping people has been supplanted by the desire to amaze them.

And astrology can do that. Given the date, time, and place of a person's birth, anyone who has done a little homework can describe with fair precision his or her general nature. There will be errors. But only the most closed-minded person would deny the fundamental validity of the portrait.

Who is helped by such a description? Certainly not the person in question. Presumably, he is already acquainted with himself. The best that can come out of such an interaction is that the client is entertained, perhaps intrigued, and the astrologer's ego gets a boost. The worst that can happen is that some unpleasant and self-defeating aspect of the person's character is further cemented in place. "Of course I am indecisive – I'm a Libra."

Astrology can do so much more.

A birthchart is a rich, living statement, full of insights, guidelines, and warnings. It describes not a static fate but a flowing life pattern, full of options and risks. An encounter with an effective astrologer should leave a person not only entertained but inspired to live more fully and confidently, with a deeper sense of purpose and a keener alertness regarding the comforting lies we all love so well.

Many years have passed since I put my quarter in the vending machine and learned all about Capricorn. For most of those years I have been studying astrology, letting it teach me. Books were my guides at first. But the more I studied people, the more I realized that the books were far more rigid than the people were. I was changing. Capricorn was not. Something was wrong. So I stopped reading and starting watching.

Slowly it dawned on me: astrological forces present us not with answers but with questions. The answers we give are our own. Those astrologers who for centuries have been trying to determine our behavior from our birthcharts have been barking up the wrong tree. Astrology supplies the terrain. How we navigate it is our own business.

Almost every day I sit down with a stranger and his birthchart. Together they rarely fail to teach me something new. Some are psychiatrists. Some are mill workers. A couple were prostitutes. I have learned, through astrology, to see the human common denominators beneath the masks of circumstance. I have learned that the most universal of those common denominators is the desire for "my life to be different." And I have learned to help people grow, to answer their own questions in happier ways.

Growth. That is the key. That is what separates true astrology from simple fortune-telling. A Libran can learn to make decisions.

Capricorn can learn to relax. Transformations like that are the goal of any real astrologer. To the fortune-teller, they are only embarrassments, unwelcome evidence of the cracks in his system.

A new astrology? Perhaps. We all stand on the shoulders of those who have gone before us. I honor those men and women who have helped create the tradition within which I practice. But that tradition has become clogged and stiff, set in its ways. We are ready now to reach a little further, to redefine the symbols yet again, to see them more clearly, more in harmony with the ebb and flow of human experience.

Anyone reading this book can learn to use astrology. Real skill comes with experience, but the aura of "occult power" that has always surrounded the art is a smokescreen. Astrology is technical, but it is the technology of life. Even someone who never heard of Capricorn until a few moments ago has already been studying these symbols for years. They are part of the human spirit.

All we are doing is learning a new language. The words may be unfamiliar. But the meaning behind them is as universal as breathing.

Then why bother with it? Only because astrological knowledge, coupled with an accurate birthchart, can boost our sensitivity to a remarkable degree. It is life's Rosetta stone. It breaks the code. The chaos, the pain, and the seeming randomness of our lives coalesce before our eyes into an orderly system. And once we grasp that system, we spend a lot less time swimming against the tide.

Learn astrology for yourself and you will make better decisions. Share it gracefully, without preaching, and you will make a better friend, able to push your own fog out of the way long enough to help people you love see through theirs. Whether you keep it or share it, I promise you an absorbing journey into that shadowy borderland, that place where cosmos and consciousness touch: the human psyche.

–Steven Forrest

Part One:
The Territory

Why Bother?

People change.

Yet one assumption runs like a virus through most astrological writing: people do not change. "Scorpios are sexy but cannot be trusted; Capricorns are industrious; Pisceans are cosmic but too spacey to balance their checkbooks." Even in advanced texts we find similar assertions: "a negatively aspected Venus suggests promiscuity." Changeless. rigid statements. From Ptolemy right up through Linda Goodman, the astrological symbols have been interpreted as pieces of psychological machinery. We are blessed or cursed with them at birth and stuck with them until we die.

It is a lie.

There is an indeterminacy, an unpredictable element in life. This wild card may be a thorn in the side of the fortune-tellers, but it is the keystone of any positive, evolutionary approach to astrology. Or to any accurate approach, for that matter.

Astrology has been so misunderstood, so misrepresented, that the real meaning of the word has almost been lost. Some of this we can blame on the usual bad guys, but the bulk of the guilt falls on astrologers themselves. Through conventional interpretations of the symbolism and through an obsession with predicting the future, much of modern astrology has become a parody of what it could be. Much of it is rightly laughable. To admit, in intelligent company, to being an astrologer has become like admitting you watch soap operas or have a subscription to the *National Enquirer*. We who practice the art can lament and protest, but ultimately we must own up to one fact: as embarrassing as that situation is, we have earned it.

Astrology is just a finger pointing at reality. Like any other language, it only provides a way of ordering our perceptions. At its best it aids us in seeing ourselves more honestly. At its worst it drops a wall between us and the rawness of our own experience. To be of value it must not only reflect the actualities of living; it must hone the cutting edge of our growth. If astrology does not give the mind the sharpness of a laser and leave the heart an open nerve, then it has failed.

How can such drama be generated? Certainly not through droning a list of "traits" associated with each celestial configuration.

We are not robots. We are men and women. We are not inalterably programmed at birth, predestined to run off our astrological tapes until our batteries run down. That choice may be available to us: we are free to be mechanical and boring, to ritualize our behavior into a haze of dullness and predictability. But we can do so much more. To be human is to be mutable. To be capable of change. To be indeterminate. To know growth.

There may be an Everest of inertia within us, but it is to that single atom of mutability that astrology must speak. It must address the life in us, not the stasis.

Each astrological symbol represents a spectrum of possibilities; each birthchart contains the roots of ten thousand personalities. This is the key to the system.

An individual can respond to a birthchart in an unimaginative way, or vibrantly and creatively. His or her response can never be known in advance. There is no such thing as a good birthchart or a bad one. There are no evolved charts or unevolved ones, no sane ones, no schizophrenic ones. Whatever measure of virtue interests us, we must look elsewhere to find it.

Astrology can help us in only three ways. It can vividly portray the happiest life available to us. It can tell us what tools we have available for the job and how best to employ them. And it can warn us in advance about how our lives will look when we are getting off the mark. From that point on, we must affirm that all choices lie in our own hands and that no planet or sign ever preordains a specific fate.

Once those points have been made, we can listen to the message of the birthchart or we can ignore it. That is our own business. And even if we do choose to ignore it, life itself will get the same message across to us sooner or later.

Then why do we need astrology at all? No reason. Many people live very well without it. Nothing can be learned from a birthchart that could not be learned someplace else. Go into psychotherapy, meditate in a Tibetan monastery, fall in love, discover a lost city – any of those might do the same thing. Astrology is just one more path to self-knowledge. And like all other paths, it has certain advantages and disadvantages.

Astrology's principal advantage is speed. Without it, we may stumble around for years trying to sort out good information about who we are from all the phony truths and empty dreams with which we have been programmed. Psychotherapy may accelerate the process. So might a dynamic marriage. So might an adventure that pushes us to the limits of endurance, stripping away everything but the barest essentials of our character.

But all those processes take time. And each has pitfalls of its own. On the other hand, an astrological reading, or reading this book, consumes only an afternoon. In a matter of two or three hours a level of self-awareness can be generated that might take years to put together in any other way.

Astrology's disadvantages? All that fine information can go in one ear and out the other. Astrology does not change people any more than psychotherapy changes people. People change themselves.

What About Metaphysics?

Go ten minutes into any discussion of astrology and chances are good you will collide with some imponderables. "My astrologer says I need to face all this stuff. Why? What if I don't feel like it?"

Those questions quickly escalate into the major leagues: What is the purpose of life? Why am I here? Who (if Anyone) put me in the world in the first place?

Metaphysics and astrology seek answers to the same questions. There is a difference, though. Unlike metaphysics, in astrology the emphasis is on the seeker rather than on what he or she seeks. Astrology is not theological; it is direct, real, experiential. It tries only to help us get our personalities into running order. To make us happier. Clearer. Behind that process we can drape any metaphysical or philosophical curtain that pleases us.

Let's try a couple of them just to see if it really makes any difference.

Curtain Number One: We are not protoplasm. We are spirit. Pure awareness. Immortal beings, incarnating in a succession of physical forms, slowly evolving toward a state of union with God. Our current existential circumstances reflect our inward condition. We select them consciously before birth, choosing the optimal astrological configurations for our evolutionary work. We may not like everything about our lives, but there is nothing random about them. Everything can be used. Everything is a blessing. Our jobs, our relationships, our hangups, the entire tableau is a conscious, purposeful choice.

Curtain Number Two: The universe is completely random. Fifteen billion years ago, hydrogen clouds condensed into stars, and stars began cooking heavier elements. Lumps of carbon formed and the lumps learned to reproduce themselves, slowly evolving into specialized relationships with their environments. What we call consciousness is an electrochemical phenomenon, utterly dependent on the physiology of the brain. When the brain dies, consciousness dies.

In the meantime, we can enjoy it. But that isn't easy. Consciousness is inefficient. It produces a lot of static: neuroses, guilt, compulsions. If we want to get maximum pleasure from our consciousness in this random universe, those energy leaks have to be eliminated.

See any practical difference?

The two models are light-years apart philosophically, but in practice they are identical. If there is a cosmic joke, this is it: no matter how we mentally construct the universe, the universe in which we actually live is unchanged. We can shift the conceptual furniture in our heads until we turn blue and still come up against the same psychological conundrums – hangups are hangups, whatever our philosophies might be.

Pick either paradigm. Our work remains the same.

Are we spirit or are we flesh? Astrologically, the proper answer is: who cares? If we are depressed or jealous or lonely or in any other unpleasant state of consciousness, changing that condition is our work whether we are nuclear physicists or Hindu pundits. Metaphysical perspectives may help us. If so, fine. But it is not the business of astrology to supply them. That is up to us.

The intensification of a person's self-awareness: in astrology, that is all that matters. In promoting that intensification, anyone who interprets a birthchart must have absolute respect for the independence and self-determination of each mind he or she touches. No would-be gurus need apply. The relationship between astrologer and client must be one of equality. We all face the same labyrinths and nobody has the master plan.

What astrology does provide is a blueprint of the lens through which we must peer into those labyrinths: the personality.

From the astrological perspective, each personality has an ideal form, a form that is indicated by the positions of the planets at the time of our birth. And while we may draw upon culture and experience in grooming that form, its flesh and bones arise elsewhere. They are rooted deep within us, at a level of consciousness far more profound than our mannerisms and styles. We can call those roots the soul, shaped and twisted by the events of a thousand lifetimes. Or we can see them as a random alignment of the genetic roulette wheel. It does not matter. The roots are there, and they represent a certain pattern of needs and predispositions that the social personality must always reflect if there is to be peace in the mind.

And peace is the objective. But peace does not arise automatically. We must work toward it, aligning our outer personality with our inner essence. We must let go of those social scripts that upset us. We must grow.

Astrology is hedonistic. Pleasure-seeking. It is immediate and amoral. All that matters to it is happiness. A mirror reflecting life, it observes but does not interpret. Fact: we hurt. Fact: we would like to feel better. Astrology helps us do that.

How? By reminding us of who we are. Ever since we learned how to turn on the television set, we have been besieged. Our society has been trying to stick us with a set of values, heroes, and mythologies. No need to criticize them. It is enough to know that many of them are unnatural to us. In the hands of a sensitive, skilled, articulate astrologer, the birthchart can catapult us beyond those traps. It helps us avoid becoming just another character out of central casting. In a flash, the whole pattern of creative tensions, blind spots, and aspirations that makes up our own unique personality comes to a focus. And it stands distinct from those unnatural values, heroes, and mythologies.

What do we gain? Glimpsing our essential self fills us with vitality. It helps us make better choices. We take care of ourselves more effectively. We learn to separate what we really want from what we feel compelled to want. And that makes us happier.

No need to talk about enlightenment or self-actualization. Happiness is enough. This, then, is the real purpose of astrology: to hold a mirror before the evolving self, to tell us what we already know deep within ourselves. Through astrology we fly far above the mass of details that constitutes our lives. We stand outside our personalities and see for a moment the central core of individuality around which all the minutiae must always orbit.

We witness ourselves.

The Seven Principles

Seven fundamental ideas form the backbone of any growth oriented vision of astrology. Any individual or text that diverges very far from them is probably more a part of astrology's bad karma than part of its future.

1. Astrological symbols are neutral. There are no good ones, no bad ones.
2. Individuals are responsible for the way they embody their birthcharts.
3. No astrologer can determine a person's level of response to his birthchart from that birthchart alone.
4. The birthchart is a blueprint for the happiest, most fulfilling, most spiritually creative path of growth available to the individual.
5. All deviations from the ideal growth pattern symbolized by the birthchart are unstable states, usually accompanied by a sense of aimlessness, emptiness, and anxiety.
6. Astrology recognizes only two absolutes: the irreducible mystery of life, and the uniqueness of each individual viewpoint on that mystery.
7. Astrology suffers when wedded too closely to any philosophy or religion. Nothing in the system matters except the intensification of a person's self-awareness.

Each of these seven principles is basic. Subtract or distort even one of them and the whole edifice crumbles into a ruin of fortune-telling.

We are free. Celestial forces and the human will function together in an open, synergistic relationship. The results of their union cannot be foreseen anymore than a child's nature can be seen in advance through a knowledge of his parents.

It comes down to this: astrological symbols are not nouns, they are verbs. I am not "a Capricorn." **I am Capricorning.** Growth. Change. Evolution. That is the heart of astrology. Leave fatalism and rigidity to the fortune tellers. Our work is elsewhere.

Symbolic Language

Signs, houses, and planets. Three distinct systems of symbols. Three vocabularies. Together they form astrology's holy trinity. Each serves a distinct purpose. Each answers a distinct set of questions. Without all three, astrology could not exist. Lacking one, it could have breadth and height, but no depth. It would be as thin as the paper you are holding.

Signs and houses work together. Let's understand them first, then go on to add the planets.

In broad terms, signs are **identity,** while houses are **the arena** within which identity operates. Signs provide the psychological framework, the needs and fears, the attitudes and biases, with which we attack the houses. Houses indicate problems and issues. They represent tasks we must face.

Signs symbolize processes that take place **within the mind,** Each is a pattern of growth with which a person becomes intensely identified: learning to become braver, learning to become more aware of other people's needs and worries; developing psychic sensitivity or meditation skills; weeding out the destructive effects of dependency.

Houses are more concrete. They represent that **which the mind observes.** Many of them are simply theaters of obvious, outward activity. One symbolizes our broad social or cultural environment. It raises the question of what role we play there. Another symbolizes the field of activity we call intimate relationships. A third shows our material or economic circumstances.

Some houses are less outwardly active. But they always symbolize something **outside** personality, something of which **we must become aware.** One, for example, refers to the existence of the unconscious mind.

Planets are the third dimension of astrological symbolism. They represent the actual **structure of the mind.** Each one symbolizes a particular **psychological function:** intellect; emotions, self-imagery, the impulse toward intimacy.

Put all the planets together and you have a map of the human psyche. It is like many other maps that have existed in history. Sigmund Freud, for example, divided the mind into ego, id, and superego. Astrologers use Mercury, Venus, and so on in the same way.

Like Freud's model of the mind, the planetary map is blank. It describes all the departments of the psyche, but it does not say what is in each department. Everyone has an ego. But not everyone's ego is of the same strength and nature. Similarly, Mercury (verbal ability) may be strong in one person, weak in another. They both possess the same mental function. But in each person it operates differently.

To understand how a planet operates we must see it in the context of a sign and a house. An aggressive planet might lie in a sign that refers to the process of developing courage. That is a powerful combination and it produces a distinctly assertive personality. But how does that assertiveness become visible? Where do we see it?

To answer that, we look at the house. That is where the sign planet dynamic is released. Perhaps that assertiveness is most clearly expressed within the career. Maybe we see it in marriage and friendship. Or perhaps that assertiveness is not outwardly visible at all. Maybe it is blazing away in one of the hidden departments of life. That question can only be answered by a house. Unlocking the interactions of these three kinds of symbols – signs, planets, and houses is the key to unlocking the secrets of the individual birthchart.

To put it all briefly, the three systems of symbols answer the questions **what, how** and **why, and where.** Always look first to the planet, which is the **what.** It lets us know which part of the mind we are considering. Then use the sign to determine exactly what that planet wants and what methods it might best use to achieve those goals – the **why** and the **how.** Finally, look at the house. It answers the **where,** telling us in precisely which department of life the battle is taking place.

Imagine, for example, that we are analyzing a birthchart with Venus in Virgo in the sixth house. How do we proceed? In chapter 8 we study that combination in detail, but let's take a quick look at it now just to focus all this abstract thought with a concrete example.

Venus is the planet, and its **what** is always the ability to **establish personal relationships.** In this case, Venus is driven by the **why and how** of Virgo. What does that mean? As we will learn in chapter 5, Virgo's **why** is the effort to **attain perfection** and its **how** involves endless analysis. Right away we know we are dealing with someone who is idealistic in relationships, but who must learn to balance that idealism against a tendency to be too critical or demanding. Responsibility in love and friendship probably comes easily, but tolerance and forgiveness must be developed intentionally. **Where** are these dramas likely to be enacted? In the sixth house, the arena of life we call work. In this case, **working partnerships** are particularly sensitive to those Venus-in-Virgo ups and downs, and it is there that the individual is most likely to encounter his pivotal developmental stresses regarding the formation of lasting emotional bonds. In other words, he tends to meet his deepest friends and life mates (Venus) through his work (sixth house) and to enter those relationships propelled by a set of Virgoan motivations and needs.

Don't worry if this analysis baffles you now. It will make much more sense after you have read the next few chapters and absorbed the basic meanings of the signs, planets, and houses. For now, it is enough to remember the following key concepts:

- **Planets** tell us which part of the mind we are looking at (the **what**).
- **Signs** let us know what needs and strategies drive that planet (the **why** and the **how**).
- **Houses** specify in exactly which of life's arenas that planet-sign combination is developing (the **where**).

Symbol Reading

The birthchart is a remarkable tool. But to use that tool you must learn a lost art. You must become a symbol reader.

Interpretation. That is the heart of astrology. Weaving together the messages of the signs, houses, and planets, interlacing them, seeing how they flavor one another, enhance one another, undercut one another – that is the astrologer's art.

And it is an art. Interpretation is not a scientific procedure. not something to be memorized. It is not mechanical. It is not a skill one acquires like learning to rebuild carburetors or to solve differential equations. The element of creativity, of inspiration, of intuition, is the vital spark at the core of the system. Without it, one can never derive meaning from a birthchart.

The mind is a living creature, just like the body. All its organs interact. If we have a headache, it may affect our stomach too. And maybe if someone massages our neck and shoulders, both problems disappear. It is the same with astrology. If our Mercury hurts, then that imbalance is reflected in one of our signs and houses too. We must learn to grasp the birthchart **as a whole,** just as a good doctor learns to see the body as an interacting system.

That is the first law of interpretation: to see wholeness. We must never read a symbol in a vacuum.

But that wholeness is complex, just as minds are. A birthchart is an intricate arrangement of multidimensional symbols. No two are alike. Many people have Mars in Aquarius or Venus in the fourth house. Those are the basic "bits" or "phrases" that go together to form the psyche, and there are relatively few of them. But their possible combinations are nearly infinite, and it is in that endlessly variable crossfire that astrology comes alive.

No book can cover all conceivable combinations of these astrological "bits." There are too many of them. To read a birthchart, we must approach the problem differently. We must learn the language. We must become familiar with all the basic vocabulary – each sign. Each house, each planet. Only then can we understand their interactions.

Learning to interpret charts is like learning to speak French. If we are going to be in Paris for just a week, then memorizing phrases out of a Berlitz book is all we need. We will be able to locate bathrooms and avoid malnutrition. But if we are serious about communicating in the language, we pursue a different strategy. We memorize vocabulary. We learn laws of grammar. And we start putting sentences together on our own.

Most astrological texts are like phrase books. They contain stock interpretations of each "bit." Have Saturn in Virgo? Turn to page 39. Neptune in the fourth house? Page 122. Each configuration is described abstractly, as if it were functioning alone. And when we put those stock interpretations together we have a mishmash. We are like the phrase-book French man who is suddenly confronted with a situation his book does not cover. We stutter.

Soon we will study the birthchart of an Englishman who was born with the sun in Libra and the sixth house. A traditional phrase-book astrological text would say that such a combination means that he is indecisive and subservient. Moving on, we find that his moon lies in rebellious Aquarius and his first house contains explosive, irascible Uranus. Turning to those chapters, the same text would teach us that he is arrogant, stubborn, and free-spirited. A strange juxtaposition of traits.

That kind of phrase-book astrology produces fast results. We don't have to learn a new way of thinking. All we need to do is look things up. We learn to operate like a computer, spitting out prepackaged paragraphs about each astrological configuration. But the results we get are bad. There is no life in them. They don't grow or change. And they contradict one another. Trying to practice astrology like that is like trying to reconstruct a personality from a dissected body. Here is an arm. Here is a nose, an eye, a tooth. We can even sew all the parts back together again. But we fool no one. All we have is flesh and bones.

A computer can construct a birthchart, but it can never effectively interpret one. To accomplish that, we must react to the chart the way we react to a living person. Intellectually. Emotionally. Physically. Intuitively. We must react to wholeness. We must learn words and form sentences. Memorizing phrases does not help us.

Learning the language really is not hard to do. All of us **are** astrologers. We just don't know the words yet. The American traveling through France with her phrase book is a competent, coherent adult. She knows what buses are. She knows all about artichokes and politics, boulevards and dark alleys. She just doesn't know what to call them. With a little instruction in the language, her natural intelligence can begin to express itself.

Like our traveler, we all have natural astrological intelligence. All of us have a Mercury function and a Pisces process. We are all built out of the same material. Our current labels may be different, but those are only words. Whatever we call those aspects of ourselves, we have been living with them, studying them, since we were born. We just need to learn some new vocabulary.

As languages go, astrology is an easy one. There are ten planets, twelve signs, and twelve houses. Only thirty-four words. Grasp them and it is as if you were off to Paris with an A in high school French. No one is going to mistake you for a native. But you will get by.

The book you are holding in your hands is not a phrase book. It is a language text. The first few chapters are vocabulary lessons. We will get acquainted with the notion of a birthchart, with each sign, each house, each planet. Then we will move on to forming sentences. By the end of the book, if you are alert, you will be doing much more than parroting lists of contradictory traits. You will be speaking a new language. An eloquent, ancient language. A precise one. One that stretches your imagination and boosts your sensitivity. One as penetrating as a dagger and as clear as a crystal held against the sun.

What Exactly Is a Birthchart?

A birthchart is a unique arrangement of astrology's primary elements: signs, houses, and planets. Even though there are only about three dozen words in astrology's vocabulary, when we add the laws of grammar and syntax they combine in nearly endless ways. A birthchart is a particular combination, taken to represent the individual.

Physically, a birthchart is simply a map. It shows the way the sun, moon, and planets were arranged in the sky at the moment a person was born. The hieroglyphics spread randomly through the chart represent the sun, moon, and planets. These symbols are called **glyphs.** Like shorthand, they save us a lot of writing.

The Planetary Glyphs:			
Sun:	☉	Jupiter:	♃
Moon:	☽	Saturn:	♄
Mercury:	☿	Uranus:	♅
Venus:	♀	Neptune:	♆
Mars:	♂	Pluto:	♇ or ♇

Let's take a guided tour of a chart we will analyze later in detail. The figure below is the chart of a person born on October 9, 1940, in northwestern England, at about six-thirty in the evening.

Sample Birth Chart

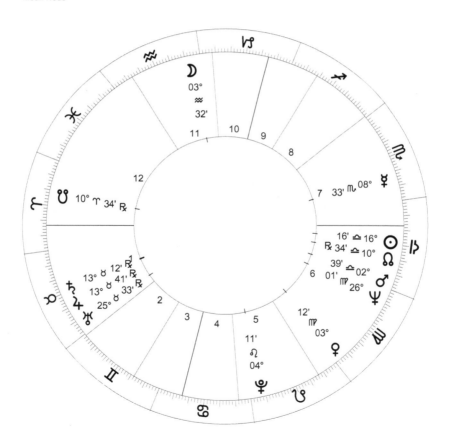

The Englishman
Natal Chart
Oct 9 1940, Wed
6:30 pm BST −1:00
Manchester, UK
53°N30' 002°W15'
Geocentric
Tropical
Placidus
Mean Node

The horizontal line that runs across the middle of our sample chart is the local horizon. Everything above it was in the visible half of the sky when the man was born. Everything below it was invisible, beneath the earth.

For reasons we will soon see, the **left** end of that line represents the **east.** It is just the opposite of the way maps are normally set up.

In the English autumn, six-thirty in the evening is just after sunset. If this map is accurate, we should find the sun just below the western horizon, having just gone down. And that is exactly what we see: the sun's glyph – the circle with the dot in the center – lies on the right side of the birthchart, just below the centerline, precisely where we would expect to find it.

The familiar crescent symbol of the moon lies in the upper left quadrant of the chart: the moon shone brightly in the evening twilight, halfway up in the eastern sky.

Little else was visible. Other than the moon, only dim Mercury shone in the half of the sky we can see – and Mercury was low in the west, probably lost in ground haze. All other planets were hidden below the horizon.

The twelve pie slices that stand out so prominently are the houses. (In the inner ring you can see numbers that correspond to each house.) In our example, the sun lies in the sixth house. That is just a fancy way of saying that it was a little below the western horizon. To say a planet is in the ninth house or the tenth house places it high in the sky. In the third or fourth houses, it is far below the horizon.

Everything else you see in our sample birthchart has to do with signs. Those numbers and symbols you see around the outer rim of the chart show where the signs were at the moment our hero took his first breath. For the detectives among you, this is your first clue to our hero's identity; he is not a woman.

Like planets, each sign has a glyph:

The Sign Glyphs:			
Aries:	♈	Libra:	♎
Taurus:	♉	Scorpio:	♏
Gemini:	♊	Sagittarius:	♐
Cancer:	♋	Capricorn:	♑
Leo:	♌	Aquarius:	♒
Virgo:	♍	Pisces:	♓

Look over on the extreme left side of our Englishman's chart, near where we found the moon. You see the number 21, followed by the glyph for Aries. That tells us Aries was rising over the eastern horizon when the man was born. Specifically, the 21st degree of Aries – each sign is thirty degrees wide.

The other numbers around the outer rim of the birthchart tell us where the signs were in relation to the houses at the moment of the man's birth. What does that mean exactly? Later we will investigate it in detail. For now, visualize the signs as great regions of space marked by stars. As the world turns, they appear to rise and set. At one moment, Aries might be rising. Twelve hours later, Aries would be setting, and the opposite sign, Libra, would be rising. Although it varies minute by minute, a particular degree of a certain sign always lies at the beginning of each house. In other words, **each sign is somewhere.** It may be above the horizon. It may be below it. Those numbers and glyphs around the edge of the birthchart tell us exactly where each sign lies.

All **signs** are the same size – 30 degrees, or 1/12 of the 360 degrees of the circle. Not so the houses. They vary in width, although for convenience most birthchart blanks show houses of the same size. Occasionally, a house that happens to be wider than 30 degrees gets lined up with a sign in such a way that the sign is completely swallowed – it does not touch either house **cusp** (beginning) at all. This is called an **interception** and is the case with four signs in our sample chart. Look, for example, at the twelfth house. It begins at 23 degrees of Aquarius (≈), completely swallows Pisces (♓), and does not end until we get all the way to 21 degrees of Aries (♈) which is the cusp of the first house.

Each planet falls into both a sign and a house. We can tell its house position just by looking – which pie slice does the planet occupy? To determine the planet's sign, consider the notation right next to it. In our sample chart, Venus lies in the sixth house accompanied by the notation, *3°W.* That tells us that Venus is in the part of the sky we call Virgo – specifically, in Virgo's fourth degree. Knowing it is in the sixth house lets us know that at the instant of the man's birth, Virgo had rotated below the western horizon, carrying Venus with it.

Some people confuse signs and houses at first. A good way to keep them separated in your mind is to remember that houses are linked to the local horizon, while signs are linked to space itself. As earth spins in space, **signs appear to spin around the earth.** And because planets are out there in space as well, they too appear to spin along with the signs, rising in the east and setting in the west. We register that rising and setting as changes in the **house positions** of the signs and planets, a factor that describes their positions only from our particular view point on earth, seen in reference to the local horizon. The houses on the birthchart, in other words, are simply empty slots – each planet and sign passes through all of them as it appears to spin around the earth every twenty-four hours.

Why Is East on the Left?

Ever notice that the sun is always in the southern sky? We think of it as rising in the east and setting in the west, but it is really always south of that line, at least until we get down toward the equator.

That is because up here in the northern hemisphere, we are "on top" of the planet – and to see the sun we need to look "down," to the south. Our Australian friends, on the other hand, need to look up, to the north. In the southern hemisphere, claiming a house has "southern exposure" won't attract anyone. That just means it always faces away from the sun, toward Antarctica.

In our hemisphere, the sun is more or less due south when it reaches the peak of its daily arc. So the uppermost point on a birth-chart is a southerly point, not a northerly one. Southern hemisphere charts look the same, but the mathematics underlying them are slightly different. Australian readers can still use this book.

With south on top, birthcharts are constructed "upside down." That seems awkward at first – but the only alternative is to have planets above the horizon represented on the bottom of the chart. That is even worse, so we just have to get used to some upside-down thinking.

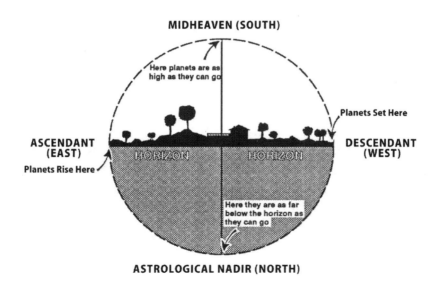

The natural inversion of the birth map puts east on the left and west on the right. So planets rise on the left side of the chart. We call that point the **ascendant.** The opposite point, the right end of the horizon line, is where they set. It is called the **descendant.**

Midheaven is the name given to the high point of the birth chart – where the sun is around noon. And the **astrological nadir** is the opposite point, where we would find the sun around midnight.

Planetary Motions

In the course of a day, the sun, moon, and planets all rise and set once. In other words, they move through each of the twelve houses. That happens only because the earth is spinning on its axis. It has nothing to do with any motion of the planets themselves.

But the planets themselves are in motion. They are careening around the sun. If we compare their positions each night with those of nearby stars, we see small changes. Put your thumbs together and spread your hands out at arm's length: that is a little less than the moon's motion **against the stars** in twenty-four hours. All the others move much more slowly. But they do move.

If we followed planetary motions over a period of years, we would discover that they all stick to the same track. They move from Aries, to Taurus, to Gemini, and on through the familiar sequence of "birth signs." We never find Venus in Cassiopeia or Mars in Orion. That is impossible. They are not on the track.

This track is called the **ecliptic** and it is divided into twelve equal segments. Those segments are the signs. Signs bear the names of constellations but don't really correspond to them. This is a complicated issue, and we don't need to be concerned with it now. For now, it is enough to remember that planets move in relation to the backdrop of stars and we measure that motion as changes in their sign positions.

Most planetary motions are erratic. Mercury stays in each sign for about a month, but that can vary widely. In that length of time, the moon passes through all twelve signs while distant Pluto has barely moved at all. It may even have lost ground.

When the Englishman in our sample birthchart was born it was six-thirty in the evening on the ninth day of October. At that time the sun is in Libra – we know that from the date alone. The sun stays in Libra until around October 21. The sun's sign position is not affected by the time of day, but knowing that the clocks read six-thirty in the evening does tell us something significant: that Libran sun had just set. In other words, it lies in the sixth house.

Had the Englishman been born a few hours later the sun would have been much farther below the horizon. The sun would still be in Libra. But now it would lie in the fourth house instead of in the sixth. During that short period of time the sun's motion through the signs is inconsequential. But its motion through the houses is enough to completely alter the shape of the birthchart.

That is why the time of birth is such a critical factor in astrology. The date alone would be enough to establish the relationship of signs to planets. but we need the time in order to add the crucial birthchart element of the houses.

OCTOBER 9, 1940

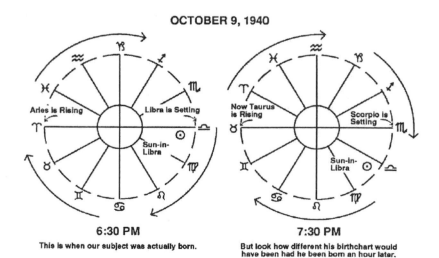

6:30 PM
This is when our subject was actually born.

7:30 PM
But look how different his birthchart would have been had he been born an hour later.

Signs have a fixed relationship to one another. Taurus always follows Aries. Gemini always follows Taurus and so on. When one moves, the others move too and in a predictable way. It is as if we were spinning a wagon wheel with numbered spokes. If we know where spoke number seven is we can locate eight and nine with no trouble.

When the sun set on that October evening Libra was setting too. At that time of year the sun and Libra are a package deal. Where we find one, we find the other.

But we know more than that. With Libra setting in the west, Aries – the opposite sign – must be rising in the east. And Pisces, the sign immediately before Aries, must have just finished rising. And Taurus, the following sign, must be just below the eastern horizon getting ready to come up.

It works just like the wagon wheel.

And that is the birthchart. Our guided tour of astrology's basic tool is over. If you have absorbed the last few pages nothing in our sample chart should be a mystery to you any longer.

As simple as this sky map is, no more sophisticated model of the mind has ever been devised. As we weave together the meanings of the signs, planets and houses, a tapestry emerges that encompasses all the aspirations and shadows, all the hilarity, all the horror of human life. And each combination of symbols, each birthchart, is unique. Like no religion, like no system of psychology, **astrology paints a portrait of the individual.**

Yet the birthchart is only a map of the sky. Such a simple thing. Its symbolism does not arise out of the pet theories of any man or woman. It stands beyond personal prejudices, beyond the mythologies of any culture. Its foundation is far deeper, far more primal. Astrology is rooted in nature just as we are.

❦ Part Two: ❧
Words

You can learn all the grammatical laws of a language, but without a good vocabulary, you will still be mute as a post. Astrological language is the same. We can memorize some practical phrases and learn to communicate a few crude ideas that way. However, if we seek fluency, our first purchase should be a dictionary rather than a phrasebook. That's what the next four chapters are: a dictionary. In them we define the thirty-four basic words in astrology's vocabulary. Later, in part 3, we add the laws of syntax and grammar. And whether you are an Aquarius or Leo, if you want to speak the language, you will need them all.

The Prime Symbol

The sky. That is astrology's **prime symbol.** The sky is the bedrock from which the elaborate language of the birthchart arises.

But what does it mean? To the astronomer, the question doesn't make sense. He or she can say what the sky **is.** But what it means – that is something for poets and philosophers to dwell on, not astronomers. Burn away all the name calling, and the difference between astrologers and astronomers boils down to this: astronomers seek to know the **form** of the heavens, while astrologers pursue their **meaning.** Astrology is the poetry of astronomy. It is not so much a study of structure as of significance. Not what the sky is. But what it says to us.

Exactly what does it say? To answer that we do not need to be an Aristotle or a William Butler Yeats. All we have to do is look and think. Who can stare at the Milky Way on a moonless summer evening, meteors streaking past Vega and Altair, without feeling a sense of wonder? Whatever cynics might say about this television – addled age such dullness of heart remains rare.

In ancient times, the sky was sacred; people were sure God lived there. This sense of the sky's holiness is a nearly universal element in early religions. Our metaphysics may have matured, but our hearts have changed little. The heavens still fill us with reverence and awe.

Astrology's prime symbol – the great sphere of space that surrounds us – is a symbol of that awe and reverence. We might choose to call it a symbol of God. It represents infinity and perfection, timelessness and universality. Americans, Russians, Europeans, Africans – we all stand beneath the same sky. Like breathing, like sex, like death, it binds us together. It reminds us of our common humanity. The sky represents the vantage point deep within us from which we sit and watch impersonally and indifferently, as our lives unfold.

Close your eyes. Empty your mind. Go beyond habits thoughts, prejudices. Feel that indefinable, vast awareness that marks you as human whether you are a Bantu tribesman or an astronaut. You are experiencing the prime symbol: the undifferentiated background of consciousness out of which emerges that far more fragile and arbitrary structure, the personality.

We might call it our **soul.** But astrology is not a study of the soul. It is a study of the personality. The power of the astrological language lies in its particularity, the way it addresses the uniqueness of each individual's personal reality. This, rather than metaphysics, must always be its focus. Yet, permeating the system we find the scent of that most primal of human perceptions: a sense of the presence of the Absolute, a sense of the possibility of self-transcendence. Heady stuff!

To make the prime symbol relevant to everyday life, we must step down its voltage. We must break it up into smaller pieces more suited to the narrow scope of our daily experience. Our first effort in this direction is to reduce our imagery from three dimensions to two, from the sphere to the circle.

The Circle of the Year

Two physical motions, both circular, lie at the roots of astrological symbolism. One is the rotation of the earth on its axis. The second is the revolution of the earth in its orbit around the sun. The first motion produces the **houses.** We discuss those in a later chapter. The second circle gives rise to the symbolism of the signs. And it is through the signs that the prime symbol comes down to earth.

If we wake each day before dawn and study the sky, we quickly notice a pattern. Every morning the sun rises into a patch of stars. Over several weeks we see that while the sun keeps rising in the east, the stars that its light first touches are gradually changing. On a particular morning it rises into one constellation. A month later it rises into another, then another, and so on until a year elapses and it is back where it started.

Objective reality is very different, but those are the facts of perception. That is what we see. What is really happening is that earth is orbiting around the sun. When we are on one side of our circular orbit, we look toward the sun and see it projected against a certain backdrop of stars. A little further in our yearly path, we see the sun against another backdrop.

The scale of the solar system is bafflingly large, which may confuse us. Let's visualize the same thing in more familiar terms. Imagine we are photographing a friend. We stand her in the middle of the floor and focus the camera. From where we are shooting she is standing in front of a tall bookcase. In soft focus, the books are a distracting riot of color. We walk across the room. From this new perspective she appears to be standing before a blank wall. The composition is improved and we snap the picture.

It is the same with the solar system. The sun, for our purposes, is stationary. We move around it like a photographer searching for the right angle. Yet our perceptions tell us we are standing still and that the sun is in motion. Why? Because the sun's starry background changes as we swing through our orbit, just as our friend appeared to be standing against a bookcase, then against a wall, even though she never moved.

Earth's "hunt for the right angle" is constant, our orbit never varies. And so the sun's apparent "orbit" around us never varies either. It travels from constellation to constellation in an endless, orderly progression. The path it follows has been mapped since antiquity. In modern times we call it the ecliptic, but it has a far more ancient name: the **zodiac.**

The zodiac is a two-dimensional translation of astrology's prime symbol, the sky itself. Like the sky, this circle is a metaphor for the eternal and the infinite, simpler than the sphere but still far too all-encompassing to be of any practical value.

We are left with a classic problem: Where does the circle begin? How can we break it down? The solution lies where it always must in astrology: with our eyes, our hearts, and our common sense.

Earth's orbit is visible to us through the varying relation of the sun to the background stars. But that's fairly subtle. Astronomer-priests might notice it. Sailors would too. But the rest of us need not have such an eye for detail. The year hits us over the head in a way that is harder to ignore. The weather turns freezing cold. Then it gets blazing hot. Seasons change. And those changes are propelled by our yearly trajectory around the sun. An astronomical "crisis" marks the outset of each season. And those four "crises" carry us beyond the prime symbol. They begin to break down the Absolute, to make it accessible. Through them we divide the circle.

Winter brings a low sun, short days, and long nights. In the summer this is reversed. If we follow the variations in light through-out the year, a distinct pattern emerges. At one point the length of the day and the length of the night are equal. Then the day begins growing. Precisely three months later we reach a crisis. Day is in the ascendency; night is at its weakest. But darkness rallies and slowly begins to erode the day. Gradually the two move back toward equi-librium. This balancing takes another three months. When it is com-plete, day and night are again equal.

Over the next three months, darkness continues to overwhelm light. Then another crisis is reached; day begins to fight back. It is feeble at first, but the momentum has shifted. In three months light equals darkness and we are back where we began.

This slow breathing of the earth's light is the rudimentary astrological rhythm; without it, we could go no further than the abstraction of the prime symbol.

Seasons, Not Stars

Astrology really has nothing to do with the stars themselves. It is based solely on these variations in light, or, more simply, on the seasons. But what about Aries and Taurus and Capricorn? Those are constellations. They are stars. If they really have nothing to do with astrology, why do we talk about them?

Millennia ago, astronomer-priests noticed that on the morning of the day when light at last began to make inroads into the darkness, the sun rose into the stars of Capricorn. The constellation served as a convenient visual marker for the location of the sun along the ecliptic. Such knowledge helped our forebears in practical ways, such as timing the planting season. The convenience turned out to be temporary.

Due to a slow wobble in the earth's axis, the position of the sun on the first day of winter gradually shifted backward through Capricorn toward the constellation Sagittarius. Traditions die slowly, though. The priests were accustomed to saying that when earth entered winter, the sun entered Capricorn. They kept right on saying it, even when Sagittarius was truly the winter's constellation.

This slip-up produced no serious problem for astrology itself, but it has been hard on public relations. Astronomers are fond of saying, "Even if there were something to astrology, all you Arians were really born with the sun in Aquarius, so you're reading the wrong sign. "The problem here is one of communication. When an astronomer says "Aries," he or she means a certain group of stars. To the astrologer, Aries means something entirely different. It refers to a certain phase in earth's orbit around the sun, or, more simply, **to a certain season.**

Seasonal changes, then, not stars, are at the heart of sign symbolism. Through variations in the length of night, we mark four critical points that help us divide the circle. Infinity is broken down into four finite phases, each with its own distinctive character.

We call these four phases **elements.**

The Dance of the Elements

Fire, earth, air, and water. The elements. Images from antiquity. Four primal states of being. Four faces of the universe. Within us they exist as states of consciousness. Beyond us they function as templates for all physical and metaphysical processes. How are they connected with seasons?

The first element arises in the **equilibrium of light and dark,** but at a time when light has the momentum, when light is increasing. Astronomically, this moment is called **the vernal equinox,** but most of us know it simply as the first day of spring. Astrologically, the vernal equinox symbolizes the birth of the element **fire.** This is the principle of **action.** Like springtime, its spirit is one of outrushing energy, charging into the cosmos, shattering all that stands in its way. Uncompromising invincibility of purpose – that is fire. Soon we will see how it comes to permeate the signs Aries, Leo, and Sagittarius.

Earth follows fire in the traditional order of the elements. This second life principle emerges out of the heart of night. It is associated with the **winter solstice,** the point in the yearly cycle at which darkness reaches maximum power. Winter time. All through nature we see a spirit of grim, enduring determination. Earth symbolizes stability and continuity. Its emphasis is on making peace with a hard, unyielding world. Practicality and resourcefulness arise here. Earth is the sustainer, the giver and maintainer of form. Embodied in Taurus, Virgo, and Capricorn, it is endlessly building, crystallizing, and perfecting.

After earth comes **air.** Air appears at another **equilibrium point** in the cycle of light and darkness. This time night is in the ascendancy, getting ready to overwhelm day. We call the moment the

autumnal equinox. It marks the beginning of fall. In anticipation of winter, there is a feeling of foreboding in the autumn atmosphere. All creatures sense the coming of darkness. They sense death, and its specter heightens their alertness. In air, we find perceiving, reasoning, connecting – the mental functions. Its tone is one of unending curiosity, of detachment and clarity of perception. More than any other element, **air is aware that beyond itself lies the unknown.** The questing spirit of air animates Gemini, Libra, and Aquarius.

Water is the last of the elements. It arises when light attains maximum power, the first day of summer. Astronomers call this moment the **summer solstice.** In summer, the land itself seems to favor life. Nature becomes a protective womb. Even weak life forms are granted a few unharried moments. Water is the principle **of nurturance and protection.** Outwardly, its spirit is one of warmth: inwardly, of imagination and intuition. With its penetrating, sensitive quality, **water's prime function is to feel.** Cancer, Scorpio, and Pisces are the signs conditioned by water.

All of us embody each one of these four faces of the prime symbol. They interact within us, defining our individual personalities. The kaleidoscope of human character types reflects the infinite diversity of relationships among the elements.

When a man or woman is born under the predominant influence of the fire signs, he or she is developing will. Courage or willpower is simply the translation of the fire principle into the language of psychology.

In a similar way, a person conditioned by earth is here to learn **patience and self-discipline;** one shaped by air, to develop **alertness and clarity of perception;** one influenced mostly by water, to learn unconditional love **in the face of extreme vulnerability.**

No one is a pure incarnation of an element. No one finds all his or her lessons in one arena. It is when we find the airy need for detachment married to the emotional rollercoaster of water or the fiery need for stimulation and change bound to the earthy structures of stability, that we begin to see in the symbolism some reflection of the poignancy of human experience.

Fire, earth, air, and water are still abstractions. From the incomprehensible perfection of the prime symbol to the level of the elements is a great leap, but we are still far beyond the range of everyday life. To bring them closer to the reality of our daily experience, we must introduce another basic set of syllables into the language of astrology. Then we can begin to turn those syllables into words.

The Modes

Everything born must die. Life teaches no more primary law, nor one more inviolable. An unstable atom is created in a particle accelerator. In a millisecond it breaks down. So fleeting is its existence that we know of it only through conjectural evidence. A child is born. Seven decades pass. An old man's body is buried in the ground. Pyramids are raised; a civilization is created in the Nile valley. Over three millennia it lives and bears its fruit. Gradually it decays.

Atoms, people, cultures – what is the difference? Only time. The core features of any life cycle are identical. Something is born. Something exists for measurable time in some relatively distinct form. And something dies. These three archetypal phases of any life cycle constitute another essential ingredient in astrology's symbolism: the **modes.**

The first mode is called **cardinal.** It refers to birth, the beginning of a cycle. Cardinality is the principle of initiation. Out of nothingness, something arises. It is the creative push that allows fresh life to manifest itself in a universe that may already be stable and closed.

Once existence is achieved, life cycles move into their second phase. Astrologers call this the **fixed** mode. Fixity has a spirit of solidarity and continuity. While in this mode, an entity is most recognizable. It is in its maturity. But fixity can also refer to stubbornness or unresponsiveness. It is the antithesis of change and the quintessence of strength.

Such stability may endure for an instant or for an aeon, but never for eternity. Life is corrosive. Bodies die. Metals rust. Civilizations become corrupt. The final mode, which astrologers call **mutable** reigns over the ending of lifecycles. Its spirit is one of change and adjustment, many times of utter dissolution. Mutability has one paramount virtue: it is adaptable. It can respond to a changing environment by changing its own form. The price it pays for this capacity is that it can lose all definition, become shapeless. It can die.

The Twelve Signs

Elements and modes. Essence and change. How do they interact?

Fire and earth, air and water – these qualities exist beyond our calendars, light-years past anything we can grasp within the normal framework of consciousness. We exist in time; they exist outside it. A wall of misunderstanding must forever lie between us.

With the modes we introduce the dimension of change. As modes interact with elements, the prime symbol is brought down to a tangible level. It is synchronized with our own rhythms. The modes force the four elemental states into the fluxing, careening trajectory of time. Out of that marriage twelve children are born. And those children are the lifeblood of practical astrology. They are the signs.

How are they formed? Each element can express itself through any of the three modes. Water, for example, can come into existence. It can take a stable form, easily recognizable and resistant to change. And it can pass away. Fire can do the same. So can earth and air. Four elements. Three modes. Weave them together and the twelve signs emerge. Through them, the prime symbol at last begins to function in the everyday world, expressing itself as Aries, Cancer, Libra, and so on.

But it is a two-way street. Signs are avenues of expression, but they are also **roads back to the source**, back to the prime symbol. They offer effective descriptions of personality. They form a useful catalog of human character types. But they are also **evolutionary methods**, ways of growing. Read signs as a typology and we are back to square one. We are still telling fortunes. "You are an Aries. That means you are brave and adventuresome." Read them as methods of growth and everything is transformed. We add the spice of possibility, of a larger destiny. "You are an Aries. You must become more courageous. You have come into the world to strengthen the power of your will. Challenging, frightening experiences have pursued you since you were born. They will pursue you until you die. Facing them bravely is your destiny. You must rise and meet them. Fail and you will meet only terror."

Growth. Risk. The uncertainty of the still-unresolved battle. That is evolutionary astrology. No one is simply an Aries. That is a myth. Signs are psychological processes common to all of us. Each one of us embodies all twelve. We differ only in the degree to which they are emphasized. Again, the prime symbol is a circle. Every birthchart is a circle – the same circle. In some way each sign is activated in every one of us.

Fully to grasp even one sign strains the intellect. Yet, compared to people, signs are as one-dimensional as Batman and Robin. Each of us is a synthesis of all twelve. To imagine a person with no Arian energy, for example, is like imagining someone with no emotions. An impossibility. People may be born without arms and legs, they are still unquestionably human. But to be born without some Taurean qualities or some Geminian ones – that would make us as otherworldly as a creature stepping out of a flying saucer. The process we call Leo may dominate someone's personality. But the other processes are there. Cancer may lurk in the shadows, never visible. Pisces may seem completely absent – until money matters hit a snag or until the person falls in love. Each sign is always present, awaiting **the right trigger.**

Useful insights may be generated by isolating the central themes of a given character. But when we say "I am a Taurus," we identify ourselves with one process to the exclusion of all others. We reduce ourselves to paper dolls. We forget the prime symbol. So why is there so much fascination with sun signs? Why do we hear so much about how "I'm a Pisces and you're a Scorpio?"

Despite the protests of the purists, if that system did not work to some extent, it would have died out. However, like any simple typology, sun signs are broad categories. To call someone "a Leo" is about as valuable as calling him "an extrovert." We learn something; but there is much that we do not learn.

The temptation to simplify ourselves like that is enormous. But the cost of succumbing to it is high. We may gain a kind of Cliffs Notes clarity about ourselves, but we sacrifice astrology's real treasure – the capacity of the symbols to evoke the theater of the mind with its many ambivalent characters.

None of what follows in the next chapter is intended to describe a specific person – even though by this point in the book many a Sagittarian will have already flipped ahead to see what I have to say about Sagittarius. Each sign is presented as a "personality," but the personality is no more believable than the hero of a 1930s western: only a type, a representative of some universal theme. Later we see how signs weave together with houses and planets to paint human portraits of unparalleled subtlety. But for now we must focus on something far more elemental than the psyche – the symbols themselves.

We must begin to learn the language.

Signs

ARIES THE RAM

Element: **Fire**
Mode: **Cardinal**
Archetypes: **The Warrior**
The Pioneer
The Daredevil
The Survivor
Glyph: ♈

Love God and do what you will.
-St. Augustine

The Symbol

The Ram. Horns down, charging. Fierce. Unyielding. Will the Ram crack his skull? He doesn't care. Nothing can intimidate him. Nothing can force him to swerve. Victory – or self-destruction in the effort to attain it: two destinies. One will claim him.

Aries is the **life force**, the will to exist. First there is nothing.

Then there is something. Life thrusts itself out of nowhere, claiming a place in the void. The tone of the process is unflinching, explosive, violent. It conjures up pictures of volcanoes of white-hot stars bursting into tattered nebulas.

A rabid dog backs you up to a precipice, fangs bared, mouth foaming. You have a hunting knife in your hand. He moves in, growling, eyes glaring red. You brace yourself. No more veneer of gentility and education. No more language. Nothing left but the animal rage to survive. You scream. You drive for the throat.

You have found Aries.

Endpoint

Aries teaches **courage.** It represents the ability of the **will** to triumph over any intimidation, any obstacle, any doubt. The Ram is the part of us that does exactly what it wants to do. It chooses and it acts. Nothing else matters. Wrestling crocodiles blindfolded? Yes – if that is what we want. But that kind of activity is beside the point. Aries is the sign of daring, of any act of sheer adventurousness, regardless of how smart the act might be. But its real meaning is deeper. It refers to **existential** courage.

What is that? In a word, it is selfishness. A delicate art. Not insensitivity. Not narrowness. Not manipulation. But the ability to say: "This is **my** life. I have the right to seek whatever experiences I need to have. Nothing will stand between me and my growth. Not another person. Not any circumstance. Not even my own fears."

The endpoint for Aries is the perfect mating of our desires and our actions. It is freedom. No getting lost in feelings. No fascination with the psychological underpinnings of our decisions. All that binds the Ram's attention is the power of the will to shape a life.

Strategy

Courage must be scared into a person. It cannot be attained through any other means. Stress and courage are a matched pair. Scary situations will not always make us braver, but we can never become braver without them.

Aries seeks courage. Thus, it is a magnet for stress. How the Ram faces that stress cannot be predetermined. He may respond creatively and with determination. Or he may run like a rabbit fleeing a bulldozer. All we know in advance is that the stress will be there.

Crisis follows Aries like a shadow. The boldness to do exactly what one pleases is hard to attain, and the crises it creates are fierce ones, Friends are often alienated. Figures of authority may crack down. Many times we must sneak up on existential courage, practicing it first in safer, less threatening ways. We are talking about adventures.

Let's imagine we are hanging by a rope halfway up the side of a sheer granite face. If the rope has no internal defects and is well anchored and if we make no mistakes, we have a reasonable chance of being alive that evening. In such a situation, if we are not frightened, we are stupid. Most mountain climbers, I suspect, would agree with that. Yet the mountain climber learns to control fear, to work efficiently in spite of the emotional static that his sport produces. In other words, he develops courage.

To scale a peak takes nerve. No question there. But that is a static statement. It captures none of the developmental dynamics of the process. The astrologer would express it differently. He or she would say that to climb a mountain **evokes** courage. Natural emotions are overcome; the structure of consciousness is altered. And all that is brought about through the classic Arian evolutionary strategy: the intentional selection of a crisis.

By whatever means they are attained, such transformations are the essence of growth. Mountain climbing is the paradigm, but each of us chooses his own mountain. For one, it may be learning to swim. For another, it may be a confrontation with an overbearing boss. For a third, quitting smoking may be the issue. Whether or not the Ram is willing to pick up the gauntlet, life will make the identity of the mountain plain enough. Then it is up to him to start climbing.

The Ram wants something. Certain experiences, usually risky, haunt it, tug at it like sunrise after a long, cold night. That desire, whatever it may be, is hidden. It is wrapped in veils of fear. The Arian strategy is to unveil the need, however fearsome it might be. And then to satisfy it, at whatever price. To live in the presence of fears, but to act clearly and decisively anyway – that is the Ram's art.

Resources

Nature prepares Aries for its mountains. The Ram comes into the world armed with belligerence, vitality, and an instinct for survival. Its spirit is intense and direct. Honesty, feistiness, enthusiasm, independence, a distaste for external authorities – these are the Ram's resources.

Under sensitive scrutiny, a combative streak will appear in whatever part of the birthchart Aries touches. This combativeness may be of an obvious physical nature, like a climber's struggle with a mountain. Often it takes a less readily apparent form. We may find argumentativeness. We may find the crusader for women's rights or for the protection of the environment. We may find an individual locked in combat with some inner demon – the reforming alcoholic, the Vietnam veteran battling his nightmares. A look at the birthchart often points to the target of the Arian fire. There will be fire and there will be a target, sooner or later. Of that we can be certain.

Subject even the mildest son or daughter of this sign to a sudden crisis and we observe a cold, lucid efficiency. Knees may knock in anticipation of the stress, and they might faint afterward. But under pressure the true Arian nature shines through. The Ram's resource? Whatever cloak he wears in the world, beneath it beats the heart of a warrior. It may take a crisis to flush it out of hiding. But it is there.

Shadow

A dark night. A dim alleyway. A hulking figure moving toward us out of the murk. Under those circumstances we would do well to have an Arian friend by our side, or, better, an Arian sun or moon blazing in our spirit.

But what does the warrior do in times of peace? He cannot maintain his self-image without some form of resistance threatening him from the outside world. The soldier needs an adversary. Armies will fight. If they are not challenged by a legitimate enemy, they find an illegitimate one, perhaps even turning on the country they were instituted to protect. We find precisely the same phenomenon in the Ram. He will fight. That much is certain. But no one can say whether his battles serve the purpose of evolutionary change or take the form of pointless confrontation.

Fortunately legitimate enemies abound. Again and again, Aries is confronted with frightening roadblocks. They may be powerful people who attempt to wrest away the Ram's freedom. They may be adverse constellations of circumstance. Sometimes they are inner weaknesses. Often the roadblocks take the form of interpersonal misperceptions, typically engendered by Aries's own intensity – since that quality often puts other people on the defensive. Whatever form the roadblocks take, they must be faced. If there is a cardinal sin for the Ram, it is chickening out.

Such battles hold ambiguous appeal. We may know that they help us grow. But perhaps we are very tired. If Aries chooses to follow the path of least resistance, it is free to do so. The battle must be willingly accepted.

Either way, the Ram remains a magnet for stress. Choice lies only in selecting the form the stress takes. It may be the meaningful stress of personal growth, of challenges accepted and mountains conquered. Or it may be an endless parade of empty, pointless hassles, largely brought about by the Aries's own boredom, touchiness and frustration. Down that road lies the Ram's shadow.

The warrior is full of the fire of battle. He needs it in order to accomplish what he came here to do. But, should he turn away from an evolutionary crisis, that fire still remains. It cannot be extinguished. Invariably it attacks some extraneous target with all the passion that might have been appropriately applied to the real issue.

Arguments may arise in which the emotional pitch seems out of proportion to the apparent content of the conflict. "Why do you insist on wearing that **damned** yellow shirt?"

All the fierceness, will, and courage of the Ram are then dissipated aimlessly. Friends are driven away. Marriages fail. Careers are blown over petty issues. Nobody wins. That volatile, evolutionary rocket fuel goes up like Fourth of July fireworks, full of hellfire and brimstone, empty of meaning.

The Arian who has taken that weaker path is left wounded, full of hunger and frustration. He may be self-righteous. He may be self-pitying. But his question is always the same: "Why do I seem to put everyone on the defensive?"

And the answer? Simple. The warrior fought the wrong war.

TAURUS THE BULL

Element: **Earth**
Mode: **Fixed**
Archetypes: **The Earth Spirit**
The Musician
The Silent One
Glyph: ♉

Strive for simplicity but learn to mistrust it.
–Alfred North Whitehead

The Symbol

Exhausted by the fiery furnace of Aries, consciousness seeks pools of cool water, the solace of ancient stones, the healing rustle of bird-song among green leaves. It seeks peace. It trades the harangue for the symphony, passion for silence. No longer incandescent with the fire of battle, spirit reaches gnarled hands into the earth, feeling for seeds, for clay, for the flesh of the planet itself

The symbol is a bull. Not the enraged monster furious at the red flag of the matador. Not the ferocious bull. But rather the tranquil one, standing solitary beneath a spreading April oak, quietly surveying grass and sun, cattle and earth. Nothing frightens him. Gone is the fearsome posturing of the Ram. The Bull is so in control of his world, so far beyond fear that fearlessness itself has become meaningless to him. The Arian war has been won. Taurus is at peace.

Endpoint

The top of a cliff in early May. The balmy wind slowly tatters lazy cumulous clouds. Dogwoods are blooming. Hawks float effortlessly on the rising thermals. You sit alone, feeling the sun-warmed stone beneath you, bathing in the warm air, feeling the soothing touch of spring. Before you stretches the valley, blossoming and fertile. Farmers are working their fields. Cattle are grazing. The electric green of springtime threads down the furrows and through the forests.

You sit there for an hour. Two hours. Three. Not thinking. Just feeling. No great questions haunt you. The nature of life is not your concern. In that moment, on that rock, beneath those clouds, you simply are. No words are necessary. In that vast interior spaciousness, what do you feel? What does the fertile earth teach? Timelessness. Serenity. Peace. How to be infinitely complex and yet still simple. How to be unfathomably deep and yet feel no need to talk about it.

In that moment, you have glimpsed the endpoint of Taurus. To find that serenity and to keep it: that is the Bull's task.

Strategy

Not all Taureans are nature lovers. But sitting on that hilltop is a basic evolutionary strategy. Mother Earth herself is the Bull's primary teacher. She soothes the spirit, teaches simplicity and calm. A walk in the woods, a quiet hour by a flowing stream, an evening stroll through the desert chaparral – those bring Taurus far more peace than any "talking cure."

Should destiny carry Taurus to the city, this does not imply psychological disaster. Pure Taurus always chooses the easiness and quiet of sylvan environments. Yet, no human being is a pure embodiment of any sign. Other forces may draw a person with strong Taurean components to the metropolis. Peace is harder to maintain in that setting. It is essential that the urban Taurean leave the city periodically, perhaps for a weekend of backpacking or a few days at a country inn. And it would be helpful to have a house full of plants. A cat or dog would help keep the earth connection strong too.

Mother Earth has a shadowy sister. If we find one, the other cannot be far away. She is the Bull's second great teacher. Her name is Silence. Taurus is the most taciturn of the signs. People animated by its energy find speaking a frustrating affair. Their essence is opposed to words, untranslatable into language. Silence breeds simplicity and simplicity breeds peace. Taurus knows this and intuitively rebels against too much talking.

Outer silence is not easy to attain. Inner silence, the Bull's true goal, is far more difficult. But here too a teacher arises, offering a strategy. Paradoxically, she is music. Absorbed in listening, hypnotized by the play of notes against a rhythm, what happens? For a few seconds, the constant buzz of language in the mind is silenced. Whether that flash of peace comes listening to Beethoven or listening to Led Zeppelin is immaterial: either way, the mind has stopped talking to itself. And for Taurus that is everything.

Music silences us when we listen to it. But it does an even better job when we play it. For Taurus, there is no more potent evolutionary strategy than singing in the shower or jamming away on a harmonica. Playing Chopin etudes before a full house will do it too. But only if we drown all the pride and pretense and nervousness of public performance in a cascade of notes.

Of all the signs, the Bull is the most physical. He seeks to ground out all the roaring tension of runaway mental imagery in the material world. The feel of flesh on flesh. Hands reaching into the earth. Fingers caressing the wood of a fine old violin. Working in clay, with paint, even cleaning the house or chopping vegetables are acts of self-healing for the Bull. His path is through the body. He does not transcend the flesh. He revels in it, glows in it, celebrates it.

Taurus must touch. That is basic. He finds the world through his senses, through his skin, through his fingertips. He can never find it through his mind alone. We feel the earth beneath our feet. We hear the music in our ears. We feel the warmth of our mate's body pressed against ours. The nature of life? Who knows? Who cares? Who can even think about it? That perfect moment **is** the nature of life. Talking about it only drops the veil again.

Resources

An aversion to drama. A suspicion of complexity. Those are the Bull's resources. Instinctively, he seeks out circumstances that allow him to find his silence and his simplicity. A stable job. A reliable network of relationships. Patiently, with absolute practicality, Taurus spins a cocoon. Inside it, his work proceeds as methodically and inexorably as the slow growth of a stalagmite.

Janie has a new psychologist. He's into neo-Freudian reincarnational vitamin therapy. She is greatly relieved to have found The Answer after all these years exploring blind alleys. Billy is now Bhagwan, which is even harder to say than Spotted Feather, which is what he was last month. Sam has found God. Ann has found orgasms. Joe has found himself.

To Taurus, it is all madness. He shrugs his shoulders. He lives. He lets live. He settles back in his leather chair. He feels the crisp taste of a perfect apple crunching in his mouth. He sees his children. He feels the solidness of his house and the efficiency of his body. And in some unspeakably deep, impenetrably silent part of himself, he feels something no other sign can feel in quite the same way.

He feels reverence.

Shadow

Enduring, massive objects like mountains and great oaks are metaphors for the peace Taurus seeks. They guide him. But he can lose sight of that and gather material security for its own sake. This is the Bull's shadow. He seeks the peace bred by inner security. But he may be fooled by its reflection in the outer world: money, possessions, land, the retirement plan.

Security is not evil; that is not the point. But it can constitute a kind of fool's gold to which Taurus is fatally attracted. Should the Bull succumb to security's lure. all the timeless serenity of the sign can be squandered. And in its place arises only a numbing. spirit-killing stability. Taurus can bore itself to death.

There is a crossroads for the Bull. Sooner or later he must face it. On one hand, he is presented with a path of material security. of predictability and stability. Chances are good it is an honest and moral path, harmless to everyone except himself On the other hand, he sees a path that excites him, that promises growth and change. Uncertain, insecure, yet alluring, it presents the Bull with a fundamental decision: Is life an offensive action or a defensive one? Am I here to grow or to be safe?

Security can become stagnation on the mental level too. Here we find the proverbial stubbornness of the Bull. Like all fixed signs. Taurus is determined, though that is not always immediately evident. Many times he appears quiet and noncommittal on the surface. Never mistake this for wishy-washiness. Beneath the silence there is an iron will. That gives the Bull the capacity to do anything he is resolved to do. But it can also produce inflexibility.

Stubbornness can result in narrow, unimaginative responses to experience, a failure to take those existential leaps of faith that are a primary element of a full life. We grow and change and as we do, our self-image and its halo of attitudes and opinions must change too. Taurus may fail here. Like the ancient hills that guide it, the Bull may come to say, "I am the same yesterday, today, and tomorrow."

And then everything is lost.

GEMINI THE TWINS

Element: Air
Mode: Mutable
Archetypes: The Witness
The Teacher
The Storyteller
The Journalist
Glyph: Ⅱ

Behead yourself! Dissolve your whole body into Vision;
become seeing, seeing, seeing!
-Jalalu'l-Din Rumi

The Symbol

The Twins. Who are they? Brothers. Sisters. Soulmates. Lovers. Two beings, irrevocably bound together, fascinated with each other. Two beings, each hell-bent on unraveling the other's mystery yet separated by an impenetrable wall of misunderstanding.

What do they do? They talk. They listen. They scan each other for clues, for meaningful gestures, for half-hidden innuendos. Nothing escapes them. No detail is too minute. No trail is too cold.

A bomb goes off in the puzzle factory. A thousand puzzles, blasted to smithereens. A million pieces scattered like confetti. Two mad geniuses, both on Methedrine, attack the problem, each one swearing to have five hundred puzzles assembled by dawn.

Imagine it. That's Gemini.

Endpoint

Turn to the Gemini chapter of any sun-sign book. Somewhere in the first paragraph you will read the word *communication*. Speaking and listening are certainly key issues for the Twins, but to understand them we must go further. The psychic process to which Gemini refers includes much more. It is the whole issue of *perception,* the way the world communicates with us. The way we see, feel, hear, and smell all the phantasmagoria that surrounds us. Listening to words is just one thread in that much vaster tapestry.

Gemini is born to perceive, to gorge itself with observations. The stasis so characteristic of Taurus is antithetical to the Twins. This sign must remain in motion all the time. There is so much to see and know. Not a minute to waste. Like a child suddenly granted ten minutes to pillage a toy store. Gemini rushes through experience, sometimes frantic, often without any apparent master plan, but always with gusto.

Alert intelligence is basic to the Twins. But concentrating on intelligence clouds our understanding of what is born here. To Gemini, thinking is epiphenomenal, just a side-effect. The thrust of the sign is not intellection. It is raw perception. Not thinking, but seeing. Gemini is not so much a philosopher as a journalist. The undigested facts of perception, not their meaning, are its food. It only wants to see, to witness the world. Ideas and understanding may arise, but they are not the point.

To unravel the secret of the world. To gather all the clues. To see everything. That is Gemini's endpoint.

Strategy

To see everything! The task is impossible. Give a person a million years to live. Give him X-ray vision and bionic ears. Give him the mind of a computer and the energy of a hyperkinetic four-year-old. What could he see? How much of life could he penetrate? It would be like dipping a thimble in the ocean. And yet that is Gemini's task.

How can the Twins proceed? One key strategy is to live as intense and varied a life as possible. To live three or four lives in one. To treat predictability and boredom as unpardonable sins. Never to let the mind stop growing. Very difficult.

We all create pictures of the universe that we carry around in our heads. And we don't like experiences that don't fit the picture. The doctor doesn't like to see the faith healer get results. The white racist has little use for a brilliant black physicist. We create a picture. Then we look for evidence to support it. Gemini must violate that instinct. It must strive to see clearly, regardless of how incomprehensible its perceptions might be. The Twins must **give the universe permission not to make any sense.** If they are confused, they are right on target. That just means the information they have gathered is ahead of their ability to figure it out. Maintaining that wide open, totally receptive state is a prime evolutionary strategy for this sign. Once again: not thinking so much as seeing.

Living is one way to gather experience. But there is another. The world is swarming with experiencers. It is swarming with people. Each one of them has a unique set of perceptions. Each one has digested them, turned them from crude observations into a far more refined form: thoughts. But how can we get at them? They are locked behind a wall of bone and brain matter.

The Twins know the answer. To get at those treasures hidden in the minds of those around us, all we have to do is ask. Make inquiries. We must master the art of speaking. For Gemini, that is a critical evolutionary strategy. The Twins are born to talk.

They are also born to listen. But that does not come as automatically. Quick wit, even eloquence, is far more available to the Twins than attentiveness. In the context of a hard, direct birth chart, they may interrupt and finish other people's sentences for them. In a softer, more interpersonally sensitive chart, the pattern may be less obvious. We find them quiet, appearing to be fascinated by our ideas. But their minds have raced ahead. Despite the eye contact and nodding head, they are oblivious to what we are saying. In reality they have already decided what we are going to say. They are now absorbed in studying our nose, thinking of how much it reminds them of a nose they once knew in high school.

Communication is a two-way street. Gemini must remember

that. We speak what we know. But we sometimes hear something we don't know. To listen. To absorb the world. That is the Twins' strategy. Speaking is useful to them only if it accelerates that process.

Resources

Curiosity. That is the ultimate Geminian resource. A sense of the world's wonder. A childlike appreciation of each dewdrop, each teardrop, each unprecedented flake of snow. Without that, the Twins are nothing but chatter.

Vitality is a Geminian resource too. The Twins' curiosity drives them ceaselessly. So much to see. So much to know. Few signs live so tirelessly, function on so little sleep. To live three lifetimes in one leaves no time for laziness. Once their enthusiasm is fired, the Twins blaze through life like a pair of meteors.

Physical vitality functions mentally too, giving the Twins a third key resource: intelligence. They combine all that curiosity, all that energy, to produce a huge, undigested library of raw information. And Gemini threads through it at the speed of light, making connections, drawing parallels, noting discrepancies. No sign has a quicker mind.

Finally, the Twins can talk. Like no other sign, they probe other people's minds, sifting through strata of falsity and fiction, prospecting for nuggets of insight, crystals of experience. For Gemini the substance of the universe is not molecules or atoms. It is information. No sign is so hungry for it or so adept at gathering it, correlating it, broadcasting it. And that is their most precious resource.

Shadow

Gemini in its pure form is beyond opinions. With no more judgmentalness than a mirror, it simply observes. Suspicious of grand schemes, of ultimate Truths, the Twins piece together a web of clues, always hesitating to draw a premature conclusion. Intuitively, they sense that anything can be proven with the facts.

The adaptability so characteristic of this phase of the zodiac arises here. Unfortunately, when married to baser motives, this same flexibility produces horrors. Pressed to face an unpleasant truth, the adaptable Geminian mind can reconstruct the information. There is little real lying involved here, only a shifting of emphasis, a few strategic silences, and a barrage of words. Often the new montage of ideas makes sense. However false, it may be convincing, or at least persuasive enough to put anyone off the track. Only the most cunning and single-minded individual can penetrate the maze the Twins weave once they are put on the defensive. Right or wrong, they rarely lose an argument.

There are physical dangers for the Twins too. The continual buzz of the Geminian psyche inevitably overflows into its nervous system. An accumulation of tension in the mind can produce jumpiness. This difficulty in relaxing often leads to insomnia and can aggravate the sign's tendency toward nervous chatter. Should the inner buzz go unchecked, circumstances begin to reflect the same pattern: busyness, overextension, and finally, emotional exhaustion.

Tension such as Gemini can develop must be released. Quiet talk with penetrating and yet relaxed partners is a big help. No mind-wars with intellectuals here. No verbal jousting. Simply heart-to-heart communication with no one taking notes and no one looking to sell a point. Physical exercise also aids in the release of the Twins' tension. Typically they need more of it than they want. Walking, running, a friendly game of volleyball, all these can be helpful. No push-ups, though. Remember: Gemini is not here to be bored.

The Twins are in the world to gather experience, to let the miracle of life work directly on their hearts. There is no room in them for complacency, for dogmatic opinions that shield them from chaos and mystery. With their insatiable curiosity they can pack a lifetime with experiences. But the horse they ride is wild. It can carry them to a far horizon or it can dance around, full of motion, going nowhere. "All tactics and no strategy" has been the epitaph of many a Geminian. It comes down to this: The horse needs a rider.

CANCER THE CRAB

Element: Water
Mode: Cardinal
Archetypes: The Mother
The Healer
The Invisible Man (Woman)
Glyph: ♋

*Those for whom not to be seen is non-existence are not alive;
and the kind of existence they seek, the immortality they seek, is spec-
tral; to be seen is the ambition of ghosts, and to be
remembered the ambition of the dead.
–Norman O. Brown*

The Symbol

The Crab. A vulnerable creature. A succulent piece of meat. The food of gulls. How can he survive? What hope is there for him? He is only a morsel awaiting the predator's mouth.

To live, the Crab must grow a shell. He must grow a wall between himself and nature. He is too delicate to protect himself in any other way.

With this armor the Crab endures. He is at peace with his environment. But that success holds the seeds of a perilous transformation. The Crab eats. He matures. And soon he outgrows his shell. It must be shed. If he is cunning and lucky he may live to grow another one. One that is larger, more suited to his expanded state. But only if he is cunning and lucky.

Endpoint

Dizzied by Gemini's spinning carousel, confused by the chaos of life on the midway, awareness now turns inward toward its roots. To the Twins truth is "out there" somewhere. They search the world, filling the psyche with alertness and wonder. And yet the search yields nothing. Life is more mysterious than ever, more full of loose ends and undigested details.

Cancer sets out in a new direction. Instead of rifling through the universe, the Crab reaches tendrils of consciousness inward, probing deeply into the underpinnings of experience, pressing toward the heart.

The fabric of the world to Cancer is feelings. A mammoth subjectivity animates this phase of the zodiac. The terse, journalistic awareness of Gemini gives way to a tapestry of impressions, of personal responses. There is no longer an objective universe. All that remains is a pattern of reactions.

Those who are born under the mark of the Crab have come here to penetrate dimensions of inner life inaccessible to any previous sign. They arrive fluent in the language of the deep self, the language of emotion. Fascinated by the reactive, subjective aspects of the mind, their lifeblood is a protracted process of psychoanalysis, usually self-administered.

To **feel** consciousness. To **feel** every nuance of life. To shed the shell of numbness that armors us against this slaughterhouse of a world. All that is the Crab's work.

Cancer's endpoint? To see the hellish discord of life. To see the cauldron within. And, against all odds, against all common sense, **to love, trust, and accept** all that existence offers.

Strategy

An automated bathysphere. Its purpose? To map the seabed four miles below the ocean's surface. To extract samples from the sediment. And to return intact to the mother ship.

One strategy supersedes all others: The bathysphere must survive. The sea presses at it, sounding the walls for any weakness, any flaw. In that unmitigatedly hostile environment, defense is everything. Without armor, the delicate sensing devices within the vessel would be crushed in a microsecond.

Yet, there must be gaps in the defense. A solid wall of steel two feet thick would protect the ship perfectly. Too perfectly. Without breaks in the armor, the bathysphere could not interact with the environment it was designed to explore. There must be windows for the cameras. Wires must run from the interior brain to the exterior eyes and ears. There must be internal storage bays for material gathered from outside.

The bathysphere's designers face a difficult problem: if they defend the machinery too well, the ship will not do the work for which it was created. And if they do not defend it well enough, the vessel will be destroyed by the environment it was designed to penetrate.

It is the same with the Crab.

Cancer's "sensing devices" are the most delicate in the zodiac. No sign **feels** with such intensity. And **feeling** is what life is all about for the Crab. But those emotional circuits can be overloaded. They can burn out. Life must be let in slowly, in a controlled way. Simply to drop all defenses would be suicidal.

Cancer's goal is to maximize the intensity of its interactions with the world while simultaneously protecting its finely tuned emotional sensibilities. To surround them in a shell of steel would allow the fragile mechanisms to endure. But life is more than endurance. The Crab's strategy is **to create the minimal defenses consistent with survival.**

Shyness is one such defense. Especially in early life, daydreams and reticence are Cancer's cloak. The person initiates only the most barely essential interactions with the world. A mask is worn, a mask of anonymity and disinformation. Like an Apache in the desert, we can look straight at such an individual and see nothing but chaparral.

Later the defenses may become more sophisticated. The Crab learns to project a plausible, three-dimensional hologram of a human personality into the social arena. Perhaps even a gregarious one.

Within that disguise he lurks like a spy, snapping X-ray photographs, secretly penetrating the souls of those around him.

To wear a mask or to stand naked and revealed: Cancer has little choice. His inner processes are so delicate and life is so jarring that without insulation his nervous system would shatter. The danger is that the defenses can become so efficient that safety can be put ahead of everything, even growth.

For the Crab to evolve he must shed his shell. But the shedding must be calculated. No one touched by this sign needs to stand on a soapbox during rush hour and pull down his psychological pants. The audience must be carefully selected and timing must be flawless. With his extreme vulnerability the Crab is playing for high stakes.

But he must play. He must open up. He must trust. Love is always a gamble, and that is a risk Cancer must learn to take.

Resources

Put Cancer on a slow bus for Tierra del Fuego. For most of us that would be about as appealing as a dose of leprosy. Cancer reacts differently. He settles down. He closes his eyes. And in ten seconds he is trekking through Middle Earth.

For Cancer, the outer world is pale compared to the one generated by the imagination. And that vivid inner life is the Crab's key resource. Like no other sign, he is at home in the fairyland we carry between our ears.

Imagination, subjectivity, feelings – these are the raw materials of the Crab. And they come to a focus in that most primal of all emotions: Love. Look at another person. Feel tenderness. Feel the desire to help, to heal, to nurture. Feel no competitiveness, no fear, nothing but support. Your Cancer circuits are illuminated.

Kindness and concern are unpremeditated reactions for the Crab. They are the only forces more potent than the sign's self-protective instincts. The meekest person in the world can drink a couple of beers, get a little rowdy, and start coming on to Cancer. He may as well be trying to get into Fort Knox with a church key. But let Genghis Khan show up with a broken heart and the doors are flung open.

That kind of loving comes naturally to Cancer. It is one of the sign's resources, not its endpoint. To be supportive. To be helpful. To be protective. Laudable traits, but they are not the same as shedding a shell, not the same as standing naked. They are a special kind of loving. A relatively safe kind.

Mothering – that is the Crab's resource. That is what arises automatically. To love truly is far more difficult, far more perilous. And it never happens without effort.

Shadow

Mothering is Cancer's highest expression – and its potential downfall. Nine times out of ten it is a tender expression of human love, commendable in every way. Other times, it is just another hiding place, another shell.

People, especially people in pain, are drawn to the Crab's soothing womb. Cancer draws out the sensitivity and suffering in everyone it contacts, encouraging them to feel safe enough to laugh and weep. Cancers seem to wear astral T-shirts emblazoned with the word **Mother.** Anyone can read the message. Let the Crab sit down on that bus to Tierra del Fuego. Within ten minutes there is someone sitting next to him, pouring out his heart.

No sign can wear the mask of the mother as convincingly as Cancer. We get understanding and compassion. The Crab gets safety and invisibility. And no one gets anywhere, at least not in an intimate relationship. Mothering works fine with strangers on the bus. But it cannot be allowed to become the dominant theme of a marriage or friendship. If that happens, the natural equality of such a bond is disrupted. Both partners are robbed of their humanity.

Cancer must vigilantly guard against the tempting dangers of the mother role. He must guard against shrouding himself in so much wisdom and forgiveness and understanding that his own turbulent inner life, his own needs, become invisible. The Crab may gain security and stability that way. But it is just another shell game. And the minimum bet is loneliness.

Emotional nakedness is frightening to Cancer. But equally frightening are insecurity and instability in the outward side of life: change, adventure, experience.

For the Crab, a little bit of experience goes a long way. The existential fireworks that propel Aries and Gemini are like a horror movie to Cancer. But even Cancer needs a modicum of variety and change. Sadly, his naturally prudent instincts may undercut that. Like Taurus, he may descend into a spirit-numbing pattern of boredom and predictability. Jobs may be worked mechanically, long after their value to individual growth has been exhausted. Relationships may wither into ritual – all to avoid the uncomfortable ciphers of change. And, safe within its shell, the Crab's romantic, creative spark may lapse into decades of dormancy.

LEO THE LION

Element: Fire
Mode: Fixed
Archetypes: The King (or Queen)
The Performer
The Child
The Clown
Glyph: ♌

We are what we pretend to be.
–Kurt Vonnegut, Jr.

The Symbol

Not a lion, but a rock band from Sioux City, Iowa. Six kids long on energy, short on experience. Lightning strikes. They get a recording contract. In two months they have an album rocketing up the charts.

They open in Madison Square Garden. The house is packed. Thousands of eyes rake the stage. In the dressing room, the band is terrified. Butterflies. Stage fright. They step out into the lights, knees weak. Eyes rivet them. They strike the power chords. The soundman redlines the volume controls. The audience is on its feet, cheering, clapping hands.

Eyes wide as saucers, the band gets the message: everybody loves them. They play harder and tighter. The audience goes wild. The band picks up that juice, blasts it back. Pretty soon nobody is thinking about Sioux City, Iowa.

Endpoint

In Cancer, the preceding sign, the veil is drawn aside to reveal the glittering, shifting depths of mind. Consciousness is mesmerized. It cannot turn away. The mirages of the inner eye fascinate awareness, collapsing it inward upon itself. Attention turns away from outward activity, dissolving into passivity, watching and feeling, projecting very little.

Leo is a reaction against the inwardness of the Crab. Fertilized, enriched by its encounter with the roots of consciousness, life now seeks a more palpable expression. Blazing magma may have flowed beneath Cancer's shell. But in Leo it roars forth with all the grandeur of a volcano. And sometimes with as much subtlety.

Expression – that is the key to understanding the Lion. The contents of the mind are made visible. Nothing is chained in the dungeons of imagination. Everything is given form. Everything is expressed. **Leo must leave tangible evidence of its internal processes in the hands of the world.** Cancer needs secrets. For the Lion, they are anathema.

To express the mind. To create outward symbols of our inward state. To weave a transparent clue whose unraveling leads anyone to the center of our most intimate mysteries – that is Leo work.

And what is that clue the Lion must weave? It is Leo's endpoint: The development of a spontaneous, unabashed openhanded style. It is the development of a behavioral surface that conforms to the shape of the mind's interior like a leotard clings to a prima ballerina.

Leo's endpoint? The development of personality.

Strategy

The Lion must learn to say yes to life. His path is one of affirmation, of positiveness. He must banish all pettiness, all pickiness and narrowness, from his mind. Fear and suspicion have no place in his vocabulary. Nothing that inhibits his self-expression can be tolerated.

What if people laugh? No matter. Leo must still affirm who he is. He must still say, "Life. I love you! I celebrate you! I am not afraid of you!"

Ego transcendence is one of our primary metaphors for spiritual growth. We often imagine "evolved beings" as pale creatures who sit around in the lotus position with their bellies full of bean sprouts, fearing nothing, hoping for nothing, harboring no opinions. Anyone hooked on that model is going to look askance at the Lion.

Leo refers to the **development of** ego, not its transcendence. And sitting in the lotus position is no help there. The Lion must accept the essential absurdity of ego, then revel in it, letting ego flow unselfconsciously into the world. He must wear a plaid shirt with purple pants and walk down the street whistling "The Star Spangled Banner." And if people stare, he must whistle louder. To perform for the world is to trust it. That unquestioning trust of life is Leo's holy grail. All the creativity, all the warmth, all the playfulness and drama of this sign are simply methods used to attain that goal. Anything inside should appear on the outside. And if the Lion has really arrived he is not concerned with his reviews.

Poetry, painting, decorating – all the traditional creative outlets are valuable centering devices for Leo. Any inclination along those lines should be pursued. Such skills provide vehicles for the expression of our inner life, and that kind of self-expression is evolutionary dynamite for the lion.

Leo shines even more brightly when the creative avenue chosen is a more direct one. Dancing, singing, storytelling, and above all, drama, are the Lion's natural turf. There, little distance remains between performer and audience. Feedback is instantaneous. Energy goes out and immediately finds its mark. And for Leo that is heaven.

Art is not the only place where imagination can manifest visibly. To have an impact on the form of an organization, or an event or even another person, is certainly self-expression. Whenever we leave the stamp of our own thoughts or values on the world, we express our creative drive.

Leo's spark must flare out in more spontaneous ways too. Simple playfulness is an evolutionary strategy for this sign. Without premeditation, imagination bursts the bounds of "maturity" and floods out into the theater of life.

To the old astrologers, Leo was the symbol of kings. Its charisma and presence justify that title. But deeper truth is conveyed when we see the Lion as the sign of the Child. The self-dramatizing, present-tense spirit so universal among children is Leo's essence.

Strategy? To celebrate one's self. To create. To keep no private secrets. To maintain the innocence, the spontaneity, and the freshness of a child.

Resources

Instinctively the Lion roars.

Anyone whose birthchart contains many Leo components has the soul of a performer: Offer the slightest encouragement and you are regaled with a torrent of good-natured self-expression. It may be jokes. It may be a tune on the piano. It may be a true story, somewhat embellished and told with conspiratorial fervor. Whatever form it takes, every Leo circuit contains an act or two. Clap your hands and the curtain will rise.

Often it is in the creative directing of raw human energies that Leo finds its niche. The Lion's radiant, magnanimous personality gives him a natural knack for leadership. He can often bring to a focus otherwise chaotic cross-currents in a disorganized group of people. Napoleon is history's most obvious example of that side of Leo, but a similar one could be found in almost any successful sales office or baseball team.

Creativity and charisma are Leonine resources, but there is a far greater one: the lion knows how to be happy. His attention is on the present moment, and in that moment he is king. Yesterday may be a web of busts and pratfalls. Tomorrow the politicians may really start those fireballs flying. But today, my body works, my spirits are high, and I've got twenty bucks. Let's dance.

The Lion's resource: like no other sign, he knows that he is alive right now. The past is gone. Tomorrow may never come. He knows he must seize this shifting moment and wring it for every atom of joy it contains.

Shadow

Madison Square Garden behind them, the six kids from Sioux City pack up their amps and take the limo out to Kennedy International Airport. Next stop: Peking.

They are on a good-will tour of the People's Republic, playing provinces where western music has never been heard. The lead singer struts up to the microphone. The guitar player does a knee slide in from stage left. The smoke bombs rain pink wisps on an audience of ten thousand Chinese, each one with his hands folded politely in his lap, utterly baffled. Who are these madmen from America? Why are they so excited?

The reality of their situation dawns on the band. This is not the Garden. This is China. The juice the New York audience supplied is not going to materialize here. And suddenly they are just six kids from Iowa, a long way from home.

Performing, creating, expressing – energy flows out in all these Leonine strategies. But if that were all there were to Leo, the sign would soon run dry. There must be some corresponding influx of vitality or the Lion would quickly exhaust himself. That flux may be one person saying, "I love you. I am glad you are alive." Or it may be ten thousand Chinese clapping their hands. Whatever form it takes, Leo needs applause. Without it he withers.

With all his warmth and presence, Leo certainly merits praise. But, like our Sioux City rock stars, he projects an image of self-assurance and pride. Unintentionally, the Lion seems to be proclaiming his superiority. And that is not a formula for applause.

People may react by attempting to counter Leo's apparently grandiose self-image. They may ignore him or try to deflate him. And that only whips the Lion into a frenzy of performance. He is saying, "Please love me!" And they are hearing, "I am the greatest."

Vicious Leonine circles have their roots in that kind of misperception. Leo needs love, but the more he tries to secure it by impressing people, the more he is likely to put them off. At extreme stages, the Lion may even begin to display those traits of which the popular astrology books have always accused him: arrogance, haughtiness the "little Napoleon" syndrome.

Leo's shadow? It is pride. Pride may prevent him from simply asking for love. He must learn to share the vulnerability he knows so well, to ask for support. Failing that, he is like the comedian playing to the room of granite faces. Or the rock band in the Chinese outback.

He is pitiful.

VIRGO THE VIRGIN

Element: **Earth**
Mode: **Mutable**
Archetypes: **The Servant**
The Martyr
The Perfectionist
The Analyst
Glyph: ♍

One can give nothing whatever without giving oneself —
that is to say, risking oneself. If one cannot risk oneself,
then one is simply incapable of giving.
-James Baldwin

The Symbol

The Virgin. Of all symbols, the most difficult to grasp. We think of virginity as inexperience. But this is not a symbol of inexperience. Nor of prudery. Nor of any flight from passion.

The Virgin is an image of purity. Nothing has possessed her. She is attached to nothing, wants nothing, fears nothing. Nothing holds her. She is free, unbound by any earthly drama.

Yet she is here, on the earth. What does the world offer one who seeks nothing but perfection? What can she do? She waits, aloof as the Madonna. She works on herself. And to pass the time, she helps out where she can.

Endpoint

Roaring gets old. Consciousness, tired of Leo's fanfare, reaches for deeper meaning, for a sense of purpose. Leo looms large. He shocks us to attentiveness. But gradually our circle of attention widens. The mighty lion is revealed in a new perspective: against the backdrop of galaxies, of aeons, of life and death, his pride and vanity are absurd. The lion's roar turns out to be empty.

In Leo, personality attains a pinnacle. It can be taken no further. Our next step is nothing less than a leap to a new level of experience. Out of that need, out of that despair, arises the Virgin. Awareness attunes to a new feeling: the hunger for personal transformation. The seeds of discontent have germinated; Virgo must grow.

But what must it grow **toward?** Purity. Perfection. Fulfillment. Significance. Harsh masters, and the goals they set are impossibly distant.

Virgo's endpoint? Call it perfection. But her first step down that road is a bitter one. The Virgin must learn humility.

Strategy

Two visions drive Virgo along her path. One beckons her from up ahead. The other whips her from behind. Together they give her no rest.

The first is a sense of the ideal, of what could be. It gives Virgo her perfectionism, her ethical and principled qualities. The second vision is a meticulous, scrupulously honest sense of what is really happening. That is where the Virgin gets her practical, orderly attributes, her abhorrence of inefficiency.

Traditional astrology describes those aspects of the sign in a static way: "Virgos are responsible and have analytical minds but they tend to be fussy over details." That approach misses all the Virgin's dynamic flavor. It sees rigid facts where a growth-oriented person would see an explosive evolutionary strategy.

The purpose of those two visions is to create a hunger, a need to move toward the ideal. The Virgin sees what she could be. She sees her potential, what she would look like if she shattered all the inner chains which bind her. And she sees what she really is. Clearly. Concisely. With brutal honesty. No sign can dissect itself so coldly.

Pop astrologers so often damn Virgo with faint praise: "Virgos make fine librarians and bookkeepers. Like no other sign, they can cope with tedium." The poor Virgin is seen as a boring sign, given to pettiness and idiosyncrasies.

In truth, there is no sign more exciting. Why? Because there is no sign more eager to grow. Her perfectionism pressures her to change. And her pragmatic realism gives her the means to do it.

If this were all there were to Virgo's strategy, she would be the most selfish of the signs. Everything would revolve around me, my growth, my hangups.

Egoism need not be arrogant. Compulsive personal analysis bestows upon the self a distortedly central position in the universe just as certainly as any messiah complex.

Virgo does not succumb to that trap. There is a second dimension to her personality, one that serves to balance her seriousness and self-absorption: this is the sign of the servant.

To the old astrologers, Virgo suggested servitude in the menial sense. That is very misleading. The Virgin symbolizes our capacity to be of use to other people. And that service is a method of self-discovery, never a form of self-abasement. The point is not simply to serve. It is to **express the self through** service.

Virgo must choose some aspect of her being. She must polish it, educate it. She must get it certified. And then she must offer it to the world.

Out of kindness? No, not really, although it often looks that way. The giving of that gift is part of the Virgin's strategy. It is part of her effort to perfect herself.

Virgo is not here to serve other people so much as to serve **the principle of** service. In doing that, she transforms herself. She takes the most perfectible part of herself and becomes **utterly identified with** it. She becomes her work.

If she is a counselor, she must try to become infinite love and understanding. If she is an artist, she must become a source of flawless beauty. If she is a garbage collector, she must be a symbol of the imperishability of human dignity. And everything else, every other more limited aspect of her consciousness, must fade. The Virgin becomes the service she offers. And as that service grows more perfect, so does she.

To perfect the self through relentless idealism, humble self-assessment, and an unyielding desire to offer a gift to the world: that is Virgo's strategy.

Resources

The Virgoan psyche is like high-resolution film. Every nuance of life stands out as starkly as glare on water. No romantic veneers cloud her vision. She sees only what is really there, and she sees it in minute detail. When that X-ray mind turns in on itself, the images it produces are even more precise. The Virgin sees herself with merciless clarity. It is as if she has taken out an insurance policy against delusions of grandeur.

If she detects a distortion in herself, she does not rest. It must be ripped out. The Virgin is never complacent. Laziness is not a part of her repertoire. The insurance policy she carries against delusions of grandeur also functions as a pitiless spur, driving her ever onward. No matter what heights she attains, her goal is always further down the road.

To say that the Virgin cannot be lazy captures half the truth. To find the other half, we must only twist the words a little differently: Virgo cannot be satisfied. For her, there is no time to waste. She has set her sights on a star. And stars are very far away.

Meaningful work is a key issue for the sixth sign. If Virgo's great aunt Winifred dies and leaves her an oil well, she may retire to the Riviera, but give her six months and we find her working harder than ever. She may not be frying eggs for a living anymore, but she is busy. Leave those millions to Leo; the Virgin is not here to relax.

Competence, especially at tasks that require patience and precision, comes naturally to Virgo. So does a sense of responsibility.

Typically this is expressed through the profession. But her helpfulness is far broader than that. Even after a terrible week at work, let a distant friend call looking for help moving a refrigerator. Virgo is there in half an hour. And if the friend asks for advice as well as muscle, cut that down to ten minutes. Virgo's counsel will be good, too. But it may include the history of refrigeration in the Western Hemisphere. With her careful mind, the Virgin would hate to leave any detail open to misinterpretation.

Shadow

For the first time in the unfolding mandala of signs, we encounter the capacity for self-sacrifice. New realms of consciousness await us down that road. But so do some cunning bandits.

The Virgin may sacrifice herself too much. She may tear herself to shreds on the reefs of her own honesty: "That is what I should be ... this is what I actually am ... oh my God..."

Perfection is a ferocious and uncompromising teacher, and many a Virgo has scars to prove it. The Virgin can fall into patterns of doubt and uncertainty. Negative, undermining self images can plague her, crippling her natural vitality. She may limit herself. She may play second fiddle to a fool in an ill-fated marriage. She may find herself stuck in a boring, menial job. In extreme cases, Virgo is capable of self-destructiveness.

Purity, perfection – they are abstractions. For the Virgin they serve as goals, but ones that remain forever ethereal. Should she lose sight of them, all is lost. Her life is dissipated in a blither of minor hassles. She becomes the comic book fussbudget of the pop astrologers.

But to actually move toward that perfection, Virgo must learn to defend herself against the dangers of the tool she is using. **The Virgin's self-criticism must be tempered by absolute self-acceptance.** She must learn to love herself unconditionally. And she must do that in the most difficult way imaginable: with an honest mind.

Once again, the Virgin must strive for purity. But the process is delicate; she must not yield to the temptation to hate her impurity. She must love herself for what she is, not for what she could be. Only then will she **avoid the trap of feeling she must make up for some inner deficiency through continuous self-sacrifice.**

The close, sharp focus of Virgo's consciousness may blind her to larger patterns. Details may overwhelm her. She may become so lost in cataloging the stress points in her life that she loses track of how good it feels to be alive. Fretting, nitpicking, self-abnegation – those are the hazards that arise when her clarity is untempered by perspective and self-acceptance.

Should the Virgin fall prey to that shadow, a second one is never far behind. Like a jackal tailing a lion, attacks on other people follow attacks upon one's self. If the Virgin frowns at what she sees in the mirror, she will also frown at what she sees in the world.

With perfection as her guide, Virgo can climb like a missile or be shattered like a piece of blown glass. The key is self esteem. Whatever happens, she must love herself. She must stop judging herself by what she has accomplished. The other side of that coin is always the road ahead, and no sign is more aware of how far it stretches. Despite her tendency to plot and plan, she must learn to live in the present, and to live there lovingly. And if she must judge herself, let it be only by the intensity of her life processes in the endless now. Nothing else matters. And nothing else leads so efficiently or so quickly to perfection.

LIBRA THE SCALES

Element: **Air**
Mode: **Cardinal**
Archetypes: **The Lover**
The Artist
The Peacemaker
Glyph: ♎

Only in silence the word,
only in dark the light,
only in dying life:
bright the hawk's flight
on the empty sky.
-Ursula K. LeGuin

The Symbol

Scales. Not the modem kind. No springs. No digital readout. Just a simple seesaw, straight out of the marketplaces of Babylon and old Egypt. Put an ounce of lead on one platform. Pour gold dust onto the other. When they balance, you have an ounce of gold.

Libra symbolizes harmony. Equilibrium. The reconciliation of opposites. Lead meets gold. Birth meets death. Love contacts fear. No light without shadow, no shadow without light.

Endpoint

Libra teaches serenity. It represents the capacity of the mind to gain conscious control over the nervous system. The Scales symbolize that part of ourselves that is bothered by nothing, offended by nothing, shocked by nothing. It has signed a perpetual peace treaty with chaos.

A bus station in Georgia. Our car is ditched three miles away in the rainy night with a burned-out engine. To our left, the pay TV exhorts us to use more deodorant. To the right a ghetto blaster is screeching out three-year-old disco tunes. An announcement comes over the PA system. Our bus has been delayed another two hours. Do we care? No: it is just life. No reason to get upset.

The goal for Libra, as for all the signs, is a transformation of consciousness. In this case, it is the attainment of an unbreakable inner harmony. From now on nothing distorts the balance. Nothing shatters the equilibrium. Hurts come. Hurts go. Joy and sorrow spin like night and day. And at the center of the carousel, aware but unmoved, stand the Scales.

Libra's endpoint? So simple to say, so hard to do. It is to calm down.

Strategy

Other signs have a kind of equilibrium built into them. No matter how cacophonous life becomes, they continue to focus their undivided attention on the business at hand. Their task has nothing to do with calming down. It lies elsewhere. And if they were easily flustered, it would be that much harder for them.

Not so for Libra. The attainment of tranquility is the essence of this sign's work. **And that tranquility must be achieved through the action of the will on the structure of consciousness.** Numbness and inattention do not count. The Scales have **no natural defenses** for their equilibrium. Their peace must be sustained through indefatigable effort. It never happens automatically.

This is the paradox: Libra, the symbol of calm, stretches the nerves as taut as the strings of a violin. And its art is not so much to loosen them as to see that they are never plucked. To be utterly vulnerable. To be pitilessly sensitive. And to be calm anyway. That is the task.

How? Libra must learn to recognize the early symptoms of

emotional imbalance. You are ten minutes late for a meeting. The phone has rung one too many times. And you spy your old college roommate. Madame Depresso, heading up your driveway for a surprise visit. Time to take a deep breath. Time to meditate for five seconds. That is the heart of the Libran strategy: never letting tension fire up a chain reaction. Stop it before it starts.

There are other methods. But that one is the key.

Read any of the popular astrological books and you soon run into the idea that Libra is the sign of artists. There is validity to that notion, but we must take it further. This sign often does elevate aesthetic sensitivity. What is less understood is that the appreciation and creation of beauty both serve Libra's evolutionary purpose. Both promote calm.

Turn a comer on a mountain trail. Step from a dusky pine forest into a wide meadow overlooking mile after mile of blue-green ridges. See the delicate pinks and reds and blues of a flawless sunset. Feel the surprise. Feel the pleasure. And what happens? Involuntarily, our mouths open. Our muscles relax. We sigh. The same mental and physical reactions occur when we watch a ballerina pirouetting across a stage. Or see an attractive painting. Or look at our bedroom when we have finally gotten around to cleaning it up.

The perception of harmony in the outer world translates into calm in the inner world. And that is one of the keystones of Libra's evolutionary strategy: it must constantly beautify its environment. Learning to paint may do it. So will traveling to visually dramatic places like mountains and galleries. And so will making the bed.

That harmony enters consciousness in more ways than through the five senses. It comes in through feelings, too. And our feelings are so dependent on the quality of our relationships with other people. For no other sign is the question of friendship and marriage so central. Libra is half of something. And the peace it seeks comes partly through locating its other half.

Popular books imply that Libra is lucky in love. Often the opposite is actually the case. Relationships are a growth intensive area for this sign. And that means work and probably turmoil.

The aim for the Scales is to form deep, harmonious bonds. The strategy is to learn **to compromise idiosyncrasies without ever compromising essence.** And the danger is to get so nervous **maintaining the semblance of harmony** in a relationship that all real peace is lost.

Resources

A sense of harmony is Libra's resource. But that harmony goes far beyond the colors, shapes, or personalities. It is an awareness that all wholes are composed of complementary halves. Female completes male. Light completes darkness. Evil creates good. Good gives meaning to evil.

Feed Libra any rigid, dogmatic opinion and the sign quickly generates an opposing view. Tell it that the political left holds all the answers. Libra extols the wisdom of the right. Tell it that the conservatives will save the country. It points out the virtues of liberalism. Truth, for this sign, is always a balancing act. Intuitively, the Scales sense that gold must balance lead, that every truth is balanced by an equal but opposite truth.

This is Libra's treasure. Not just artistic sensitivity. Not just amiability. Not just social grace. But something deeper, something that permeates all those virtues and a dozen more. Like no other sign, **Libra tolerates a paradox.** It does not need the world to make sense. Opposing philosophies, opposing people, opposing alternatives – the Scales accept them all.

Mary thinks Jack is selfish. Jack thinks Mary is manipulative. Their friends are divided. One of them must be right. But which one? Only Libra understands. They are both right. Truth lies in the balance of the two. To Libra, **every truth is composed** of two **half-truths.** And no sign is less content with a half-truth.

Shadow

Truth is inherently ambiguous. If we can accept that, our perceptions are less clouded. But that knowledge is a terrible burden. We come to crossroads. We need to make decisions. And yet every decision is a definite step. Bridges burn behind us.

Want to go to medical school? That means you cannot go write poetry on Crete. Want to be married? That means you must stop being single. The mind is vast, it can hold both possibilities. But life is far narrower. There we must choose.

In the realm of the mind, a tolerance for paradox is wisdom. But in everyday life, it often means nothing but indecision. Libra can stand at the crossroads, shell-shocked by the realization **that no path is unambiguously** correct. Take the high road; you are haunted by the ghost of the low road. Take the low road; you meet the ghost of high road.

All the Scales can do is flip a coin and then **act as if they passionately believed there were no alternative.** Without commitment, life is nothing but a long wait. We cannot keep our options open forever. But Libra may try, and in that attempt it meets its shadow.

Once captured, the Scales can only bide their time. They drift. They smile sweetly. They make no enemies because they hold no position. And yet beneath the peaceful exterior, tension is mounting. Something is fundamentally wrong. What is it? No threats. No pressures. No problems. Nothing is happening.

And yet somewhere an ancient clock is ticking. With or without decisions, life goes on.

SCORPIO THE SCORPION

Element: **Water**
Mode: **Fixed**
Archetypes: **The Detective**
The Sorcerer
The Hypnotist
Glyph: ♏

The ally we *must cultivate* is *the part of* our *enemy*
which knows the truth.
–Mohandas **K.** *Gandhi*

The Symbol

You lie in your sleeping bag, rigid as a corpse. The desert sun creeps higher, threatening to turn the fillings in your teeth to molten gold.

One move and you die: a scorpion stands motionless on your belly.

Tension in your marriage. Critical politicking in your profession. Yesterday those thoughts crowded your mind. They were the center of your world. Today, with that scorpion standing there, they seem as irrelevant as a dim red star in a distant galaxy.

With that scorpion on your belly, only the awesome intensity of the present moment remains. Everything else – all pretense, all vanity, all ambition – is ripped away. Only essentials remain. And mind, naked and alert, focused sharp as a cut gem, stands ready to live or die.

That attitude, that state of consciousness, is Scorpio.

Endpoint

Here you sit reading an astrology book. Your mind is intent on it.

Presumably you are calm, reasonably comfortable. You forget your birth. Your death is an abstraction down the road. Somewhere between the two, you are floating along, taking what comes and making the best of it.

But think: you live on a planet hurtling around a gargantuan nuclear bomb. Million-ton stones blast randomly around you at a hundred miles per second. You are protected only by a thin haze of gas. And within that airy shield, you share living quarters with madmen bent on destruction. Some have a thirty-eight special. Some have neutron bombs. And even if you escape them, it does not matter: you are bound to a physical body as doomed and fragile as an orchid in a buffalo stampede.

That knowledge frightens us. We would rather not look at it. So we make our plans, buy our life-insurance policies, and avoid thinking the unthinkable. But what if we dare to think it? What if we have the courage to undo the taboo surrounding death? What happens then?

Like the person sharing a sleeping bag with a scorpion, our priorities are clarified. The future disappears. The past evaporates. We are utterly focused on the present moment. Nothing else matters. And in that present moment, all our posturing and politeness, all our phony, comfortable answers, are stripped away. Only truth remains. Like never before, we know who we are and what we want.

Should that scorpion crawl out of the bag and off into the desert, maybe the nightmare turns out to be a blessing. Maybe we carry some of that honesty and intensity and clarity forward into our lives. Maybe we are less likely to get strung out over an irredeemable past and a chimerical future.

That is the Scorpion's endpoint. To live with that kind of intensity. To bum away all pretense. To let nothing be hidden behind walls of fear. To make the unconscious conscious.

The aim of the Scorpion, in a word, is to **live every minute as if it were the last.**

Strategy

Imagine that your doctor told you that you would be dead in six months. What would you do? Let's throw in a million dollars, just to make it more interesting. Now you have the freedom to do what you please, but you had better do it quickly.

Some of us might frantically arrange a world cruise. Others, equally frantic, might try to make up for all the ignoble deeds we had done in the past. But the ones who adapted successfully would all have one behavior in common: each of them would sit down quietly, get centered, and try to **feel** what they wanted to do. They would not be thinking. They would know instinctively that logic and deduction and rationality were the wrong tools for the task, fine in their place, but inappropriate here.

They would be following the Scorpion's principal strategy to the letter: basing their actions on feelings rather than on reason.

Why? Because logic is too general, too impersonal. At life's crossroads there are typically many logical alternatives. Logically, for example, each of us could have many different careers, marry many different husbands or wives. Logic serves only one purpose: to weed out the impossible and the ridiculous. After that, the Scorpion must **feel his way through life.**

Happiness comes, in large part, from getting what we want. And we **feel** what we want, never deduce it. Scorpio knows that.

It is always that way; death just makes the principle stand out more starkly. Always, if Scorpio is to live each minute as if it were his last, he must **create a perfect alignment between his feelings and his actions**. And to accomplish that, he must destroy whatever walls prevent those feelings from entering consciousness. He must have the courage to **feel anything**, no matter how terrifying those feelings might be or what implications they might have for his life.

Thinking about death helps the Scorpion to arrive at that level of self-knowledge. Its shock value brings emotional clarity.

Morbidity is not the point; that is a distortion of the process.

The strategy is to **fully accept into consciousness the reality of one's own inescapable death.** To let death serve as a counselor. To feel the fear, to let it stir up emotions, and then to ask death the critical question: "Given that my time here is limited, what should I do next? What is **really** important to me? Which of my commitments and behavior patterns are based on the insane assumption that I am physically immortal?"

"Scorpios are sexy" is a commonplace observation in pop astrology circles. There is truth in that assertion, but it is often misinterpreted and overblown. The key is to remember that a vast reservoir of emotional energy is tied up in our sexuality and we must define sexuality here in an emotional, personal way, not just in a physical one. It is much more a need for intense emotional encounters than a need for orgasms.

To live each minute as if it were our last, to bring that kind of intensity to bear upon the present moment – this is impossible if we have lost track of our sexuality. Too many of our emotional needs, too much of our actual psychological reality, is then lost behind a wall of suppression. **And suppression creates a disharmony between actions and feelings**, the antithesis of the Scorpion's aim.

Accepting one's sexuality, feeling one's own feelings in that department, is an elemental Scorpio strategy. To get past all the glamour girls and Marlboro men telling us to "do it." To silence all the preachers and prudes telling us not to do it. To gracefully, sensitively **let one's sexuality be what it is** – that is the Scorpion's way.

But sex is not the point. Feelings are the point. Feelings that are often twisted and distorted by the alternately moralistic and hypersexualized training we receive. Feelings that we must uncover if we are to live happily and decisively in a world where everyone dies.

Resources

A guard stands on the border separating the conscious mind from the unconscious. His function is to hold out of awareness any realization that might upset us or undercut our self-image. He is conservative, judging, prudent. In the language of psychology that guard is labeled the **repressive mechanism.**

In Scorpio the repressive mechanism is defective. It works. But not well. Overwhelming emotions, disruptive thoughts, shocking, painful interpretations of circumstance erupt explosively into the mind.

Strange as it may seem, that **defective repressive mechanism is Scorpio's prime resource.** Without it, the brutally clear self-analysis so essential to the Scorpion's work would be impossible. An awareness of those shattering, sometimes life-warping feelings simply could not arise.

Failure of the repressive mechanism fills the mind with emotion, turns it inward. Consciousness becomes unrelentingly honest with itself. Endlessly, it maps its own interior terrain, searching for lost nuances of awareness, seeking to pull away the veils behind which we hide the unthinkable.

No sign is so mercilessly introspective.

Such inward intensity has outward effects as well. Just as the Scorpion penetrates so deeply into his own mind, he turns the same piercing gaze on the world around him. Instinctively suspicious, he mentally delves into the minds of those who surround him, grasping for understanding, for a knowledge of each person's innermost motivations and darkest secrets. And typically he succeeds in finding them.

The Scorpion's resource? A mind as sharp and silent as a stiletto, bent on tearing away every comforting lie, every soothing half-truth, every phony, idyllic description of our lives. A mind utterly committed to knowing itself.

Shadow

Scorpio is caught between two shadows: too much self-knowledge and too little. Each has its own pitfalls. Each is as deadly as the other.

Should it succumb to either, immediately all the aspiration, intensity, and wisdom of the sign are changed to venom.

Too much self-knowledge? To the Scorpion, that is a difficult concept to swallow. Automatically, sometimes blindly, he digs into ever-deeper strata of consciousness, always pursuing that final fact or ultimate realization that will transform his life.

Sometimes what Scorpio uncovers is too much for him to face. That repressive mechanism is there for a reason. When it is defective, awareness is confronted with grave peril: it can become hypnotized, held enthralled by feelings too complex to unravel.

Should that occur, **Scorpio collapses into moodiness.** Mind cannot tear itself away from its depths. It broods. It mentally tape-records descriptions of impossible, irresolvable situations – and plays those tapes over and over again until awareness is devitalized and exhausted into a state of despair.

Too much self-knowledge is dangerous, at least if it comes so quickly that we lose perspective. But too little can be just as corrupting, especially if that lack arises because we intentionally hold something fearful or unpleasant out of consciousness.

Should Scorpio, for example, choose to avoid thinking about death, its instinctive knowledge of its own mortality does not simply disappear. Rather, it is forced to operate outside the conscious mind, in the unconscious. The feelings remain. They continue to pressure the Scorpion's behaviors and attitudes. But he can **no longer understand the source of the pressure.**

What happens? Mind is oppressed by the certainty that "something awful is about to happen." Free-floating anxieties plague consciousness, attaching themselves to any convenient target: my car is about to break down, my boss is planning to fire me, I think I have a brain tumor.

Suppressed sexuality works the same way: the feelings remain, but we lose track of their source. Scorpio, succumbing to that shadow, finds himself endlessly hungry, endlessly unfulfilled. **But mind does not know what it wants.** It cannot understand its hunger. And, once again, a convenient target is selected: money, power, a fault-lessly clean house. Obsessively, compulsively, the Scorpion pursues those goals, only to remain unsatisfied.

Dark, brooding, sometimes treacherous, the Scorpion who has taken that road lurks glumly in his own shadow, gnawed by devils he can never see, until death draws the curtains on his self-absorption and his despair.

SAGITTARIUS THE ARCHER

Element: **Fire**
Mode: **Mutable**
Archetypes: **The Gypsy**
The Student
The Philosopher
Glyph: ↗

It is not entertainment I am seeking. It is understanding.
Understanding, understanding, and more understanding. I will stuff
myself with it, sniff it up with every pore, cram it into every orifice.
Someday it will pay off. Everything will fall into its proper place,
and I will, at last, understand.
–Laurel Coldman

The Symbol

Not the archer but the arrow. Fingers quivering with tension, the marksman releases the taut string. The curve of the bow snaps back, sending the feathered shaft darting into space.

The arrow. It flies faster than sight, whipping through the air, speeding toward the clouds. If it had eyes, it would see the archer's form grow tiny, fading to an insignificant speck in the landscape. And it would see that landscape laid out like a map, simple and schematic.

If that arrow were suddenly given a mind, what thoughts would occupy it? Like a man on a mountain peak, it would think thoughts of perspective and experience, driven by exuberance. Who fired me into this luminous sky and for what purpose? What is my place here? Where am I going? What is the reason for my existence?

Endpoint

To medieval astrologers, Sagittarius had three destinies. It symbolized the gypsy. It symbolized the student. And it symbolized the philosopher. The three were arrayed in a good-better-best hierarchy, with the philosopher on top.

Once we drop the idea that one expression of the Sagittarian energies is better than the others, those three destinies are still an effective way of understanding the meaning and purpose of the sign.

Gypsy. Student. Philosopher. What do they have in common? If each is a manifestation of Sagittarius, their common denominators must be the sign's essence.

In each one, mind projects itself outward toward a new horizon, just like our flying arrow. In each, we observe **actions that expand awareness through the gathering of unfamiliar experience.**

That expansion is the lifeblood of Sagittarius.

In the gypsy, the expansion results from a physical activity – she moves about geographically, entering new and exotic environments. The student accomplishes it intellectually, absorbing new facts and points of view. And the philosopher does it intuitively, attempting to expand consciousness, always attempting to become aware of the basic laws of the universe.

The Archer's endpoint? To realize the ultimate meaning of life. To find one's destiny in the cosmic scheme of things. To arrive at the Truth. Those are the goals of the arrow. Lofty goals indeed, and in practice their attainment is harder than walking up a flagpole.

The Archer's endpoint is perhaps the most difficult of the twelve to define at a practical level. For Sagittarius there is no clear ending, only an endless process. It is a moving, fluid state of being. An image of life as a perpetual quest. A recognition that the elemental human task is the search for meaning – and the realization that in this world of impermanence, no sacrifice of safety or security counts for anything if it stands between a man or woman and that unceasing quest.

Strategy

Gypsy. Student. Philosopher. The medieval formulation contains coded instructions for the evolving Sagittarian. The three manifestations of the Archer are not rigid descriptions of the sign's nature. They are evolutionary strategies.

To become a gypsy – that is the first step. To release the bonds that tie one to a particular culture with all its attendant values and customs. The point is not so much the need to travel as it is the need to **remain open to foreign ways of thinking.** The literal journey is simply a method Sagittarius can employ to enforce that openness.

A month in India is far more than entertainment. We are confronted with a society that operates in a way fundamentally alien to our own. If we can let go of the judgments and attitudes with which we were brought up, traveling there can teach us to **look at life from a different point of view** – and for Sagittarius, that is like lighting the fuse on the evolutionary skyrocket.

Journeys to the East are expensive and sometimes impractical. No matter. The gypsy's path is broader than the brochures at the travel agency. To make friends with an Indian living in this country – that works the same way. So does getting close to a poor person if you are rich, or getting close to a black person if you are white.

The gypsy's strategy is not simply to collect a lot of exotic passport stamps. It is the expansion of awareness through willing, openhearted contact with cultures outside our own, even if the journey is no more than a trip across town.

The way of the student is similarly deceptive if we take it on face value alone. Certainly, formal education can expand awareness. Sagittarius is fed by courses and lectures. But books do the same, even if they are read outside the auspices of an educational institution. So does any experience that compels us to look at life in a fresh way.

Standing poised on a tall sand dune, a hang glider strapped to your back, you prepare to leap into space. That too is the way of the student. Mind has opened itself to a new experience, a new opportunity to learn.

Just as the gypsy blurs into the student, the student blurs into the philosopher. All that happens is another shift in the focus. Now we have moved our attention away from eyes and ears and placed it on that deepest of human perceptual functions: intuition. We attempt, intuitively, **to grasp the wholeness of life and to find our place within it**.

The philosopher's way is dependent on the insights gathered by the gypsy and the student. Without them, he is nothing but a dried-out old pedant with a head full of bloodless hypotheses. **The philosopher's intuitive leap must be fueled by experience**. Otherwise, it can have no roots in reality.

Christianity, Buddhism, existentialism – the philosopher's strategy is to absorb all of them, but never to let any such system do his thinking for him. He must constantly seek to gather more experience, perpetually modifying and deepening his vision of life.

The Archer's strategy, in a word, is to live life as an adventure. He must surrender all notions of safety. He must willingly set aside any idea or opinion as soon as he sees himself hiding behind it. He must go unhesitatingly forward, expecting miracles, forever ready to perform that classic Sagittarian masterstroke: the leap of faith.

Resources

Personal freedom is essential to the Archer's strategies. The gypsy would wither without it. The student would be captured by mind-dulling routine. The philosopher could not gain a grand perspective, nor check it against the realities of differing circumstances.

Appropriately, a pronounced love of freedom is a basic Sagittarian resource. No sign is so fearful of constraint.

Enthusiasm, buoyant spirits, adventurousness – those are Sagittarian resources too. Whatever life throws at the Archer, he is ready. He is adaptable and resilient, able to bounce back from any adversity.

Strong Sagittarian components in an individual are like an ironclad insurance policy against the blahs. Sadness and depression are possible. But in the Archer they are temporary conditions, ready to dissipate at the hint of an adventure or a new possibility.

Sagittarius may not be born with a ready-made sense of the meaning of life. But he is born with the certainty that life means **something**. For the Archer, that is an unquestionable premise. It is as if he came into the world with an empty altar in his head – instinctively, he sets out to provide it with an icon. It may be Jesus. It may be literature. It may be world revolution. In his free-spirited way, he chooses his own gods regardless of what pressures are brought to bear upon him. But choose he will.

The Sagittarian resource? **Faith in his ideals**. That faith can take a thousand forms, but the Archer lives by it, whatever form it takes. No sign operates so unquestioningly at **the level of principle**. Regardless of costs or impracticalities, Sagittarius does what is right. That "rightness" is self-defined and not everyone agrees with it. But once we know the Archer's god, his behavior is as predictable as the course of a planet around the sun.

Shadow

There are times when prudence can be our salvation. Life is dark and tricky sometimes, full of deadly traps wearing masks of innocence. Hesitation and suspicion may save us. But hesitation and suspicion are as alien to Sagittarius as a bathing suit to an Eskimo.

In his bright-eyed, trusting enthusiasm, the Archer has blundered into many a morass. Over-optimism, overextension, and plain bad judgment are his shadow. Like a friendly golden retriever who thinks all those cars whipping down the interstate are nothing but playmates, he has often been crushed beneath the wheels of life.

He may put too much trust in the strength of those rickety steps. He may pass on a blind curve. He may follow some self-appointed guru to a mass grave – all in the name of faith.

Nowhere is the Archer's precipitous shadow so obvious as in

intimate human relationships. Freedom is precious to Sagittarian evolutionary work, yet few signs are in such peril of throwing it away for the promise of eternal romance. Once again, it is that trusting, wide-eyed attitude that snares the arrow in mid-flight. "Married in haste, repented at leisure," has been the epitaph on many an unhappy Sagittarian tomb.

Robust faith, a sense of humor, a willingness to take a plunge – those traits help us live more fully, and the Archer has them all. But unless they are balanced by a sense of how frail and fleeting our lives are, and an awareness of how easily the spark can go out of them, bright-spirited Sagittarius can become the sign of tragedy.

CAPRICORN THE SEA-GOAT

Element: **Earth**
Mode: **Cardinal**
Archetypes: **The Hermit**
The Father
The Prime Minister
Glyph: ♑

You thought, as a boy, that a mage is one who can do anything.
So I thought, once. So did we all. And the truth is that as a man's real
power grows and his knowledge widens, ever the way he can follow
grows narrower: until at last he chooses nothing,
but does only and wholly what he must do.
-Ursula K. LeGuin

The Symbol

The Sea-Goat. A mountain goat with a fish's tail; an impossible creature. A dog paddler at sea and a waddler on land – except in the world of symbolism. There, the Sea-Goat loses all clumsiness and vulnerability. He becomes a symbol of ultimate, absolute power.

He is the master of two worlds: the sea and the stony heights. The Sea-Goat scales the most treacherous peaks, breathes the most rarified air. He swims the widest oceans. Nothing can stop him. Once his mighty will is fixed on a goal, he is invincible.

He must only choose. Nothing can stand against him.

Endpoint

Ambitious, materialistic, power hungry – the faceless, gray-flannel Capricorn of popular literature is a sly devil indeed. Calculating, manipulative, quick to exploit any weakness, he is typically represented as the epitome of slick, insidious opportunism.

Such descriptions are fair pictures of Capricorn's shadow. But they have little to do with its endpoint.

It is true that the Sea-Goat symbolizes worldly power. But that does not mean money. It does not mean having your face on the cover of *Newsweek*. So many seemingly powerful people live their lives as hostages, bound by the strictures of their public roles. Their role has worldly power; they don't. And that is not the Sea-Goat's path. For Capricorn, worldly power has a different meaning. It does not signify glory. It signifies freedom. In the arena of the world, the Sea-Goat must act only according to the dictates of his essential character. **The marriage of one's nature and one's public identity** – that is Capricorn's endpoint. It is the oneness of the inward and the outward, proven and expressed in the forum of society.

In a word, Capricorn is the symbol **of integrity**. In the sign's highest expression, there are no lies and no pretenses. Only a flawless mating of visible public behavior and invisible personal essence. One's job and one's life become indistinguishable. The two are one.

To accomplish that, the Sea-Goat must be utterly immune to applause. He must never play to the crowd, although his work, being public, must invariably be executed before a crowd. Should he get hooked on social approval, everything is lost. Yet, he cannot flee from it. Those clapping hands are always there, tempting him, flirting with him.

To avoid the seductiveness of power, Capricorn must become a **master of solitude**. The point is not that he must spend time alone, although that is a legitimate strategy. The point is that he must seek approval **within himself**. To succeed, he must become indifferent to success and failure, to praise and vilification. He must stand alone.

Capricorn's endpoint? Integrity and solitude. Both must be attained, for if one fails, the other collapses with it.

Strategy

Spending time alone is an effective evolutionary strategy for Capricorn, especially in the early stages of development. The Sea-Goat must learn that he needs no one's approval, that if no one appreciates him or praises him, he can still be content with his thoughts and his projects, whatever they may be.

This is far from saying that Capricorn is a loveless sign or a cold one. The Sea-Goat can love and be loved. That in no way violates his strategy. He must only avoid **needing** another person.

Capricorn's strategy is dependent on finding practical supports for his self-sufficiency. Solitary walks. Private daydreams. Solo skiing or singlehanded sailing: anything that can be done alone can help him – reading books, meditation, any habit or avocation that transforms solitude from a burden to an opportunity, something to be pursued with enthusiasm.

Only when that inner state of solitude is attained is it safe for the Sea-Goat to turn his eyes on the world. If he does so prematurely, glamour and glitter blind him more surely than staring into the heart of the sun.

Capricorn is a climber. He looks at the glittering world, and it is as appealing and challenging to him as Everest to a Sherpa. He knows that he must ascend the peaks. The horror is that he could choose the wrong one.

This is a critical juncture in the Sea-Goat's path. Just when the world opens up before him in all its color and drama, he must fall back on his solitude. He must find the strength to look away, to tear his eyes from the presidential suite and turn them inward, toward his roots.

That turning away is not a permanent condition; the Sea-Goat must climb. He must face the world. To resist its temptations by hiding from them accomplishes nothing. He must only look away long enough to remember that he does not **need** the personal affirmation that comes from other people's praise. He already **has** his self-respect. He already knows who he is.

So reassured, Capricorn casts a cold eye on the world of celebrity and renown. He enters it, but with his mind implanted firmly on a single goal: to do only what comes naturally to him. **The Sea-Goat must select a public role that expresses his own personal values, interests, and whims**. Perhaps that role is a job. Perhaps it is something voluntary. Maybe it is a public service. Maybe it is just a personal predilection – like playing the clarinet in a Dixieland band. Whatever form it takes, people may cheer him, hold him in awe, call him master. Or they may write him off as a washout. No matter. Either way, the Sea-Goat must remain as indifferent as a galaxy. All that counts is whether he is being himself.

Resources

To plug into the success machine is not terribly difficult. One must learn some skills, smile at the right people, and stick with it for a few years. There is no shame in that, but it is not Capricorn's course.

To hack out one's own place in society as the Sea-Goat must, is far more challenging. Defeats, uncertainty, long periods with meager rewards – all those obstacles plague him. But Capricorn is prepared. He has two resources that enable him to withstand relentless pressure: patience and self-discipline.

Like no other sign, Capricorn can wait. But his waiting is not indecision. It is not vacillation. It is the intensity and stillness of a cat as he sits frozen with concentration eight feet from an unsuspecting mouse.

The Sea-Goat's self-discipline is unparalleled as well. Regardless of pressures, once he has made up his mind he sticks to his course. Fear, frustration, resistance – nothing can sway him. He may feel those forces, but **Capricorn's actual behavior always reflects his intentions, not his emotions**.

Capricorn has another resource: **an instinctive practicality**. When he adds two and two, he gets four no matter how badly he wishes they made five. Fantasy has a place in his life but only if there is a logical possibility that the fantasy can be made real. If that chance exists, the Sea-Goat works efficiently and with absolute persistence until the dream is a reality. And if the chance does not exist, he tosses it away like yesterday's newspaper.

Capricorn's resources? In a nutshell, it is an iron will. His solitude, his determination, his patience, his unerring logic – all enable him to weather the storms and discouragements of daily life while never once losing sight of his dreams. He may be slow. He may look as if he has stopped dead in his tracks. But in the end, he gets what he wants.

Shadow

The Sea-Goat's path requires enormous self-control. Applied correctly, it enables him to scale any peak. He chooses and he acts. If he meets failure, he persists. But should that self-control be misapplied, the Sea-Goat meets disaster.

Capricorn's self-control must always be applied to the objective world. It must be reflected in the nature of his **actions**. But should the Sea-Goat experience a failure of nerve, should his resolve waver, then that self-control becomes distorted. It no longer bears upon behavior. It now manifests subjectively as a suppression of one's emotional responses to the issues and developments of life.

The Sea-Goat can turn to stone.

No sign can appear so icily unemotional. While his life careens out of control, Capricorn can look as cold as a block of obsidian. Down that road, the Sea-Goat meets his darkest shadow. It is a corruption of his natural solitude. It is **loneliness**.

The lonely, unexpressive Capricorn is still a formidable creature, but now a twisted one. With his own course lost, he seeks to determine the courses of everyone around him. He becomes dictatorial and tyrannical. He develops a patronizing attitude toward people with whom be ought to be sharing his life as an equal.

And he seeks power in the world like a hungry wolf seeks carrion. Everywhere he goes he seeks to extend his authority.

Blindly, he pursues outwardly the approval he should be finding within himself. And he succeeds. He claws his way to the top with all the persistence and determination of a weasel in a rut. But when he arrives there, he is still unsatisfied. So he pushes harder. He becomes the workaholic, driving himself unmercifully, losing touch with the howling of his physical body and the aching of his heart. And he dies a victim of his role and his responsibilities, powerful, perhaps wealthy, and lonely as a grain of sand floating motionless in the void between the stars.

AQUARIUS THE WATER-BEARER

Element: Air
Mode: Fixed
Archetypes: The Genius
The Revolutionary
The Truth Sayer
The Scientist
The Exile
Glyph: ≈

If you meet the Buddha in the road,
kill him.
–Zen Buddhist saying

The Symbol

The Aquarian glyph – a pair of parallel wavy lines – is often mistaken for water. That is not the case. Those lines are serpents, symbols of knowledge.

In Eden, the serpent tempted Eve to eat the fruit of the Tree of Knowledge. She did, and God threw her and Adam out of the garden for it, setting into motion the history of the world.

But in acquiring that knowledge Eve did something more. In that single rebellious Aquarian act, she gave birth to a quality far more precious than safety, far more precious even than wisdom.

She gave birth to human freedom.

Endpoint

Freedom – that is the Aquarian endpoint. What is it? Individuality. The ability to choose our own path. To do what we want to do. To take orders from no one, be that person father, mother, president, priest, or any other authority figure.

Easier said than done.

Enormous forces are massed against our individuality – forces that can stream-roller us if we let them, turn us into dancing monkeys. Peer pressure. Conformity. Socialization. The desire to be accepted. Let them take hold, and we serve two masters: our own nature and the vagaries of those around us. Immediately, our freedom is compromised.

For Aquarius, that compromise is anathema. **The Water-Bearer's mortal enemy is the tribal instinct.** If she succumbs all is lost. She becomes just one more familiar character in the endless sitcom of our daily existence.

Aquarius and conformity: they mix just about as well as peace and nuclear warheads.

To conquer that tribal instinct, the Water-Bearer must cultivate an **absolute loyalty to truth.** She must say what she sees, regardless of consequences. She must stand firm when her freedom is challenged, whether by direct coercion or by insidious persuasion. And she must willingly accept her destiny: that of the exile, forever ordained to be out of synch with the values and motivations of her community.

The Aquarian endpoint? The flawless, uncompromising expression of self. Individuality perfected.

Strategy

Picture the Water-Bearer as one of those walled cities in the Old Testament. Times are violent. Each city-state is a separate culture, and the tension between neighboring cities is constant.

Should the Water-Bearer's walls collapse under the pressure of a siege, her culture is crushed. The victorious armies kill the Aquarian king and tear the temple gods from the pedestals, installing their own.

There can be no surrender. Once the enemy passes through the gates, holocaust ensues, with oblivion on its heels. For the Water-

Bearer, there is only one strategy: keep those defenses intact at whatever cost. No deals. No compromises. Only the hard certainty of stone and mortar.

The city-state metaphor is apt, only now we are not speaking of the cultural integrity of a historical society. We are talking about the freedom and individuality of a single human being.

The enemy is arrayed outside the walls. They mass before the gates. They prepare the battering ram.

For Aquarius, that battering ram takes many forms, but in essence it **is the pressure brought upon us by our culture to conform to an established pattern of behavior.**

Inwardly, we have a certain unique set of predilections and values. But our society has other plans for us. Ever since we could talk, we have been programmed with descriptions of what constitutes success, decency, and sanity. For most of us, plugging into those patterns is natural, even helpful. For Aquarius, it is a death sentence.

The Water-Bearer must resist the battering ram. **She must resist the coercions of her culture.** Her strategy is to follow the dictates of her own individuality, making her own choices regardless of the rage or hoots of disbelief those choices produce in the people around her.

"I will be sane, even if that means everyone else thinks I am crazy." That is the Aquarian motto.

If she follows that strategy, society may threaten to take away her freedom by force: jail or the asylum. But those are the real battering rams. Usually, cultural pressures are more subtle: "Keep on acting like that, and you will never keep a job. We will starve you, make you insecure and uncomfortable." Or: "Keep that up, and we will all laugh at you. We will label you the crazy one. We will never take anything you do seriously."

As if those rams were not enough, the Water-Bearer's enemies have a second ploy. They have already established agents within the city walls, spies whose task it is to open up the gates from inside. For the Water-Bearer, those spies take the form of **people who love her.** And they do love her, deeply and sincerely. That, unfortunately, is a far cry from saying that they understand her.

These spies have already cut through the Aquarian defenses. They are inside the walls. They may be husbands or wives. They may be friends. Often they are parents. And when the Water-Bearer makes her choices, they apply enormous pressure on her, pressure aimed at forcing her to reconsider, forcing her to **conform to their expectations**.

How? Their hearts may be in the right place, but, whether they know it or not, their methods are treacherous. These spies lead the Water-Bearer to believe that **she has a responsibility to betray herself,** that if she truly loves them she would not put them through the turmoil of watching her take the heat that goes along with being a square peg in a society full of round holes.

Facing those spies is the ultimate Aquarian test, far more difficult than resisting the battering rams. In defending her freedom, the Water-Bearer must steel herself to meet a chilling, often embittering challenge: she must be prepared to break the hearts of people who love her. No matter that their disappointment and pain come only from their thwarted desire to crush her into a mold she was never meant to fit. Their hurt is real. With one compromise, Aquarius could assuage it. And yet she cannot compromise. She cannot pretend to be other than what she is.

Is the Water-Bearer coldhearted? No. but she often looks that way. Her path is an austere one, leading her into the clear, thin stratosphere of true individuality. And if her ascent there disappoints the ground dwellers, she must sometimes live with the hurt, taking what comfort she can in the knowledge that those broken hearts are the inescapable price of freedom.

Resources

"Every year before we plant the com we sacrifice a virgin to the rain god. Every year he sends us rain in return. Yet you say that this year we must not sacrifice anyone, that the rains will come of their own accord."

Some Aquarian ten thousand years ago heard those words and stuck to her guns anyway. If she was not killed for her convictions, then her certainty changed the course of human history.

Why? Because she **saw the truth** and no one could convince her otherwise. She looked at the obvious and saw something that nobody else could see.

There is a word for that radical independence of mind – a word that describes the most critical Aquarian resource. That word is **genius.**

Genius – we are taught to think of it as extreme intelligence, but that is misleading. Intelligence is only a tool of genius and can exist without it. Genius is the capacity to think freshly, to view old problems in new ways. **Genius is the ability to think in ways we have not been taught to think.** The Water-Bearer has that quality in abundance.

Let's not sacrifice a virgin this year: the woman who first had that rebellious Aquarian thought was immediately placed under unrelenting pressure. Perhaps there were a thousand people in the village. If so, nine hundred ninety-nine of them thought the idea was madness. **But our Aquarian heroine knew it was the truth** – and that certainty sustained her. And it sustains Aquarians today in exactly the same way. They know their choices are right even if nobody else agrees.

The Water-Bearer has a second resource. Without it, her genius would be of little use. Mere knowledge alone does not prepare one to resist a thousand accusing fingers. Her second resource is an implacable, unbending stubbornness. When she plants her feet, she makes the Matterhorn look like dust in the morning breeze. Nothing can move her.

Shadow

Such stubbornness serves the Water-Bearer's strategy. To resist the crushing weight of the tribal instinct, she must have an unflinching certainty about herself. Somewhere, deep in the core of her psyche there has to be an unshakable conviction that **her perceptions are valid**, regardless of how violently or eloquently her foes argue against them.

But that same stubbornness can destroy her.

The Water-Bearer can invent some artificial statement of her independence and defend it with all the stubbornness of Davy Crockett at the Alamo. She may refuse to wear anything but blue jeans. She may insist on her right to use four-letter words in front of the minister. She may categorically refuse to listen to anything except classical music. Those eccentricities are harmless enough in themselves. The horror is that they sidetrack the far more fundamental Aquarian process, that of individuation.

That quirky stubbornness is the Water-Bearer's shadow. Instead of defending her right to shape her own life, she acquiesces to the pressures of society. She follows a fundamentally conventional course, side-stepping legitimate developmental issues. And then all that Aquarian rebelliousness and freedom are bled away into some essentially safe arena.

The genius disappears. There is no rebellion, no revolutionary thinking. All that remains is one more nameless face in the crowd, leading a predictable life, colored only by a few exasperating but ultimately harmless peculiarities.

The Aquarian shadow is darker yet.

Conventionality is no sin. The vast majority of us are inherently conventional people. When we fit in with society, we fit in with ourselves too. Not so with the Water-Bearer. For her, conventionality is a mask. She may choose to wear it, but if she does, she pays a terrible price: the life she leads is not her own.

An Aquarian traveling that dark pathway may have the outward appearance of success. She may be poised. She may be graceful. She may be affluent and witty. But she feels like an outsider, like a foreign agent who has flawlessly adopted a false identity.

The Water-Bearer feels **alienated**.

Then, even the people closest to her never know her. They go through the motions of relationship. But they sense that there is something aloof about her. She seems distant, perhaps cold or un-feeling. Her words are right. She fulfills her responsibilities. She laughs at the right jokes. She makes jokes of her own. But no one is fooled. Everyone knows that something essential is simply not being revealed.

Behind those eyes, as clear and penetrating as a dagger of ice, there is nothing. Only a missing person.

PISCES THE FISHES

Element: **Water**
Mode: **Mutable**
Archetypes: **The Mystic**
The Dreamer
The Poet
The Face Dancer
Glyph: ♓

... we are luminous beings. We are perceivers. We are an awareness:
we are not objects: we have no solidity. We are boundless.
–don Juan Matus, quoted by Carlos Castaneda

The Symbol

Ocean. Not Fishes, but the home of fish: Mother Ocean, the realm of undersea sierras, of luminous plankton, of lost cities. Ocean: mother of life, brooding symbol of all that is impenetrable, all that can be felt but never known.

Ocean: washing the shores of continents, carrying art and thoughts among the nations, carrying war, carrying disease and pestilence, carrying wine and food, poets and musicians, endlessly mixing and blending the cultures of earth.

The Piscean ocean: liquid, flowing symbol of the unutterable mystery that binds us all together. The symbol of life.

Endpoint

Buddhist teachers in high Tibet counsel their students to regard the world as a dream. People, events, relationships, even the mountains themselves – all are to be seen as mirages, only a play of insubstantial images in the mind.

In the West we often misinterpret the Buddhist idea. We take it to mean that the world is not real, that its atoms and molecules are illusory: a tough notion to swallow, especially when you have just stubbed your toe on an "illusory" bedpost.

To those Buddhist teachers, the reality or unreality of the world is not the issue. The point is deeper: it is a recognition that we do not experience the world directly – **we experience an awareness of the world**.

An awareness: something cerebral, something in our heads. What we take to be the world is an electrochemical phenomenon occurring in the folds and creases of our brains. Only a play of images. Only a dream.

For most of us, that kind of knowledge is of no practical use. Whether we were bitten by a dog or bitten by the illusion of a dog does not concern us: we hurt either way.

For Pisces, that knowledge is everything. Why? Because Pisces is the symbol of **consciousness itself**. Traditionally associated with mysticism, the Fishes' evolutionary pathway represents a fundamental alteration in the way the mind operates. A shifting of gears. Instead of observing the world, **Pisces observes the mind observing the world**. The objective universe evaporates. All that remains is a vast network of subjective reactions.

All that remains is a dream.

The Piscean endpoint? A realization. A subtle reorientation of the mind. A reorientation that changes nothing and yet changes everything. It is the knowledge that wherever we go, whatever we do, whatever we see, we can meet only one inescapable reality: our own consciousness.

Strategy

Relentlessly, the events of our lives pressure us to believe that the world is "out there," that there is an objective reality independent of mind. Cold wind howls through our clothes, making our bones ache.

Hot grease pops on the stove, burning a scar into our forearm. Our lover disappears and we have a sickness in our stomach for months.

Action and reaction.

Every Piscean strategy revolves around subverting that belief in the objective universe. The Fishes must lose their certainty. They must let go of the world.

How? One strategy is to spend a few minutes each day focusing on the mind itself. To close the eyes, slow the breathing, still the thoughts, and simply **experience consciousness.** Not the contents of consciousness – not the worries and theories and noise that normally fill the mind – but consciousness itself. Empty. Formless. Peaceful.

One name for that process is meditation. But that word has become loaded. It conjures up images of incense and austerities – of Hindu gentlemen with long white beards and cryptic smiles. None of that is necessary. For Pisces, meditation is a natural, organic function. It implies no theology, no metaphysics. We might just as well call it "spacing out."

Whatever name we give it, meditation is an essential Piscean evolutionary strategy. Through it, mind becomes aware of itself. It loses some of its fixation on the barrage of information that continually floods it through the five senses.

Creativity works the same way. As the Fishes unleash their creative powers, the outer world recedes from center stage. The next line of the poem, the next note of the sonata, the next image

in the painting – all arise in the mind, not in the objective realm. They direct attention away from physical reality, toward awareness itself.

The evolutionary strategy? Pisces must play out its creative inspirations, whether in the form of art or in the pure fantasy of secret daydreams. Why? Because in the **free play of imagination, we experience the inner world as solid and real**. We grant our subjective lives, however temporarily, the same reality that we normally accord to the world of events and circumstances. And for the Fishes, that is like giving eyesight to the blind.

Realistically, we cannot take up permanent residence in our imaginations. We have our relationships and our responsibilities. We have our physical bodies to maintain. The Fishes, like the rest of us, must live in the world. But living in the world need not slow down their work. Living in the world vivaciously and colorfully, can be a Piscean evolutionary strategy too. They do not need to withdraw to a Tibetan monastery. **The Fishes must only change the way they look at the world**. Nothing else requires alteration.

Austerities? Pisces does not need them. Austerities are just more outward behavior, and no sign benefits less from believing that behaviors have any significance. It must only avoid any mindset in which **objects and events are granted existence independent of mind**. Compassion, helpfulness, non-competitiveness – if the Fishes can sustain those attitudes, observing with equanimity the ebb and flow of their terrestrial fortunes, then even the most active and stimulating of lives can support their evolutionary strategy.

The Piscean strategy? It is letting go of the world. It is a recognition that consciousness itself is the only reality we can ever contact and the only reality that ever needs to be adjusted.

Resources

Where do we go if we let go? That question alone is enough to keep most of us clinging desperately to our circumstances and our fictions, furiously attempting to do the impossible: to create a safe, stable niche for ourselves in this roller coaster of an existence.

Not Pisces. Instinctively, the Fishes are aware that personality is only a cork bobbling on a far vaster sea: the sea of consciousness. Whenever they feel the urge they can take a deep breath and plunge into the territories submerged within the mind.

For Pisces, the **mind itself is a primary resource**. It is the sign's refuge, its escape route from the insults and pressures of life. A fairyland. A world of wonder and peace, of endless fascination. A world that is always available.

And it beckons them.

Images arise spontaneously out of the depths, filling awareness with fantasy and inventiveness. Like no other sign, Pisces can **imagine**. Whether that imagination leads to artwork or to daydreaming is not important: either way, attention is pulled inward, away from its instinctive preoccupation with circumstance.

Empathy and gentleness are Piscean resources too. Personality is flexible in the Fishes. It bends and flows, adapting to changing situations. Understanding other people, feeling compassion for them, comes easily. The Fishes simply imagine that they were in the other person's position. Effortlessly, they seek to locate that **alien subjectivity** within their own fluid awareness. It is as if Piscean consciousness possesses the property of containing all possible human viewpoints simultaneously.

Finally, the Fishes have an **instinctive awareness of higher levels of consciousness**. From childhood, they busy themselves mapping the territory of mind, stretching out toward the frontiers of the psyche. Some become religious. Others develop a fascination with psychology. Many become interested in clairvoyance and other paranormal phenomena.

Whatever form that exploration takes, it represents another key Piscean resource: **a sense of the possibility of self transcendence**. The Fishes may express themselves in countless different ways, but all of them come into the world with three core insights: life is mystery, circumstances are its veil, and consciousness itself is the key to unraveling it.

Those three resources are given. From then on, the Fishes are on their own.

Shadow

Pisces must be fascinated with its own consciousness. Without that bewitchment, all evolutionary work would be stymied. And yet that fascination of itself is insufficient. It must be directed and disciplined. Failure there leads to horrors.

The Fishes can become shell-shocked.

Their minds flood with images and impressions. An overwhelming tide of emotion, a tide of fear and vain dreams, rushes through awareness, overwhelming the personality. And Pisces just sits there, eyes wide as saucers, while the cellars and dungeons of the mind erupt, shattering the individuality.

If those explosions from the deep self cannot safely be channeled into creativity and meditation, they are more fatal than the guillotine, and more brutal for their slowness.

First, the Fishes simply drift. So much effort goes into maintaining some semblance of a normal personality that little is left over for life strategies and commitments. A job is accepted. Relationships are established. And from that point on, Pisces follows the path of least resistance.

Soon, life takes on a logic of its own. It runs away with the Fishes like a spooked stallion, with them trying only to avoid being thrown. Increasingly they view their lives in the third person, as if they were only characters in an incomprehensible film.

That emptiness, coupled with Piscean sensitivity, leads to the ultimate pitfall: **the Fishes attempt to escape from the objective world into the subjective one**. No insight is involved. No recognition of the dreamlike qualities of life. Only a search for numbness.

Pisces may begin to drink. They may develop a dependence on tranquilizers or hallucinogens. Those Piscean shadows are well documented in the popular astrological literature.

But there are other shadows, less understood.

The Fishes may flood themselves with books, or television or music. They may become obsessed with food or with sex. They may sleep ten hours a day.

None of those activities are wrong. That is not the point. It is only that they can be used to stimulate subjectivity to such an extent that objective reality is temporarily blotted out. There is no transformation of one's perceptions or cognitive processes. All that happens is that the evolutionary issues are forced into the background, replaced by shallow and meaningless surrogates.

Pisces's shadow? It is **escapism.** Mind, in all its imagination and creativity, hides from the world, biding its time, turning away from every obstacle, and waiting for fate to deal it that last bad hand.

Planets

Aries. Virgo. Aquarius. Put them together and we are back to the prime symbol: the perfect circle. And that circle is passive. It just sits there, eternal as the sky.

For signs to touch us, an active force must be introduced. Some mediator must stand halfway between heaven and earth, translating celestial language into human terms.

Planets do that. They ignite the system. Without them, there could be no astrology, only deadness and abstraction. It is the planets that touch us, not the signs. It is the planets that carry the zodiacal energies down to us, implanting them in our cells and tissues, shaping our lives.

But how? On the face of it, the idea is crazy. Mighty Jupiter is a half-billion miles away. When a baby is born, even the doctor's gravitational effect on him is far greater. How can a planet have any effect on us? How can it possibly be **symbolic** of anything?

How does astrology **work?** It is a knotty question. I could point to the established correlation between crimes of passion and the full moon. I could point out impressive statistical studies linking career choices with the rising and setting of certain planets. If you are interested, you will find references to that kind of material in the appendices. But I am not writing this book to prove the validity of astrology. Hopefully, you will be able to check that out for yourself after reading these pages.

Still, it bothers me when people say planets cannot possibly affect us. Science aside, in one way at least a planet's touch is real and undeniable. Go out on any clear night. Find Venus or Saturn in the sky. Stare at it for a while. What is really happening? Electromagnetic vibrations are plunging across millions of miles of void, hitting our retinas at 186,000 miles per second, creating **biochemical** changes in our eyes and brains. At least in the visual sense, planets touch us *every* day. The wonder of the process is simply veiled by familiarity.

Light is not the only form of energy arriving on earth from planetary sources. There are radio waves, microwaves, X-rays, infrared radiation, and so on. Any might ultimately prove to be the carrier of the mind-shaping astrological forces. Or perhaps those forces are of an utterly alien nature. We just don't know. At this point in history we have not yet arrived at anything like a coherent *theory* of celestial influence. The loss to individuals is slight. Even without understanding the mechanics of the process, a sensitive astrological reading can be of invaluable **practical** help to a person facing life changes.

Who cares if we don't yet understand precisely what is going on? That kind of uncertainty is perfectly acceptable in hard science. Physicists, for example, still do not have an airtight *theory* of how gravity functions. All they have done so far is learn how to describe the phenomenon *very* precisely. Astrology is in exactly the same position. We don't comprehend **how** the planets work, but we have learned to predict and describe their effects.

And the effects are quite real. Planets are power lines that link us somehow to forces we do not yet understand. Each one is like a filter transmitting light, but also coloring it. Mars adds one tone, Mercury another. When a planet passes through a sign it conducts **something** down to earth. But in so doing, the nature of that **something** is distorted. The planet affects it. Changes it. No planet, then, ever allows us to see a sign **directly.** Mediation means distortion. It is as if we must gaze at the signs through colored glass.

How does it work? Again, we don't know yet. But here is a picture that is probably not far from the truth. It is only the bare skeleton of an idea. Perhaps before we are much older, science will hang on it the flesh of facts and observations.

The zodiac is a vast wheel of light. A prismatic spectrum with twelve color zones, it encircles earth like a halo. Beneath that halo move the planets. These operate like tinted lenses each of a different hue. They traverse the signs at varying speeds, sometimes stopping, sometimes moving backward. Always they take the zodiacal light and **focus** it, training it down on the earth, much like a child igniting fallen leaves with a magnifying glass.

But the **light is corrupted in transmission;** planets distort it.

Now it is far more complex than the simple reds and greens of Aries and Taurus. Saturn may add a hint of gray to the red; Jupiter may tint the green with wisps of purple.

There are many of these light streams. We know often – the sun, the moon, and the eight planets. There may be more. All of the streams fuse on impact with earth, much like floodlights of varying tones bathing a stage in a single color.

And planets never rest; the light streams are constantly shifting. Always they are moving against the zodiacal backdrop, always transmitting different hues.

What arrives here on earth is a melded rainbow of planetary rays, varying minute by minute. And somehow that infinitely variable, eternally renewed tone is crystallized within us at the moment we are born. It is unique. It is as unrepeatable and as fleeting as a moment. And it is our identity and our purpose, to be unraveled over a lifetime.

Two Solar Systems

None of this has much to do with the way an astronomer would describe the solar system. It is almost as if there were two distinct systems of planets. One is for astronomers; the other is for astrologers. Both are composed of the same elements: Mercury, Mars, Jupiter, and so on. But differences in perspective make the two look quite different.

The astronomer's point of view is not the earth. It lies on the observation deck of a starship a billion miles above the sun. From there the solar system appears to be laid out like a diagram in a sixth-grade science text. In other words, the astronomer sees it objectively. And what he sees is an orderly system. All the planets move in the same direction. Each of them keeps to a certain path, a certain distance from the sun, more or less. Each moves at a fairly constant speed. Near the center of the system, there are four "terrestrial" worlds – small, rocky planets whizzing through their orbits at relatively high speeds, all packed in close to the sun. Then there is a wide gap filled only with a haze of stone: the asteroid belt. Beyond the asteroids the astronomer sees another quartet of worlds. These are the "gas giants." Much larger than the terrestrial planets, the giants are great mush balls of methane and ammonia. These four are spread out over a vastly greater volume of space than the innermost worlds, and their pace is much less frenetic. Finally, right on the edge of the system (as far as we know) lies Pluto. This is the joker in the planetary deck: a dwarf among the giants, following an erratic orbit.

The astrologer sees the solar system differently. He does not see the planets as they are, nor does he want to. He sees them only as they **appear to be.**

The astrologer's viewpoint is not some starship hovering halfway to Orion's belt: it is right here on earth. He seeks a different truth. Not the abstract truth of the astronomer, but an experiential truth. Not the way things are, but the way they look.

What does the astrologer see? Chaos. Some planets whip through the zodiac. The moon, by far the swiftest, passes through a sign in just two or three days. For many planets the journey around the ecliptic consumes decades. Pluto, for example, requires 248 years to complete the circuit.

This variety of orbital speeds insures that the solar system is continuously changing.

At one moment we may find Saturn in Virgo and Pluto in Sagittarius. In twenty-nine years the ringed planet has completed another passage around the sun and returned to Virgo. But by then Pluto has moved only as far as Aquarius. While Saturn in Virgo has certain specific significance, the fact that Pluto is now in a different sign makes the two situations quite distinct. If we wait two and a half centuries, we again find Pluto and Saturn where they were originally – but by then Uranus and Neptune have altered their positions and again we have a unique situation.

Countless millennia must elapse before a given pattern of planets appears a second time. Even then, gradual shifts in planetary orbits due to the interaction of gravitational fields within the system introduce slight variations. For all practical purposes we can say that at any given instant the alignment of astrological influences within the solar system is a new event, unprecedented and unrepeatable.

Our terrestrial vantage point confuses the picture even further. Earth is the third planet from the Sun. Two planets lie closer to the center of the system; all others are deeper in space. Earth races among them at about sixty-five thousand miles per hour. And it spins on its axis like a top. Watching planets from a platform like that is like watching a ballet from a rollercoaster. All the soothing orderliness of the astronomer's solar system is lost. Nonsense, confusion, and illogic replace it.

Retrogradation

Our moving platform produces even stranger illusions: planets stop and go, change course, reverse themselves. When a planet appears to be going backward, we say it is **retrograde.**

Why does it happen? What makes a planet appear to turn in its tracks?

Let's imagine we are driving along in our car. Up ahead, running along the roadside, we see a horse. While we are still far behind him, our eyes tell us exactly what is happening: the horse is moving forward. At the moment we overtake him, everything changes. For a couple of seconds, we observe the horse moving backward against the scenery. It is just a trick our eyes play on us. But that is what we see.

Precisely the same illusion occurs in the solar system. But, unlike the situation with the horse, our brains are not nearly so quick in figuring out what is really happening. Earth is our fast car. Only two planets, Mercury and Venus, move more quickly. All the others are slow horses. As we pass them in our orbit, they appear to stop and move backward for a while.

Even the two speedsters, Mercury and Venus, exhibit retrogradation, though for different reasons. Like us, they orbit the sun, only much closer in. But our eyes don't tell us anything about orbits. All we see are lights moving in the sky. As the two inner planets spin around the sun, we observe them oscillating from side to side. It is as if we were watching a child on a carousel. As we follow him, our head turns first to the right, then to the left. It is the same with Mercury and Venus. When they pass in front of the sun, they appear to move one direction. Passing behind the sun on the other side of the orbital carousel, the direction is reversed. So, even though the reasons are different, the bottom line is the same: Mercury and Venus go retrograde just like the outer planets do.

Only the sun and moon are immune.

The sun never goes retrograde simply because it is the center of the system. We always orbit it in the same direction. And that produces the illusion that it orbits us-again in the same direction.

The moon is the only important body in the solar system that really does orbit the earth. Its path through space never changes and we watch it from a steady platform. So there can be no retrogradation.

What does retrogradation mean? We will look at that later in this chapter. Right now, the point is that to the astrologer, the solar system is an unpredictable, disorderly place. Imagine a mechanical shooting gallery in a maze of mirrors – that's close. Planets speed up and slow down without warning. They approach us, grow dazzlingly bright, then fade off into the distance. They stop in their tracks. They move backward and forward. They form clumps, then spread out across the sky. What we see is totally different from the astronomer's orderly universe with its immutable laws.

Astrology and astronomy. Are they natural enemies? All too often it looks that way. Reputable astronomers go on national television, read a couple of sentences from one of those silly astrological newspaper columns, and purport to have thereby debunked astrology. Astrologers retaliate by pooh-poohing the "coldness" of astronomy, implying that it has fallen into the hands of men and women with microprocessors where their hearts should be.

It is a shame, because even though the astrologer and the astronomer are so often cast as rivals, they are really of the same blood. The raw material of their work is the same: space and the human mind. The real difference between them is that to the astrologer, space-and specifically the planets it contains – has an impact on our experiences here on earth. Astrology is just astronomy inside out. Instead of the mind trying to comprehend the universe, we use the universe as a key to comprehending the mind. And strange as that seems, it works. Why? Once again, we don't know. But we can prove it. And so can you. Just learn the language. Take it on faith at first. Absorb the words. Form the sentences. Then judge for yourself.

Introducing the Players

Each planet has a unique personality. Each symbolizes a certain compartment in human consciousness. Intellect. Personal power. Emotional bonding. A sense of self-transcendence.

None of these compartments is ever completely absent in anyone: every birthchart contains all ten. We vary only in terms of which compartments are emphasized and how we choose to express them. If we can openly and willingly face the issues the planets represent then they can guide us. They can teach us how to make ourselves happier. But if we resist learning, then they are as harsh as wind-driven sleet on raw flesh. It is up to us. We do have an inside track: if we choose to learn the language, the lesson plan is ours to read. It is the birthchart.

So far we know of only ten planets in our solar system. With the advent of orbiting telescopes, we will very likely meet more. But for now, ten are plenty. Let's meet them.

THE SUN

Glyph:	☉
Function:	The development of a coherent, operational self-image. The focusing of one's willpower and capacity for positive action. The creation of ego.
Dysfunction:	Selfishness, insensitivity, tyranny over the lives of others, vanity, pomposity, inflexibility; imperiousness.
Key Questions:	Who am I? What kinds of experiences help me strengthen and clarify my self image? Where can I find and expand my personal power? What unconscious biases shape my view of the world?

A warm salt breeze. Our backs on the sand after an hour's play in the surf. Sunlight pouring down like molasses, relaxing every cell in our body. What does the sun mean? To answer that one, you don't have to go meditate in a Tibetan cave. You don't even have to read this book. All you have to do is go out and lie on the beach on a bright August day.

The sun's meaning? Simple: it means **life**. Instinctively, we know that. No scientific arguments are necessary. That is a truth so obvious that we can **feel** it. The life-giving sun is the center of the solar system. Everything orbits around it. The gravity produced by its enormous mass holds the planets in their tracks.

Astrologically, the sun works the same way: it is the **gravitational center of the human personality**. It is the focal point of all the varied functions that coexist in each of us. Our sense of identity. Our sense of being a distinct person with certain ways of feeling and seeing, of shaping a life.

Without the sun a person would be lost, paralyzed by contradictory whims, staring blankly out into the cosmos.

Focus. Organization. Those are the sun's tasks. But how does the sun organize the nine remaining planetary functions? How does it take qualities as hostile to each other as our need to dominate and our need to dream, and make them get along together in the same personality? The same way it accomplishes that among the planets in the solar system: with its gravity. But the gravity in this case takes a psychological form. It is that endlessly fascinating, irresistibly attractive faculty at the core of each of us: ego. **Ego is the focal point of the mind just as the sun is the focal point of the solar system**. The mechanisms are precisely parallel.

Sun creates ego by slipping a set of assumptions into the unspoken dimensions of consciousness, assumptions about the purpose of life, assumptions we may never acknowledge but that underlie every breath we take.

We all face the same blank slate: birth and death with nothing but question marks in between. One person fills the slate with work and career. Another sails around the world. A third becomes addicted to heroin. A fourth enters the monastery.

Why? Each reflects his unconscious assumptions about life, assumptions that always seem **natural and obvious** to him. Each reflects the form of his ego. Each reflects the sun.

Those ego-shaping solar assumptions are always arbitrary.

They vary strikingly from one person to the next. But they don't feel arbitrary. To us they always seem like the natural order of things. The businessman cannot quite grasp what motivates the junkie; the adventurous sailor scratches his head at the thought of choosing thirty years in the monastic cell. Our own assumptions always make perfect sense – to us. We cannot understand why everyone else fails to see them.

Sun, in creating ego, also creates blindness and insensitivity.

We get trapped in our individuality, insulated from the overwhelming array of options life affords. **But the sun is what enables us to** act. Without it, we would turn to jelly. Consciousness itself cannot interact with the world; its function is only to observe and react subjectively. Never could it positively seek a specific kind of experience or shield itself from another kind. That is the domain of ego. It is the part of the psyche that makes **choices.** And without choice, nothing happens.

But for choice to occur, ego must first coalesce. A personality, with all its hungers, all its visions, must take form. A myth must be created, and to us it must be an utterly convincing one. That is the work of the sun.

From some cosmic viewpoint, our solar identity may be a vanity, an absurd posturing. It may be a myth. But it is not a totally groundless one. That myth arises from deep within us. It has roots.

The condition of the sun in the birthchart helps us see those roots, but even once we see them they must still be nurtured. Despite its superficial bravado, ego is timid, hesitant to take form. The sun must be carefully fed, made to feel safe. All the while we must guard against allowing it to cloak its uncertainty in delusions of grandeur. The process is delicate; if we err, we must err in the direction of indulging the sun. Life will correct that eventually. But if ego fails to emerge confidently and vigorously, then all is lost. We become nothing but a disorganized pattern of psychological fragments, devoid of unity, will, or purpose. A space case.

How do we feed the sun? Later we go into detail. For now let's have a look at a simple example. Say the sun lies in Sagittarius. As we saw in the last chapter, that sign refers to the ability to break up routines, to gather experience from outside the boundaries of our accustomed environment. With the solar myth rooted in Sagittarius, such a person would realize deeper feelings of well-being and psychological integration as a result of seeking Sagittarian kinds of experience – adventures, leaps of faith, journeys, and so on. That remains true even if the rest of the chart suggests all the fire and gypsy spirit of Dagwood Bumstead.

The other eleven signs operate the same way. Each prescribes a specific experiential "vitamin" guaranteed to vivify the psyche. Swallow the vitamin and the sun shines more brightly. Know someone who has a perpetual case of the blahs? Who watches endless television? Whose behavior is as ritualized and boring as an automatic elevator? You know someone who is suffering from a starved sun. Those are the symptoms: fail to feed the sun and spirit dies.

THE MOON

Glyph:	☽
Function:	The development of the ability to feel or to respond emotionally. The development of subjectivity, impressionability and sensitivity. The development of what we might call a soul.
Dysfunction:	Emotional self-indulgence, timidity, laziness, wishy-washiness, overactive imagination, indecision, moodiness.
Key Questions:	What kinds of experiences are most essential to my happiness? When moodiness and irrationality overtake me, how are they expressed? What unconscious emotional needs motivate my behavior?

The half-empty bottle of Bordeaux glistens in the firelight, neglected. On the sofa, before the stone hearth, you sit with your new flame. Conversation has stopped. Awkwardly, expectantly, eyes meet, turn away, return. Just then, the moon emerges from behind a cloud, pours through the windowpane. It startles both of you, filling your eyes with yellow light. You reach for each other.

You are not in love. But that's good for another five seconds. The moon. Queen of Mysteries. We all know what meaning it has romantically. Astrologically its significance is about the same. The moon symbolizes **feelings**. To understand the moon, we begin where we did with the sun: our eyes. After that, all we have to do is put two and two together. We interpret the universal poem, much as did the original astrologers. All the clues are there. We must only find them and bind them together.

Apart from its sheer luminosity, the most striking clue the moon offers is its variability. It is always changing, always passing through phases. Unlike the sun, we never know exactly what shape it will take. Nor do we know where or when we will see it. The moon surprises us. We glance up and there it is, hanging pale as a ghost in the bright blue sky. Or poking up through the pines at four in the morning. Or simply hiding, not visible anywhere at any time. Always the moon seems to be reacting to something outside itself, registering those reactions in its appearance. The sun dominates its environment. The moon's way is not like that; it adjusts and responds, always giving and taking.

Luna symbolizes the part of consciousness that reacts and responds, that is sensitive to its surroundings, melding into them rather than shaping them or resisting. It represents the **mood** of the psyche, the way life feels. It represents the impressionability, the irrational, emotional substratum of mind. Heart: that is a key word for the moon. Pure emotion. It leaves the rationality of the "head" to other planetary functions.

Far more fluid than the sun, Luna fertilizes the imagination, filling awareness with imagery and fantasy. To fulfill its visibly more dynamic function, the sun must screen out a great deal of unconscious material. It must guard the ego. Not so the moon. It erupts out of the unconscious, reveling in the richness of the psyche, censoring nothing. And sometimes the intensity of the feelings it creates can be too much for us. We get overwhelmed. Moody. Depressed.

Hard, linear, Monday-morning reality holds little allure for the moon. Its function is to feel, not to act or make decisions. It can, as a result, look lazy as a stone. Left alone, the moon would do no more than dream. Making choices means burning bridges behind us. The moon would rather live in the imagination, where all possibilities can be kept alive all the time simply by never choosing to live one out.

Still, the moon is the soul of life. Without it, all experience would be mechanical, a pointless meshing of gears. It is the moon that gives happiness and fulfillment. Despair and ennui are its gifts too, for they are the other side of the same coin. The moon is love; it is fear; it is human warmth and human depravity. The sun may build pyramids and space shuttles, but it is the moon that puts the sparkle in our eyes when we behold them.

To feel happy, we must enliven our moon. Like the sun, it must be fed. And the birthchart gives us the formula. Although interpretation is a subject for later chapters, let's look briefly at one example. Imagine that the moon lies in Leo, a sign of self-expressiveness and creativity, as we saw earlier. With the moon in that sign, there is an emotional need to perform and to receive applause. Such a configuration promises playfulness, an entertaining, engaging quality. But it may backfire. The vigor and intrusiveness of the performance may put people off. Then, without applause, the moon's timidity may take over. Feelings of being unappreciated and unloved, however groundless, may cripple the person. Life will **feel** empty and pointless, regardless of how full it may look on the surface.

The moon makes no sense. It doesn't care to. It is only an emotion, a need to love and be loved. And if the moon withers, the heart of life becomes the heart of darkness. We become no more than broken-hearted cogs in a random universe. The moon is that most fleeting and delicate of creatures. It is our joy.

The Significance of Retrogradation

The sun and moon can never turn retrograde. The concept is irrelevant to our understanding of them. But from now on we investigate planets that have the capacity to stop in their tracks and actually appear to reverse their motion through the heavens. Before we go any further, let's grasp the astrological significance of this astronomical phenomenon.

Planets are channels for the **expression** of signs. In that sense, all of them are extroverted. But when a planet is retrograde, it is going against the ordinary currents. Its polarity is reversed. Instead of flowing outward in the normal extroverted pattern, a portion o its vitality is directed deeper into the mind, toward the unconscious, away from the world.

Traditional astrologers often claim that it is "bad" for a planet to be retrograde, that it has a harder time expressing itself. There is a kernel of truth in that assertion, although whenever we hear the word **bad** in connection with any astrological configuration we should immediately be suspicious. A retrograde planet often leaves that aspect of an individual's personality tinged with shyness or backwardness. But that is only half the story. Such a planetary function often possesses extraordinary depth and sensitivity.

Retrogradation, above all, leads to independence.

When planetary force is directed away from the world, it does not just evaporate. It continues to function as powerfully as ever. All that shifts is the arena. Safely hidden deep in the mind, insulated from much of the social programming that shapes more extroverted planets, the retrograde planet grows up like a wild child. It is completely, and perhaps dangerously autonomous. The problem is how to coax the wild child in from the forest. He is suspicious of civilization, uncomfortable there. If he comes back from the woods with his gifts it is because he chooses to.

A retrograde planet represents an aspect of a person's character that lacks confidence in itself. It feels awkward and insecure – unworthy – although those feelings may wear a cloak of bravado and defensiveness.

When you see a retrograde Mercury or Neptune or any of the others, treat it as you would a foreigner. Remember that it feels out of place, afraid of doing something wrong. That planet is a gold mine of fresh ideas, but they are buried deeply. Unearthing them takes patience and diplomacy.

The main point to remember is to avoid getting carried away about the importance of a planet being retrograde. It is certainly significant. But the fundamental meaning of the influence is unchanged. Mercury is still Mercury. Jupiter will not turn into Saturn just because it is going backward. The main effect is that the planet is quieted down.

One more related note: when a planet is about to turn retrograde or to resume its normal direct motion, we say that it is **stationary.** Being stationary does not alter the core meaning of a planet any more than being retrograde does; it just turns up the volume on the influence. That compartment in the person's mind is handling extra-high voltage. It often becomes a dominant feature in his character, and almost always a stubborn one.

Let's meet some more planets.

MERCURY

Glyph:	☿
Function:	Intelligence. Transmission of information; talking, teaching, writing. Reception of information; listening, learning, reading, observing.
Dysfunction:	Nervousness, rationalization, worry, flightiness, intellectualism, chattering, inconsistency, hyperactivity.
Key Questions:	What are my intellectual and communicative strengths? What are my intellectual and communicative weaknesses?
If Retrograde:	Mind turned inward, freed to think in independent, imaginative, innovative terms. Possible difficulty in self-expression; words do not form.

A stroke of luck: you have been chosen as a contestant on a TV quiz show. If your good fortune holds, you walk away with a classy new car and a week in Hawaii. If it doesn't, you look like a jackass in front of ten million people. You have been prepped. Made up. You walk out under the lights, smiling like Miss America, feeling tense as an astronaut at T minus one.

You get through the pleasantries with the emcee. Who are you? What do you do? You greet your opponent. Now the pressure. Who was Bogart's leading lady in *The Big Sleep*? Tick, tick, tick ... better think fast ... Buzz! Your opponent will be driving home in that new Chevy if you don't act quickly. Where is Tasmania? What is a quahog? Where did the name bikini come from? On and on. Beads of sweat. Think, think, think. Who was the first man to set foot on the moon? What was that name? The clock is ticking ... That's it! Hit the buzzer!

Pack your bags for Hawaii. Mercury has come through for you. This is the planet in charge of the library we keep in our heads. Its function is to think. To know. To deduce. To reason. And when it is on center stage, our minds are clear and quick. Our intelligence is working at its limits. And we are as jumpy as a smoker watching a show about lung cancer.

As planets get closer to the sun, their orbital tethers shorten. They move faster and faster. Even distant Pluto, the slowest, covers three miles each second. Most terrestrial traffic courts would call that a moving violation, but as planets go it is almost standing still. Earth, by comparison, averages a little over eighteen miles per second – six times Pluto's velocity. But Pluto's orbital tether is forty times longer.

No planet is closer to the sun than Mercury. And no planet moves with more alacrity, screaming along through space at thirty miles per second. It completes an orbit in only 88 days, compared to Pluto's 248 years. That is over a thousand times faster.

If your head is starting to spin, that's good. You are getting on Mercury's wavelength. This is the planet of the mind, of the linear, logical functions. Just as it moves more quickly than any other planet, it refers to the part of our consciousness that holds all the psychic speed records: the thoughts, the second-by-second firing of our mental circuitry.

In the old myths, Mercury is the messenger of the gods. Traditionally, it is associated with speech and written communication. Those connections are valid, but pure Mercurial energy is more primal. It is the disorganized, free-associative play of imagery in the mind, the response of consciousness to the stimulation of the senses. Words come later. They are a cultural artifact, only a way of imposing order on the confusion of our perceptions.

Language is only Mercury's playground. Still, a strong Mercurial influence usually indicates a talker. And it always indicates a thinker. Those thoughts may be lofty and abstract. Or they may be no more than fretful recitations of mental grocery lists. Either way, they cascade through the mind at breakneck speed. Thirty miles per second. But so often going in circles.

Looking at Mercurial people, one often feels as if they are doing 78 rpm in a world where the rest of us are doing 33.

That speed is both Mercury's strength and its main liability. It absorbs impressions faster than any other planet, so deep is its fascination with the shapes, sounds, and ideas of the world. And it may process those impressions as clearly and unjudgmentally as a mirror.

But those perceptions may also pass through the mind undigested. Like a book collection belonging to an illiterate medieval baron, they may accumulate on the mental shelves like so many colorful, meaningless objects.

Do you have an acquaintance who can tell you the years in which Beethoven wrote each of his symphonies, but who never smiles or taps his feet when he is listening to them? He has a runaway Mercury. This planet can rev up to a redline pitch and still not have much to show for it. Just a lot of words. A lot of pithy one-liners. It can turn a person into a trivia addict.

Another Mercury risk: our thinking and perceiving functions can easily be warped by the fears and biases built into our own egos.

Astronomy itself warns us of that Mercury pitfall. How? Visually, Mercury is tied to the sun. The two are never far apart in the sky. Astronomers have known that for millennia, but it was not until the sixteenth century that they understood the reason: Mercury's tiny orbit is so much closer to the sun than ours that they can never be separated by more than 28 degrees. We stand so far away from the two of them that they always appear to be right next to each other.

Mind orbits ego just as Mercury orbits the sun.

Without care and humility we may see only what we want to see. We may gather our perceptions selectively, always in an effort to support the model of reality with which our ego is most comfortable.

That kind of rationalization and defensiveness is another of

Mercury's traps. This planet can prove anything with the facts. And even if it can't, it can still talk so fast and furiously that we miss the holes in the argument. And the only behavior belying Mercury's certainty then is nervousness. It can twitch like no other planet.

We must have perceptions. They are to the mind as food is to the body. The position of Mercury on the birthchart helps us see how best to hone and refine them. But it also warns us of prejudices and blind spots. The task with Mercury is to turn it from the sun's yes-man into his prime minister. Mercury need not know the meaning of life. Its concerns are more immediate. It must only gather raw information and feed it to the sun. Observation. Information transfer. Those are the Mercury functions. Nothing else is necessary.

VENUS

Glyph:	♀
Function:	The restoration of equilibrium to the shattered sensitivity. The stabilization of a network of supportive emotional bonds. The development of the capacity to make an aesthetic response.
Dysfunction:	Indolence, manipulation, vanity, spineless-ness, chronic abandonment to sensuality.
Key Questions:	How can I calm down? What do I need in a partner? What can I bring to a relationship?
If Retrograde:	May produce shyness or social backward-ness. Feelings of "goofiness" around potential romantic partners. Doubts and insecurities about worth as partner. Creative mind can be free and inventive.

The sun sets over a snowy field. All moisture frozen out of the air, the sky is clear as blown glass. Distant branches and twigs stand out like filigree. Our eyes rest now. The dazzling glare of stark sunlight on bone-white snow is abating. Shadows form. Sharp lines and edges appear. Subtly, grays and blacks begin to dominate the landscape. The brilliant blue floodlight of sky takes on depth. Cobalt fades to azure, azure to the indigos and violets of incipient night.

Suddenly there it is. In the blue aurora of the earth-fallen sun gleams a diamond. Luminous. Resplendent. Soon it will be radiant enough to cast faint shadows. Worshipped for millennia, it is the evening star. And it can still take our breath away.

If the sun is king and moon is queen, then the princess of the heavens must surely be Venus. Her light is dim compared to them, but she outshines everything else in the sky. Imagine a pearl heated to incandescence: that's Venus. White as lightning, but with a hint of something softer. Golden. She is the most exquisite jewel in the celestial storehouse.

If you find yourself touched by the poetry of these words, then you are also touching the part of yourself that astrologers call Venus. This is the goddess of beauty. Balance, harmony, equilibrium – these are the keys to the Venusian vibration. She may lead us to create harmony between colors, shapes, and sounds, or to respond to a harmony that is already there. Venus gives birth to our aesthetic perceptions. It is she who puts the tear in our eye as we watch the sun set over that snowy field.

When Venus plays a prominent role in a birthchart the individual is not always a Michelangelo or a Claude Monet. But he or she almost invariably has paintings on the living-room wall or an interesting collection of music. Asked about their own personal creative work, Venusian people may claim a tin ear or ten thumbs – but somewhere up in the attic is a collection of poetry or an old guitar. And if you can beguile them into playing a tune, get ready for a shock: you will feel as if you are seeing who they really are for the first time.

Saying that Venus gives artistic inclinations is not enough. That is still fortune-telling. It is far more useful to suggest that people born under her influence must actively develop their creative abilities. The more they accept an image of themselves as "artists," the more they feel in harmony with themselves and their world. They are the painters and musicians and actors and poets who delight us all. If they deny that, they come adrift from their deep psychic moorings.

Venus is more than the cosmic artist. She can also harmonize all the warring factions that exist within the individual psyche. Inner serenity is her gift. In the old traditions she is the goddess of peace – peace of mind as much as any truce between nations. Her position on the birthchart always suggests a kind of experiential input that can calm us down. She is heaven's answer to valium.

To go further we must return to some astronomy. Venus is the closest planet to earth. Our other neighbor, Mars, never gets nearer than twice Venus's distance from us. All the others are much farther away. The Venusian closeness to earth extends into other areas: in terms of mass and diameter she is our planet's twin. Were it not for the dense atmosphere of sulfuric acid and the 900-degree temperatures it produces, Venus would very likely be a tropical version of our own planetary home.

What could all that mean? Let's recap our clues: Venus is physically close to us. She gives the appearance of "empathizing" with us. She is perhaps the most lovely planet in the sky.

Could she be anything but the symbol of our ability to form relationships? Could she be anything but the goddess of love?

Relationships: we are all born feeling like half of something. Much of life is spent looking for the other half or coping with it once it is found. For virtually all of us, relationships are pivotal life issues. Just as Venus is the brightest of the planets, the questions she represents are perhaps the most compulsive ones we face. And the most confusing.

We cannot make much progress learning about love without some input from outside ourselves. We must have partners. Venus knows that, so she advertises for us. Often she grants us physical beauty, advertising the fact that we are doing relationship work. Or if she does not grant us beauty in the movie star sense, then she gives us a kind of irresistible animal grace. And she offers attractiveness to the personality as well. Poise. Courtesy. Elegance of speech and motion. A Venusian is never pushy. Instead he or she just washes over us like the tide. Before we know it we are overwhelmed.

Since our interactions with those we love are such profound developmental themes, the situation of Venus in the birthchart is a critical piece of information. Her sign gives us some sense of a person's needs, of what he or she finds attractive. If she lies in Gemini, there is a profound need for mental stimulation from the partner – not necessarily lying in bed discussing Kierkegaard, but fresh, stimulating conversation and a willingness to try new experiences. There is also a need for a variety of partners – if not lovers, then friends. With Venus in Cancer, the situation is utterly different. Here the needs are quieter, more purely emotional. Monogamy comes more easily and is more readily acceptable.

Like Mercury, Venus is an inner planet, closer to the center of the system than earth. That means that from our viewpoint, she too never drifts very far from the sun. The maximum separation possible between them is 48 degrees. And again, like Mercury, that binds her to ego. She can descend into vanity and self-possession, turning human love into a series of soap-opera vignettes. Her grace can decay into slickness, her attractiveness, into manipulation. She can be the playboy or the femme fatale, collecting scalps. She can become filled with lassitude and passive, sybaritic sensuality.

At her worst, we can imagine Venus as a faded movie queen – lying back on her divan, surrounded by yellowed old publicity shots, fat and vainglorious, eating chocolates.

We are all born hungry, although the cure for the craving is not easily known, let alone found. Sating that appetite, even if only temporarily is the Venusian art. Her methods are diverse, but her goal is always the same: to help us find a moment's peace. It may come in the arms of a lover or in the adagio of a string quartet or in a transcendent flash on the peak of a lofty mountain. Wherever it lies, Venus will guide us there if we only listen. We can heed her advice or we can ignore it. The choice, as always, is our own.

MARS

Glyph:	♂
Function:	The development of will. The expansion of courage. "Assertiveness training."
Dysfunction:	Touchiness, rage, selfishness, insensitivity, cruelty, sadism, bombast, irritability, a "chip on the shoulder."
Key Questions:	What battles must I face? Where must I be more assertive if I am not to suffer pointless conflict and strife? How can I sharpen my will? How do I express my aggressiveness?
If Retrograde:	Tremendous staying power. Hesitant to assert oneself or make demands. Passive demeanor. Anger controlled but internalized.

There you sit, enraptured, with this book in your hands. What a sucker! I can tell you that now that you've already paid your money. My editor and I are going to be eating caviar and drinking Saint Emilion, thanks to you. A fool and his money are soon parted...

Feel some anger? Some surprise? A new, threatening reality to adjust to? I hope so, because if you do, you are also well on your way to understanding Mars.

Once again, we meet a symbol that should not be new to any of us. The label is foreign, nothing more. The feeling, the aspect of consciousness to which it refers, is as familiar as gravity. It is aggression.

Mars is the first planet beyond earth's orbit. Mercury and Venus are closer to the center. In a sense we spin around them. Visually, that binds them to the sun; they can never appear very far from it. Not so with the red planet. It can go where it pleases, independent of any other influence.

That simple astronomical observation tells us a lot about Mars. It is the planet of freedom. Of independence. Of self-determination. A blood red eye in the night sky, the ancients grasped its meaning right away. They knew Mars as the god of war, and they feared him. Arrogant and touchy, when he moved, they trembled.

Aeons have passed, giving us new models of reality. We now know Mars as a tiny, third-rate world, a chilly desert planet, protected by a wisp of dusty atmosphere. Nothing to be feared. The evidence for that view is compelling. Probes have landed there. Photographs have been transmitted back. Not a scrap of support has been found for the notion that Mars is the home of the war god. There are no herculean soldiers with bulging biceps. No Amazonian women. No testosterone flows in the canals. In fact, no canals have been spotted.

Yet, to astrologers Mars remains the symbol of assertiveness and aggression. A "god of war." Why? Simply because that is the effect that we observe it to have. Even a casual study of a few birthcharts reveals that when Mars plays an important role, the personality is feisty and direct.

The traditional astrologer's view of Mars harks back to the days when Chaldean priests would scramble to sacrifice a lamb whenever the red planet twitched. An utterly "malefic" influence in their eyes, they connect it strictly with unpleasantness. Conflict. Discord. Hostility. Terror. Those realities are Martian; no argument there. But to put them first is to miss the point. Above all else, Mars symbolizes the power of the human will. This is the planet that gives us the steam to do what we please. To shape our own lives, and to crush anything that stands in our way.

Clearly, that is a risky energy to play with. When Mars goes bad there is no planet more horrible. It can be unspeakably cruel, unpardonably selfish, insensitive beyond comprehension. If there is a "killer instinct," this planet is its symbol.

Why is there no "Let's Nuke Mars" button included with this book? Because without the red planet we would be dead. If Mars were destroyed we would all just go to sleep. This is the planet of enthusiasm. It is the planet that puts the gleam in old men's eyes and the spice in the spirits of old women. It is Mars that enables the marathon runner to sprint that last half mile. It is Mars that explodes in the violinist as she plays those lightning-quick passages out of Paganini. It is Mars that sustains the human will at Dachau, at Wounded Knee, on the streets of Calcutta.

Killer instinct? Sometimes. Survival instinct? The will to live? Certainly.

Mars cannot abide a coward. The surest way to turn the planet sour is to let fear make our decisions for us. Mars needs adventure. He needs stress. He needs the opportunity to go to his limits. A fierce, uncultured warrior, he is a good friend to have nearby when the thug stops us under the streetlight and asks for a dollar. But we might not bring him along for a quiet afternoon in the library – he might start shot-putting the *Webster's* unabridged just to get his blood percolating.

How do we insure that Mars will be the survivor instead of the killer? By feeding him what he wants. And the recipe is there for us to read in the birthchart.

Let's imagine that a woman has Mars in Capricorn, a sign of self-discipline and ambition. She has a secret dream: she would like to singlehandedly drive a dogsled across Labrador and write a book about her adventures. That would be a Martial experience in that it is colorful, scary, and requires a massive focusing of will. It is Capricornish too, because it requires a sustained organizational effort, it is solitary, and it has career implications – the book she would write.

Should she abandon her job and start looking at used huskies? No astrologer can say. But we do know that it is her destiny to experience some such Mars-in-Capricorn adventure. It may not be Labrador. It could be. If she knows in her bones that she must go there but fails to act on the feeling, then her Mars has no healthy outlet. It is cornered. We see the killer. She becomes increasingly irritable. Touchy. Argumentative. Competitive over trifles. And of course the people around her do not put up with that for long. They get angry themselves. She gets back exactly the same juice she is putting out. In other words, she gets her stress anyway. But not the kind she needs or wants. She would have been better off facing those polar bears.

Face the bears: that is everything anyone needs to know about Mars.

JUPITER

Glyph:	♃
Function:	**The maintenance of faith. The development of vitality and confidence. The lifting of spirits.**
Dysfunction:	**Overextension, over-optimism, pomposity, pretense, denial of negative realities.**
Key Questions:	**What kinds of experience will help me feel more faith in myself and in life? Where might I be taking too much for granted?**
If Retrograde:	**Deeply rooted inner faith. May produce a very serious exterior. May inhibit emotional openness.**

Rain. Cold, misty-wet rain, driven by a gusty north wind. Ten days of it. Mud everywhere. A chill that cuts through woolen socks and sweaters as if they were fishnets. A runny nose, bad enough to be an irritation, not bad enough to warrant staying home in bed. Every morning, eyes open, hunting through the cloudy curtains. Every morning, they meet the same dim, devitalizing gray. Three days, five days, eight days. Nobody is talking anymore. No laughs. No jokes. Just endless waiting.

Then suddenly it happens. The sun rises into a perfect aquamarine sky. A south wind wafts warm air through the bedroom window. Birds sing. Children play. Trees glisten as if leaves were emeralds. And it's Saturday! What do we feel? Bliss. Gratitude. Liberation. Contentment. Triumph. The astrological label for all those sensations is Jupiter.

Jupiter – the king of the gods. The most massive planet in the solar system. If we took all the other planets, all the moons, asteroids, meteors, comets, everything but the sun, and rolled them up in a ball, they would still not equal the weight of this single planet.

Astrophysicists tell us that when a planet is forming, all it needs in order to become a star is more mass. If a body gets heavy enough, nuclear processes begin and a sun is born. That nearly happened with Jupiter. Our solar system came close to having two suns.

Spacecraft have filled in the picture further still. When the **Voyager** probes flew by Jupiter they relayed back some data that scientists are still scratching their heads over. The planet radiates a great deal of energy – far more than anyone expected. It is almost as if Jupiter will not admit defeat in its bid to become a star – even now, five billion years later, it is still trying to shine using its own light.

A planet with stellar pretenses: that's Jupiter. Like an exiled king, he has set up a minor empire a safe distance from the true center of power. From there he dominates the outer reaches of the solar system and reigns over a huge retinue of moons – four of them the size of Mercury. But Jupiter is no tyrant. That is not his spirit. He is more like a celestial good king Wenceslaus. Expansive, generous, cheerful, he is considered the most fortunate of planets by traditional astrologers.

One word captures the essence of Jupiter: faith. Above all else, this is the planet of faith. Not faith in the sense of "I believe in the Father, the Son and the Holy Ghost." Not anything so formal, but rather something much more primal. A faith in life. An unshakable certainty that life is worth living. Ten days of rain, then the sun emerges – our Jupiter circuits are buzzing. When Jupiter plays a major role in a man or woman's psychic structure we typically see a high-spirited person, an individual who moves with the natural elegance of a true aristocrat. There is magnanimity, expansiveness, a contempt for pettiness and pickiness. Always there is an indefinable element about the Jupiter person – something bigger than life. We are in the presence of a star. Unfortunately, the person may know that.

Jupiter is the planet of pretense and pomposity. He can be nothing but a glamorous shell, puffed up with illusions of his own glory. Demanding and autocratic, he may hold sway over a court of ghosts like a deposed czar. And when the ghosts won't play along, he may sulk like an insulted child. He will not sulk for long. Jupiter's spirits are resilient. He always bounces back. The cosmic clown, his faith in life is inexhaustible. Nothing can break him. Defeat is just not in his vocabulary.

But defeat is in the vocabulary of life. For all of us there will sooner or later be a mountain too tall, a disease too overwhelming, a relationship too impossible. These are the demons against which Jupiter cannot defend himself. He cannot gracefully retreat. This is not out of some kind of half-suicidal bravado. That state of mind is more akin to Mars. It is simply that Jupiter cannot imagine losing.

The blindfolded fool blissfully stepping over the edge of the precipice – that is a classic Jupiter image. Wherever this planet lies on the birthchart we find an arena of life in which we are undeniably lucky – and one in which we must guard against taking our luck for granted. Over-optimism, overextension, and unrealistic expectations are the pitfalls of every monarch. And Jupiter may do a swan dive right into them.

Traditional astrologers call Jupiter the "Greater Benefic." They love him. But they do not see him very clearly. They are right when they say that Jupiter makes us feel good. What they so often fail to see is that he may lead us down the garden path. Kings and fools – such a thin line separates the two. And Jupiter balances between them, uncertain as a tossed coin.

SATURN

Glyph:	♄
Function:	The development of self-discipline. The development of self-respect. The development of faith in one's destiny. Making peace with solitude.
Dysfunction:	Depression, melancholy, cynicism, coldness, unresponsiveness, time-serving, drudgery, lack of imagination, suppression of emotion, materialism.
Key Questions:	In what arena of life must I learn to act alone? Where will a lack of self-discipline lead most quickly to sorrow? Where will my ability to dream and have faith be most severely tested?
If Retrograde:	Deeply rooted self-sufficiency. May indicate a "loner." Enormous reserves of inner strength. Emotional self-discipline. May have a hard time saying "no."

Picture a young woman. A dreamer. She has a master's degree in English, but not much use for it. For the past five years she has been waiting on tables. Waiting for anything. Her ambition is to be a writer, but so far that has been sheer fantasy. She has written nothing.

One day that changes. She is getting older, a little scared. She realizes that it is now or never. She begins a novel. The book reflects her nature. It is dreamy, romantic. A gothic *Passion on the Moors*. And lightning strikes. She sells the manuscript and four copies sit in the paperback section of every grocery store in America.

Thirty years elapse. Thirty years and fifteen more versions of *Passion on the Moors,* each with a different title. She is affluent and famous. You see her face in *People* magazine. The years have changed her. No longer the spacey little ingénue, she is now a mature woman with vision and confidence. But her books do not reflect that. And she knows it.

She has an inspiration for a new novel, a very different one. Deeper. More serious. A work she could be proud of. Her publisher is appalled, but she persists. Halfway into writing it, she goes to the doctor. Cancer. Three months left to live. The book will take twice that long to finish. Impossible. She cries. She writes her will. She plans her world cruise. A week goes by. She has a long talk with herself, shrugs, and sits back down at her typewriter. She has lived as an author. She will die as an author. Her masterpiece will never be completed. Who cares? That was not the point anyway. The point was the process.

In that moment, the woman passed the fiercest of all the planetary tests. She became a master of Saturn.

Saturn – the old astrologers sometimes called it Satan. The Greater Malefic. Even now, the ringed planet is often viewed as the cosmic Frankenstein. It is associated with depression and melancholia, with defeat, with loneliness and frustration. All that is true. It is an accurate description of the way Saturn manifests if we displease him. But that is not his purpose. No planet is there just to hurt us.

Saturn teaches one virtue above all others: self-discipline. That is the key to understanding the symbol. Like Mars, the other so-called malefic, Saturn seeks to focus the will. To teach us that most elusive of arts: how to do exactly what we please. How to make our **intentions** dominant over our fears, our laziness, our emotions. Jupiter is the planet of faith. But in a sense it is Saturn that truly deserves that title. Jupiter gives us the feeling of faith, but often by supporting us with a thousand crutches. "Sure, I've got faith. Life is great. Look at my bank account, my sexy mate, my brand new Mercedes..."

Saturn's approach to faith is not like that. He takes away the crutches. He shows us darkness, impossibility, certain defeat. Then he asks: "Do you still have faith?" Again, this faith has nothing to do with religion. It is faith in life, in oneself, in our dreams and visions, in our ideals. It is faith in the idea that we have a destiny. And only if those visions can stand alone, unassisted, in the face of absolute impossibility, can we say that we truly have faith. Until then we are still riding with training wheels. The woman in our story knew she was a writer. That was her destiny. To flee from that would have been a flight from her own deeper self. No way she could finish her book, but that made no difference. The act of writing was what counted. Not success or failure.

Saturn is often symbolized by the hermit, which is a very appropriate image. This is the planet of solitude. Wherever it lies in the birthchart, we find an area of life in which we must act alone. An area where self-sufficiency is everything. An area in which we can count on no one but ourselves. Even our rewards must be supplied by us alone.

Death would prevent our author from receiving any praise or money for her book. No one would ever see it. As far as the world was concerned, it would be as if she had never written a word. Yet she wrote anyway, purely for the satisfaction that came from doing a flawless job of being herself. And again, she was a master of Saturn. Her solitude was perfect. From now on she would perform for an audience of one: herself. She might love. But she would never really need anyone else's approval ever again.

Fail to learn the lesson Saturn has woven into the birthchart and we drift. We lose track of ourselves. Life becomes empty, meaningless. We descend into cynicism and despair. Absorb the lesson and we still may not be dancing in the streets. That is not Saturn's way. But we gain the deep satisfaction that only the ringed planet can offer us, the satisfaction that arises from self-knowledge and self-respect. Without them there may still be joy. But the joy is like papers in the wind. Rootless.

The Invisible Planets

Two centuries ago a cataclysm rocked astrology. A new planet was discovered. Two hundred years later, the system is still quivering with aftershocks. Only now is it beginning to recover, to get reoriented.

England. Late winter, 1781. Peering through his telescope, studying maps of known stars, Sir William Herschel did something no human being before him had ever done: he detected a new world. With good politics and bad poetry, he christened the faint point of light Georgium Sidus, or George's Star, after the king. Mercifully, that did not stick. The English still sometimes call it Herschel. But in the end it was gods and not men who triumphed. Most of us know the new planet as Uranus, after the Greek god of the heavens.

Why was the discovery of Uranus such a shock?

For thousands of years astrology had been a closed system. There were seven planets, counting the sun and the moon. Seven had been taken as a magic number. Rainbows had seven hues. Octaves had seven notes. Weeks had seven days. Seven kept appearing in mystical traditions: the seven chakras or energy centers of the physical body, the seven churches in the Book of Revelations. There was something right and comforting about having seven planets in the sky. For millennia that simple observation had served as a quick "proof" of astrology's validity.

That neat, tight system crumbled the instant Herschel announced his discovery. Suddenly there were eight planets. And if there were eight, why couldn't there be more? When the dust settled, astrology appeared to be dead. The Age of Science had begun.

Astrologers lost prestige, but they gained an unprecedented opportunity: the chance to unravel a fresh symbol. Uranus was out there, undeniably. It had to mean something. But what? The answer was still elusive six decades later, when Neptune was first observed. And it was fuzzy as late as 1930, when Pluto was found. What could these new planets mean? The sevenfold system appeared to be a perfect model of the human mind. Everything was there: identity, emotions, logic, love, fear. Nothing was left out. It started with the sun, the basic symbol of vitality, and it culminated with Saturn, the planet of death and finality. Saturn was a natural endpoint. With the ringed planet the circle of life closed. There were no more possibilities. Yet, deep in space, tantalizing as a second chance, hovered the blue-green globe of another world.

It took astrologers a while to approach Uranus from the correct angle. When they succeeded, astrological theory made a quantum leap. What could lie beyond the function represented by Saturn? That is to say, what could lie beyond the **final, self-actualized form** of the personality? Or, more simply what could lie beyond death?

Structures **within** personality are the domain of the visible planets. They map that territory flawlessly. With the new ones we shatter the borders of nature, of ego, and of normalcy. We travel **beyond** personality. Their meaning? We do have one hint: we cannot see them. Only when telescopes artificially boost our senses do we become aware of them. And that observation is symbolic. It is the key.

Uranus, Neptune, and Pluto represent only possibilities. They signify transcendent, unnatural qualities attainable only through intentional work on the self. Unlike the classical planets, no positive manifestation of their functions can ever be triggered automatically. Until we purposefully move to transform our being, we see only their shadows. Without effort, these three mysterious symbols remain to the spirit exactly as they are to the eye: invisible. Let's take a closer look at the first of these cosmic outriders.

URANUS

Glyph:	♅
Function:	The development of individuality. Development of the capacity to question authority. The transcendence of cultural and social programming.
Dysfunction:	Contrariness, stubborness. Inflexibility, touchiness, quirkishness, unreliability, irresponsibility, selfishness, insensitivity to others' feelings, inability to learn from others, eccentricity for its own sake.
Key Questions:	In what department of life must I be most willing to function without social approval? Where must I learn to break the rules and follow my own path? Where will I consistently receive the most misleading advice? Which authorities am I destined to challenge and offend?
If Retrograde:	Individuality may be dissipated in fantasy life while outward behavior remains safe and noncontroversial. May symbolize genius – not in the sense of high intelligence so much as in the mind's freedom from culturally dictated "obvious truth."

When Patrick McMurphy and his appealing band of schizophrenics in *One Flew Over the Cuckoo's Nest* bust loose from the asylum and commandeer a fishing boat, we all cheer. Everybody loves the underdog, especially when he challenges top dog's will. No matter how lost the cause. "I am not going to take it anymore" is a rallying cry that stirs sympathetic chords in everyone.

Hierarchies, authorities, rules and regulations – these are the basis of every civilization. Without them we would still be a pack of Neanderthals throwing stones at one another. But something inside every one of us hates those constraints. Something within us cannot bear to be told what to do. Something in us always identifies with the outlaw, with the rebel, with the rule breaker.

The astrological label for that untamable quality is Uranus. This is the planet **of individuality,** of freedom. Nothing is more delightful to it than the prospect of mutiny. It is independent, rebellious, headstrong, colorful. If there is an astrological symbol of what physicists call the uncertainty principle, this is it. No planet is more unpredictable.

Astronomical observations bear out the astrological meaning of Uranus. Most planetary equators lie more or less in the plane of the solar system. In other words, what is north for earth is also north for Jupiter. Not so with Uranus. This planet does not spin in its orbit. It rolls. Its north is nearly perpendicular to our own. Even in space, the planet of individuality dances to its own tune.

What is individuality? Language, philosophy, humor, style – those traits are not individuality. They are merely masks that arise from culture and experience. We are born in America. We watch a few Clint Eastwood films, dress a few Barbie dolls, read a little Agatha Christie, a little pop psychology and voilà: personality is formed. It is an accretion, little more than an accident of birth.

Individuality is something deeper, something wild and spontaneous, something **inherent to the structure of the mind**. It is the part of us that would have remained the same whether we were born in Brooklyn or Batsuanaland. It is the part of us that does not buy the myth of the tribe into which we happened to be born. It does not obey those rules. It respects no authority. It shows no reverence for ancestors, for priests, for presidents. It honors no pretense.

When we manifest our individuality and develop it, we catch

merry hell. Why? **Because culture and individuality, society and Uranus, have been mortal enemies since God lit the quasars**.

In that battle there are no heroes, no villains. The best that can be said is that each side corrects the excesses of the other. If culture won, we would all become robots eternally living out the same two or three basic stories. If Uranus got the upper hand, then we would descend into utter barbarism.

Uranus challenges us to be free. Where it lies on the birthchart the high drama of rebellion crackles in our mental circuitry. It symbolizes an area in which our essence makes war on the constraints imposed on us by our culture. To be true to ourselves, we must break the rules. And in breaking them, we get into trouble. **We are forced to develop and defend our individuality**.

Later we will learn how to unravel the Uranian clues woven into the birthchart. There is a battle plan there – and a horrific description of the surrender terms should we choose not to fight. But for now we must only grasp the principle: Uranus is the part of us that refuses to be steamrollered by Miss Manners.

For an "invisible planet" Uranus makes quite a racket. What is so transcendent about rebelliousness?

The first step beyond the bounds of Saturn is not a "spiritual" step in the normal sense of the word. It is a step beyond conformity, beyond impersonality, beyond automism. The personality must be perfected before it can be transcended. We must manifest outwardly what we are inwardly, with no regard, for the applause or vilification we receive. We must accept in some small way the lonely burden of the revolutionary, of the genius. We must leave the tribe.

Few prospects are more terrifying. We may squawk about our jobs, our marriages, our boring lives, but to stand naked, stripped of those supports, before this awesome, brutal universe and to still **make conscious, coherent life choices** is the highest kind of courage. That spiritual transformation is the essence of the Uranian leap.

What if we would rather not make it? That is our choice. As with all the invisibles, this planet makes no useful contribution to our character without effort. But it will not just evaporate either.

A weak response to a Uranian configuration typically involves empty, symbolic battles. Imagine a man with Uranian overtones in the part of his chart relating to career. In his heart he wants to be a clam digger. But he is a lawyer, coming from a family of lawyers steeped in the "claw your way to the top" mythology. As much as he wants to heed the call of Uranus, to toss his law degree out the window and buy a clam rake, he cannot muster the courage to do it.

What happens? All that Uranian explosiveness gets safely invested in some quirk. He insists on his right to wear blue jeans in the office. He adamantly refuses to wear a necktie. And he defends those meaningless eccentricities with all the passion with which **he could more profitably be defending his right to live his own life**. This is the lash with which Uranus drives us: if we fail his tests, we feel like a bit-part player in somebody else's movie. And the role we are asked to perform is that of a harmless but somewhat ridiculous marionette.

A fascinating footnote with Uranus and the other invisibles: we discover them astronomically about the same time that we discover them psychologically. Uranus was found in 1781 – a time of upheaval in global consciousness. The American Revolution had just occurred. The French Revolution was just over the horizon. The scientific era, the "Age of Enlightenment," was beginning. All over the planet the **dignity of the individual** and his right to **question authority** were thrust into the collective awareness.

Coincidence? Maybe. But consider this: Uranus is extremely faint, but it is actually visible to the naked eye at certain times. My own eyes are not unusually sharp and I live in the misty, humid state of North Carolina. Yet, I have seen Uranus. It was as dim as a cat's eye a mile off. But I saw it. Why was it missed by the Chaldeans, the Egyptians, the Chinese? There were centuries of painstaking observation in crystal-clear skies before electric lighting and atmospheric pollution dimmed our eyes – and still no record of this planet. Could it be that we were just not ready to see it?

NEPTUNE

Glyph:	♆

Function: The decentralization of ego in self-imagery. The creation of a point of self-observation external to ego. The weakening of the barrier separating conscious from unconscious, ego from soul. The development of an awareness of what we may call God.

Dysfunction: Confusion, laziness, daydreaming, spaciness, escapism, drifting, drug and alcohol dependence, poor reality testing, glamorous delusions.

Key Questions: Where must I learn to de-emphasize logic and to function intuitively? Where is narrow self-interest most inappropriate and destructive to me? Where am I most vulnerable to mistaking wishes and fears for reality?

If Retrograde: The psychic sensitivity is distanced from outer reality; it is easily distorted by subjective factors, but relatively free of interference from the logical function.

A man believes he is Napoleon Bonaparte. The asylum in which he lives he imagines to be the island of Saint Helena. He dresses like Napoleon. He eats like him, speaks like him. He longs for Josephine. He laments Waterloo. There are no cracks in his delusion. He believes it perfectly, plays it out impeccably.

Another man believes he is the president of the United States.

Every day he meets with his advisers. Every day he makes important decisions. Everywhere he goes he is surrounded by guards. There are no cracks in his delusion, either. In fact, it is so perfect that we all believe it as much as he does. He really is the president.

The line between madness and sanity is as insubstantial as a hair. It exists. It is real. But there is far more overlap between the two states than many of us see.

"Napoleon" creates a mental picture of who he is, believes in it, makes decisions based on it. So does the president. In both cases, an infinitely deep, unimaginably complex psyche identifies itself as a kind of paper doll. Identity is a three dimensional mask worn by a multidimensional being. The mask of the madman does not work nearly so well as the one worn by the sane person. It is out of kilter with the actual opportunities that surround him. But the parallels between the two processes are unmistakable. In both, the mind organizes itself around a myth. In both, the consciousness enters the theater of the world. And the price of admission is radical simplification. We must play a part.

Something in each of us understands all this perfectly. Something in us never gets caught by the myth, never forgets that this world is a theater. Something in us **does not identify with "identity."** It stands apart. It just watches. Astrologers call that part of the mind Neptune.

This is the planet of **consciousness itself.** Not the contents of consciousness. Not identity. Not philosophy. Not even wisdom. None of the furniture we carry around between our ears. Just consciousness, just the blank slate. Nothing more.

Traditional astrologers are divided into two camps regarding this planet. Some like it. Some do not. Those who do often bill themselves as "esoteric astrologers." They see Neptune as a mystical influence, full of compassion and visions. The ones who take a dimmer view consider the planet a weakening force, inclined toward alcoholism and delusions.

Both camps have a piece of the truth. Both refer to behaviors arising when consciousness sheds the armor of ego. Sensitivity is heightened. A feeling of unity with the world awakens. We penetrate the fictions of status and identity. Our pretenses and worries, our ambitions and fears, our style, our self-importance, all become hilariously funny.

What can we do with that awareness? Some of us may just sit with it, shell-shocked into passivity. We become dreamers. All volition, all sense of direction, melts away. We are left staring into space. We lose the capacity to take ourselves seriously. Ego refuses to coalesce. So we do nothing. And sooner or later we seek ways to numb ourselves.

Others respond more creatively. They intentionally explore this new territory, making forays beyond the normal boundaries of identity. They return full of insights, full of a sense of life's unity, full of suspicion regarding the masks of separateness and individuality. And their message is always the same: all identities are mistaken.

Some call these Neptunian forays meditation. Others call them prayer or contemplation. Religious language is natural to Neptune, but it is not necessary. A psychologist may touch that part of consciousness and call the process self-hypnosis. A cowboy may call it staring into the campfire. The process is universal and organic. Wherever Neptune lies on the birthchart we find an exposed nerve, an extraordinarily sensitive, vulnerable place. Here is a part of the mind that refuses to accept the limitations of the "real world." It is often an inspired area, a visionary one. But also an area in which the person must guard against disorganization, wishful thinking, and escapism.

The issue is always the same: Neptune asks us to go beyond the universe of ego, hunger, and aggression **without sacrificing our ability to function as a personality**. The first part is relatively simple. The second part is another story.

Mirages, dreams, illusions – these are the domain of Neptune, and they are reflected in the planet's scientific history. It was discovered by a man named Lalande in 1795, but he thought he was looking at a star, so he made nothing special of it. Neptune tricked him out of immortality. Later, astronomers noticed that newly discovered Uranus was acting strangely. Something was disturbing its orbit. They suspected gravitational interference from a more distant planet. In Paris a mathematician named Urbain Le Verrier calculated the probable position of the disturbing influence, and Neptune was finally found there in 1846 by a German named Galle.

Just as Neptune was found through its disturbing influence on Uranus, **the experiences Neptune represents come to our attention only through cracks in the ego and its armor**. They come to us only through psychic disturbances. We have dreams. We have extrasensory experiences. We are inspired artistically or poetically. We are invaded by the delusions of schizophrenia. Neptunian mental events like these point **indirectly** to the existence of a larger framework of consciousness, just as perturbations in Uranus's orbit pointed indirectly to the existence of Neptune. They point to a vast dimension of mind, a dimension on which our awareness floats like a cork.

In the decades immediately following Neptune's discovery, Neptunian values and preoccupations swept through humanity like a storm. The Romantic movement in the arts. The rise of spiritualism – séances and mesmerism. The inception of mystical organizations like the Theosophical Society. The arrival of the first wave of great Hindu and Buddhist teachers in the West as the British Empire linked Europe to India. The founding of the Red Cross and the Salvation Army. The radical increase in social awareness regarding poverty, the rights of women, child labor, and slavery. Like never before, mystical Neptunian philosophies and compassionate idealism **took hold of the popular mind**. As a species, humanity was ready to discover Neptune. Once more we see evidence that the discovery of a planet is more than a scientific curiosity. It is a deeply symbolic event. In the astrologers' universe, just as in Neptune's, no perception is unrelated to deeper events in the consciousness experiencing it.

PLUTO

Glyph:	♇ or P
Function:	The realization of one's destiny. The recognition of the absurdity of all narrow pursuits. The development of the capacity to discern truth.
Dysfunction:	Megalomania, grandiosity, violence, preaching, dogmatism, rigidity, dictatorial behavior, hunger for power, a sense of meaninglessness or absurdity, end-justifies-the-means thinking.
Key Questions:	Where can I find enduring significance in my life? Where in myself might I find wisdom for which there is a great need in the world around me? Where must I guard against dogmatic, unscrupulous, or tyrannical behavior?
If Retrograde:	May produce a fear of personal "disempowerment." May lead to a hesitation to speak the truths one sees. Can give humility in the exercise of great powers.

Adolph Hitler and Mohandas Gandhi. Monoliths. Symbols of good and evil. These two loom like colossi in the collective mind, casting stark shadows across the far more ambivalent lives most of us lead. Baal, Ra, Apollo – their temples are fallen. No lambs or sparrows bum and bleed for them any longer. We worship men and women, paying homage in newsreels and editorials.

Gandhi and Hitler. What do they have in common? Eyes? Ears?

Headaches? As much as we may resist seeing it, those two are brothers in a far deeper sense than flesh alone. Both men shaped history. Each one touched the awareness of a generation, weaving into it his own dream, his own vision. Each man became a symbol of personal power. And each wielded that power in a way that the world will never forget.

All of us dream. What is it that takes one person's dream and so magnifies it that it warps history? What drives a man or woman out of safety and anonymity to become a world shaper? Whirling in the icy black edges of the solar system, minuscule and ominous as a plague virus, tiny Pluto holds the answer.

Standing on the frozen methane plains of this celestial outpost, the sun is so distant that it shines only with the light of a bright star. That observation is symbolic: from Pluto we actually experience the fact that the sun is nothing special, that the earth is a dust mote, and that we are microbes vainly scratching out a moment's existence. How can we accept that? How can that perception be absorbed without destroying us? Only through a fundamental transformation of being. Failing that, Pluto forces us to stare into the ultimate meaninglessness of our existence. Nothing matters. How could anything matter? We are only parasites awaiting extinction in an indifferent universe.

To face Pluto is to face the elemental futility of life. The planet was discovered in 1930. It is no accident that we were discovering existentialism around the same time. Pluto ushers us into the theater of the absurd. It confronts us with galaxies and supernovas, with endless aeons of time. And it looks us squarely in the eye, pronouncing the final verdict: "You are nothing. Your life is a joke."

To live with that brutal truth we must leap beyond the melodramas of personality. We must identify with something larger, more timeless. In that desperate flight from absurdity there is only one path of escape: we must leave our stamp on eternity. We must change the world.

Pluto is the planet of vast dreams, of visions, of conquest and transformation. Driven by emptiness, haunted by anonymity, it rips through our safe routines, thrusting into consciousness a sense of mission, a sense of destiny. Mere survival is insufficient. Merely to live is nothing. We die and in moments we are forgotten. Like Gandhi, like Hitler, we must carve our initials on the tree of history.

Indian independence and nonviolent rebellion were not Gandhi's ideas alone. Hitler did not invent Nazism. If those myths did not have far deeper roots, the two men would have been mere theorists, just harmless academics. And when a theorist speaks, the earth does not shake.

How did Pluto give these men the power of gods? By letting them voice the cry that was already there in the soul of their people.

Pluto is a taproot penetrating the heart of a nation. It transmits into the individual psyche the brooding, seething force of humanity as a whole. All the dreams. All the nightmares. All the angels and demons of a race.

But Pluto does more than fill our minds with phantasmagoria. It is an active planet. Unlike Neptune, it thrives on motion and change. Through it we **embody** the visions and terrors of humanity. We represent them. We serve as a living **symbol** of some communal need or fear. And in so doing power is invested in us by the culture as a whole. Our lives are given **transpersonal** meaning. We do not lose individuality, but we take on a second level of identity: not as a personality, but as a figurehead.

This is the secret of the world shapers. The authority they wield is not their own. It is ours. They strike the chord. But we are the cathedral in which it echoes and resonates. Their power is not personal; it is collective. Hitler and Gandhi are catalysts, nothing more. Their power is our power reflected back to us.

History does not make room for many Hitlers or Gandhis. How does Pluto manifest in lives closer to our own? Not so differently. It still offers us a mission. It still challenges us to shape the world. We are still mocked in our self-importance, still tempted with the abuses of power. The fundamental issues are unchanged, whether we are on the cover of *Newsweek* or barely made it into our high-school yearbook.

Pluto represents a special wisdom in each of us. A precious gift, it must be found and cultivated, cajoled out of hiding. We may find ourselves expressing insights we did not know we had. Maybe they are connected with death and dying. Maybe they relate to what goes on in a marriage. Perhaps they can inspire friends who feel lost and directionless. The nature of the wisdom depends on the position of Pluto in the birthchart. But whatever its form, when we speak from our Pluto consciousness, people listen as if it were the voice in the burning bush.

Few experiences feel better than being the crowd stopper. That is the horror of Pluto. Its hypnotic power can be corrupted, drafted into the service of a grossly lower master: our vanity. We can become bombastic and dictatorial. We can behave as if we were charged with divine orders to preach a message to the world, or to embody it. But the message has no divinity. It is just our own opinion, resting on the skeleton of our insecurities and personal history. Frighteningly, once accelerated and intensified by Pluto's fierce posturing, it can still sway people.

Adolph Hitler is the patron saint of that path.

And Gandhi rules the other course. His way represents a far purer response to Pluto. Not because he was "good" while Hitler was "bad." Those concepts have no significance to this icy planet. Gandhi's way is better only because it worked. He really did transcend himself. The freeing of India was just his vehicle. Nothing was left of his personal vanity, his private dreams. Nothing was left to be absurd. In **becoming his mission** he left no opening for Pluto's existential mockery. He was no longer a target.

Pluto, the chilly lord of emptiness, the pitiless trickster stares blankly and indifferently down on Mohandas Gandhi. And like galaxies, like billion-year-old atoms, Gandhi stares back. In some cold, incomprehensible way, he and Pluto understand each other perfectly. And when Pluto turns his pretense-withering gaze on Adolph Hitler, he does not see the six million, he does not see the awesome Wehrmacht. He sees only the ridiculous pride, the ranting and the strutting, the vain little puppet trying and failing to flee his own desperate insignificance. And Pluto's laughter howls and swells down through the labyrinth of the ages. To Pluto, Hitler was no modem Lucifer: No devil. Nothing so glorious.

To Pluto he was a fool.

Beyond Pluto

Prospects for the discovery of a planet beyond the orbit of Pluto are good. Perhaps before this book is very old, one will be found. No disagreement exists between astronomers and astrologers on that question. Some astrologers have jumped the gun. So certain are they of the existence of trans-Plutonian planets that they have named them and even published ephemerides purporting to locate these bodies. Typically, the sources quoted for that information are "not of this world."

Personally, I would be astounded if these listings proved accurate. Uranus, Neptune and Pluto were found only when global consciousness had come to a point where it was ready to grasp them. Their discoveries were **symbolic** events. There is no reason why it should be any different with future deep space discoveries. Planets beyond Pluto? We will find them when we are ready. And until then we could not understand them anyway.

Houses

Days and years: these are the blank pages of our lives. For aeons our planet has spun on its axis and revolved around the sun. Those earth rhythms shaped the amoebas and the primeval ferns. And they continue to pulse within each of us. Like the endless roar of traffic in a city, we take them for granted. Only background noise. Yet they are always there, defining the borders of our experience. These two earth rhythms are astrology's keystones. The year we have already studied. Punctuated by the seasons, our solar orbit is the source of the twelve signs.

We are now ready to investigate the second great planetary heartbeat: the day. In so doing we introduce the third and final tier of astrological symbolism. Taking their place alongside planets and signs, we meet the houses. Apart from some fine-tuning, this completes the system.

The houses. Like signs, they are another cycle of twelve symbols. Twelve more fundamental human processes. But now the focus is different. More immediate. More obvious. More concrete.

Physically, houses are divisions of the space above and below our local horizon. As we learned in Chapter 2, they locate planets on a minute-to-minute basis. Forget the grand galactic backdrop of the signs. We are now concerned only with where a planet **appears** to be. Is it overhead? Is it dropping down low in the west? These are the questions houses answer.

Symbolically, houses represent specific fields of activity. They are life's stages and arenas, the tangible theaters in which **identity is made visible through action.** One refers to career, another to verbal skills, a third to marriages and deep friendships. Even without houses, a good map of the mind is provided by planets and signs. But that map is a museum piece. Inert. Abstract. Isolated from everyday reality. Houses add the dimension of **experience.** Include them in the synthesis, and astrology becomes more than a model of the mind. It becomes a model of life.

The Daily Cycle

We know that earth is a damp ball of stone rotating on its axis, circling an obscure star, surrounded by a thin layer of gas, and hovering a few degrees above absolute zero. But it doesn't look that way. From our viewpoint, earth is an immense flat plain, apparently circular, with a luminous blue bowl inverted over it. Every day, stars and planets lift over the eastern rim of the plain, wheel overhead, and disappear over the world's western edge. To us, it appears that we are stable and they are moving. That, of course, is not true. All those effects stem from the fact that our planet is spinning. But that is what we see.

And **what we see** is forever the heart of astrology. Eye-truth, not mind-truth. But what about science? What about the objective truth? Don't the last five centuries of progress in astronomy count for anything? It is earth that is turning, not the planets.

Certainly. Astrology does not contradict astronomy. It is just that the questions it asks are different. Astronomy studies the **facts themselves.** Not so with astrology. Astrology studies the **space between the facts and the observer.** Reactions. Feelings. Appearance.

Everything in astrology is relative. Everything is individual. Not

Truth. But rather the billion little truths that arise as a billion finite beings make their peace with life. That is why astrology must remain earth centered. We are interested in how the sky **looks,** not in how it "really" is. To make astrology objective like astronomy is to make it absolute. To dehumanize it. We astrologers are not concerned with the solar system directly. We only seek to know its **relationship to us.** And that relationship is something we **see.** No need for abstract speculation.

Nowhere is that premise so clearly visible as with the houses. These are simply sections of space above and below the place where we are standing. To say a planet lies in the first house is to say it is just beneath our eastern horizon. To say it lies in the seventh house is to locate it low in the western sky. Those observations are completely dependent on our point of view.

Move even a few miles and the house position of a planet changes. When Mercury is overhead here in America, it may be setting in London and be far below the horizon in New Delhi. Its sign position does not change. But in each case it lies in a different house. A new viewpoint, a new house. And a new house means a new set of experiences. A new birthchart.

Horizon

Twelve houses. Together they form a ring around the earth, just as the signs do. Once again we return to astrological bedrock. We return to the prime symbol: the circle. Symbol of Infinity. Wholeness. The Absolute. But now we see the prime symbol from a new angle. Not divided up by the yearly pattern of the seasons, but cut in a more immediate way: split in two by the ground on which we stand. Infinity divided by two.

Half the sky can be seen. Half is invisible. Above: six houses representing an obvious, communally shared reality, visible to all. Below: six houses symbolizing a reality known only by inference. A reality encountered only in the imagination.

Subjectivity: that is the theme of the hidden houses – the ones below the horizon. They represent feelings, secrets, the inner life. Reactions are formed here. But always in darkness, always hidden from view.

When a majority of planets lie in the houses below the earth, we do not necessarily see an introverted character. A Sagittarian with an Aquarian moon and a prominent Jupiter is not going to be shy even if all his planets lie below the horizon.

What we see is more subtle. Emotion and intuition flavor all his perceptions. His conversation tends to emphasize feelings about facts rather than facts themselves. His life is a search **for an inner state**, and he takes major evolutionary steps without creating the slightest ripple in his outward pattern of circumstances.

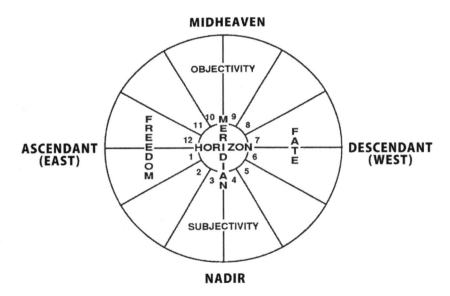

The masterpiece of work below the horizon is not the ambition fulfilled or the dream made real. Nothing so concrete. It is the **realization**. And realizations happen invisibly.

A preponderance of planets in the upper hemisphere has precisely the opposite connotation. Concrete, palpable experiences are emphasized in the houses above the horizon. The sky overhead is seen by all, shared by all. It conceals no secrets. Objective structures and communal consciousness come to a focus, balancing the privacy, mysticism, and illogic of the lower hemisphere.

A person born with most planets overhead is not always an extrovert. Again, the issue is more subtle. Signs and planets spotlighted in her birthchart determine the tone of her character, not the houses. But whether she is a bookworm or an exotic dancer, her life is a busy one. A **visible event** marks every important developmental milestone on her path. The event may be a move to another city. A marriage. A journey to the East. No way to tell. But it will be there. For such a person there is a **perceptible life ritual signaling every major evolutionary step**. No significant change occurs without an accompanying rite of passage, visible as the sky. Realizations are insufficient. She must craft an **event** through which she can project and crystallize her changing individuality.

Our first division of the celestial sphere is an obvious one. Earth itself is the dividing line, splitting space into a pair of parallel universes: the objective and the subjective worlds. Our second division is more elusive.

Meridian

Sunrise and sunset. These are clear markers. But there is at least one more milestone the sun passes each day: it reaches the peak of its daily arc. High noon. The sun stops ascending and starts its descent toward the western horizon. If we think carefully we realize the sun has still another milestone to pass: somewhere below the horizon, it must stop descending and start ascending. We call that point midnight.

The horizon is a physical line. The line connecting noon and midnight is imaginary. But its effects are real. This vertical divider, the **meridian,** separates the birthchart into an eastern and western section, each containing half the visible sky and half the invisible one. And each has a distinct significance. Six houses lie east of the meridian. And in the heart of the east, we find a single symbolic event that unlocks the meaning of all of them. The event is **sunrise**. Dawn.

Even with no sleep and a hangover and no cup of coffee, who could look at the dawn without some feeling of possibility and hopefulness? That word catches the spirit of sunrise and of the eastern houses: **hopefulness**. The new day is a blank slate. Nothing has been written on it yet. We may go on to trash it, to fill it with neurosis and fear and laziness. But we haven't yet. And maybe we won't.

Of course we could say the same for any moment. Life change does not have to occur at daybreak. Anytime will do. But back before clocks and graveyard shifts and electric illumination, dawn marked the beginning of the day's activities. It was clearly the inception of a new round of choices, a new chapter. Astrologically, dawn retains that significance.

Hopefulness, possibility, another chance – what is the common denominator here? Freedom maybe. That is certainly a part of it. But what determines how that freedom manifests itself? What is the active ingredient? The answer is the most fragile force in the universe, and the most unreliable. It is a force whose development lies at the core of any constructive use of astrological symbolism. Ethereal, uncertain, given to long sleep, that force is the **human will.**

Dawn **symbolizes** the will. Our ability to make choices. Intentionally to pursue certain kinds of experience. In the half of the sky it dominates we find our freedom. In those six houses we make the decisions that shape our lives.

With most planets lying on the eastern side of a birthchart, self-determination is everything. Such a person may not be an assertiveness-training wizard. But personal action or inaction is critical in shaping the tone of her life. Little of a purely circumstantial nature wields a decisive blow or offers an important life-shaping opportunity. Good luck and bad luck have no place in her vocabulary. Everything revolves around intentionally following through on choices. She must depend totally on the power of her will. She must create her own destiny. Her life, for good or ill, is in her own hands.

What about the other half of the sky? What about dusk and twilight? Photographically, sundown is indistinguishable from dawn. But its spirit is utterly different. Now the day is finishing. For our primal forebears, a cycle of activity was drawing to a close. It was a time of sleep and silence and waiting. Even now we experience a sense of finality about sunset. A feeling of completion. What we have is done. Fixed forever. Life may have dealt us another freedom card. But now it has been played. Maybe tomorrow we will get another one.

The western houses have a more restrictive tone than the eastern ones. They represent established forces, immutable powers, accomplished facts. We may negotiate with them. But they can never be pushed away.

In the west, freedom meets its match. It meets limits. Fate. Karma. Chance. Acts of God. Call them what we will, they are there and we must learn to live with them. A person with a western-hemisphere emphasis in his birthchart should not be discouraged from making decisions and commitments. But in looking at his biography we see more evidence of seemingly random forces striking in critical ways. Large inheritances. Chance meetings with powerful people. Alcoholic parents.

Twists of fate.

An individual operating within that framework must cultivate alertness and adaptability. He must learn to read omens, to sort out the threads of his destiny from a tangle of dreams and circumstances. Unlike his eastern-hemisphere counterpart, his life is unfolding within a larger pattern. His path can be summarized in a modern proverb: "Go with the flow." Not laziness. Not drifting. But a cooperative, pliant relationship between his will and the realities that surround him.

The Great Cross

Horizon and meridian. Two natural incisions, each sundering the prime symbol. Each cuts the sky into hemispheres. Each takes an incomprehensible unity and splits it into a comprehensible duality. Horizon gives us subjectivity and objectivity: the world within and the world without. Meridian gives us freedom and fate: the absolute power of will and its inevitable collision with other wills, equally free and powerful.

Together horizon and meridian form a cross. The cross of life. Esotericists have called it the cross on which spirit is crucified. The metaphor is melodramatic, but apt. The polarities the cross creates tear our hearts with the *Catch-22s* of life: freedom versus love, dreams versus reality, pleasure versus responsibility, and so on.

On that cross hang the twelve houses. Each is a battlefield. In each one, individuality comes out of hiding and makes a stand. In each one, the miracle and horror of daily experience interact with the raw psychological mechanisms symbolized by the signs and planets. Until they encounter the houses, those mechanisms are untempered and untried, safely hidden in the skull. They are only the stuff of dreams. After that encounter, they are transformed. Scarred by experience, taught courage and love, schooled in hope and endurance and compassion, they at last emerge from the womb of theory. They become living symbols of identity. Symbols of people. They become human.

Houses And Signs

Twelve houses, twelve signs. The two symbol systems are parallel Aries is the first sign. Its dramas are also the dramas of the first house. The same goes for Taurus and the second house. And for Gemini and the third. The correspondence holds true right through to the end in Pisces and the twelfth house. Learn one system and you are well on your way to grasping the other. Each is a twelvefold cycle of symbolism, and the phases of one correspond to the phases of the other.

The difference between signs and houses is only one of focus. Signs are psychological processes. They refer to events that happen in your head. Houses are experiential. They speak of what happens when your head is compelled to perform on the stage of life. We **are** our signs and we **do** our houses.

Aquarius, for example, may give a person a rebellious disposition. Put it in the house of career and that rebelliousness is likely to get crystallized as self-employment. No bosses could be tolerated. Put it in the house of relationships and the Aquarian theme no longer works itself out on the job front. The hub of activity is now a fear of being engulfed by a dominant husband or wife.

Meet someone. Get a feel for her. The introvert. The extrovert. The expansive, devil-may-care type. The meticulous, self-controlled type. You are tuning into her sign structures.

Watch someone's actions. See what issues keep snagging him. Always the relationship tensions? Endless concern about money? Don't worry about his character. Just focus on behavior. What part of life demands his constant attention? Is it career? Creativity? Home life? His next trip to Europe? Where **is his life happening?** You are feeling his house structures.

THE FIRST HOUSE (THE ASCENDANT)

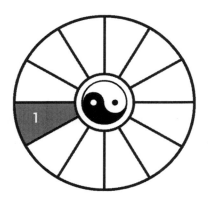

Traditional Name:
House of Personality

Corresponding Sign:
Aries ♈

Associated Planet:
Mars ♂

Terrain: The establishment of personal identity.

Successfully Navigated:
Clarity and decisiveness in one's actions. A sense of control over one's direction in life. A sharply focused sense of identity.

Unsuccessfully Navigated:
Fearfulness and lack of self-assurance leading either to inflexibility and tyranny over the wills of others or to self-effacement, vagueness of purpose, and the assumption of defeat.

Each of us is a web of contradictory feelings. We are haunted by memories and premonitions. We are tantalized by dreams. We love. We fear. We create. We know the tragedy of life. When the traffic cop stops us for doing thirty-five in the twenty-five zone, there is no way we can express all that to him. To function effectively in the world, we must simplify ourselves. We must translate all the richness of the psyche into streamlined form. That translation may be a pale reflection of what we really are. But there is no choice. However two-dimensional it seems in comparison with our true self, life requires that we have a personality – and a personality is always a role we play, always less than what we truly are. A personality is always a mask.

The first house symbolizes our optimal mask, **the outer expression that best serves our inner needs.** The more sensitively we respond to it, the stronger and more centered we feel. It gives a sense of **autonomy,** of self-knowledge, of authority over one's own life.

The ascendant does not create the outer personality. The forces that come together to produce it are far more complex. Rather it **channels the totality of the birthchart into the world of action,** flavoring and expressing the deeper material. Say a woman has a shy, indrawn birthchart – she is a Cancer with a prominent Saturn influence. Her Sagittarian ascendant alone does not make her the life of the party. But the depth of her reticence is not apparent on first meeting. Flavored by the initially distant qualities of the rest of the chart, her first house produces an aloof but breezy poise. Put that same Sagittarian ascendant on a supercharged Leo personality and she will be telling jokes at a funeral.

If we define sanity as the ability to generate a reasonable, purposeful pattern of action, then the **ascendant is the antidote to madness.** A weak response to it invariably makes a person feel crazy and disconnected. He or she is lost in role conflicts trying to be too many kinds of people all at once. Uncertainty and a feeling of illegitimacy plague such a person. Nothing comes together. For that individual there can be only fumbling and bewilderment, like an actor who has forgotten his lines.

Why? **Because he has no mask.** And on the stage of the world, a person with no mask is mute, extraneous, and invisible. When, through a failure to create an effective first-house mask, we lack clarity about who we are, life feels out of control. And when life feels out of control we get scared. A person with unresolved first-house problems – a person whose identity and direction are unfocused – often expresses his fear as a tyranny over other people. A self-centeredness. He cannot control his own life so he tries to control everything else.

Will an unsuccessfully navigated first house produce the tyrant or will it produce the spineless dreamer? To answer that we must understand the individual's birthchart as a whole. And we are not quite ready to do that yet. For now it is enough to remember that all of us wear masks. We all have social identities, "personalities." And we need them. Without them we could only stare wide-eyed out into space. Those masks, whatever form they take, are created at the ascendant. And when we see a man or woman at peace with the world, radiating assurance and poise, making no false starts and no unnecessary moves, we are witnessing its mastery.

THE SECOND HOUSE

Traditional Name:
House of Money

Corresponding Sign:
Taurus ♉

Associated Planet:
Venus ♀

Terrain: **Challenges to self-esteem. Money, and possessions.**

Successfully Navigated:
Confidence and self-esteem based on concrete self-adjustment, self-development. Effective, worry-free management of resources.

Unsuccessfully Navigated:
Materialism and the equation of self-worth with the value of one's possessions. Lack of self-respect. Fear of risk. Collapse of will-power leading to failure in world. Life-limiting concern with material security.

A kid roars down the street in his hotrod, lurid orange flames painted on the side walls, and nothing but air where a muffler might be. Strip away all our judgmental reactions, and his message is simple and sad. He is begging us to acknowledge that he exists. Something in him drives him to thrust the mere fact of his presence upon us. And any reaction will do. Hate, envy, fear, anger – if we react at all, he is satisfied. Sitting on the corner as he thunders by, anyone with an ounce of psychological understanding could sense a lack of self-esteem in the boy. And chances are good that observation would be valid. That kind of noisy, intrusive behavior usually does have self-doubt at its roots.

But how did our street racer try to resolve his lack of confidence? He sought to erase his uncertainty by **equating himself with an impressive object**. "I am this gaudy car. You have no choice but to notice me." It is an old game. The businessman who always manages to mention his big income is playing it. So is the suburban housewife with her collection of hundred-dollar blouses.

Second-house influences create a crisis of self-respect. According to the signs and planets involved, we may feel dumb or clumsy or unattractive. And the way we choose to resolve that insecurity becomes a key life theme. If we respond negatively, a compulsive kind of materialism warps our consciousness. We seek to alleviate our self-doubts through the manipulation of physical circumstances rather than through working directly on the problem. Sometimes money becomes the symbol of the confidence we need. We pursue it relentlessly. We advertise how much of it we have accumulated. But the pain remains.

Second-house issues need not revolve around the bank account or the cars and clothes it buys. We may collect prestigious friends or decorative lovers just as easily. We may even objectify our own bodies – obsessive sun tanning or body building often reflect tensions in this part of the birthchart. So does endless mirror gazing.

A successful navigation of second-house terrain always involves **proving oneself to oneself.** We compensate for inner doubts through disciplined effort and concrete accomplishment. Properly harnessed, personal insecurity can drive a person to reach toward the limits of growth.

A busy second house can be the weakest possible astrological structure or the most resilient. Everything depends on how the individual copes with the pressures it generates.

Always, a vigorous response to second house issues involves **intentionally altering some embarrassing personal trait**, while a weak response attempts to **conceal that trait behind a veil of money, glamour, or safety**. How we evaluate our own worth is the real issue. Money is just a red herring.

THE THIRD HOUSE

Traditional Name:
House of Communication

Corresponding Sign:
Gemini ♊

Associated Planet:
Mercury ☿

Terrain: Information gathering. Information sharing.

Successfully Navigated:
Clear, accurate, unbiased perceptions. Willingness to tolerate perceptual ambiguity and uncertainty. Capacity to probe the world for more information either verbally or intellectually.

Unsuccessfully Navigated:
The urge to protect a given concept of the world, leading to defensiveness, intellectualism, and verbal overkill. Scattered, unfocused curiosity, leading to chronic time wasting and disorganization.

Speaking, teaching, writing – these are the activities traditionally associated with the third house. Accurate enough, but the terrain here is far larger. Anytime we express a thought or a feeling in such a way that it can be decoded and understood by another person, we have activated our third-house circuits. Gestures, meaningful glances, body language – those expressions mark its terrain as much as anything we do with words. And even that covers only half the territory. Communication is a two-way street. The third house refers to listening, too. And to reading and learning. But words are not always necessary there either. The sky communicates blueness to us.

The night communicates darkness. The world floods our senses with an endless barrage of information. And we "listen" to it all.

House of Communication? Yes, but the title may mislead us. It is too narrow. Let's call the third house the **House of Perception**, remembering always that perception flows two ways: we gather information from the world and then we echo it back again. Two processes: we perceive. And we make our perceptions **perceptible to others**. Both are essential to this third phase of house symbolism. Both must be developed if we are to navigate its terrain successfully.

One person sees conflict everywhere. His words are bombastic and confrontational, always presented as arguments even when no one disagrees. Why? Perhaps he has Mars in his third house. Or maybe a couple of planets in Aries there. Another person may be angry as a hornet, but if gentle Venus lies in this part of the birth-chart, even those explosive energies come out softened. Polite words are chosen. Balanced ones. Perhaps even manipulatively ingratiating ones. Expressing affection and support is easy for him. His critical choices revolve around learning to be more direct when he has a gripe.

In the same way, each planet and each sign can color the tides of information that flow between us and the world. Sagittarius adds an expansive, philosophical quality. Saturn brings discipline, structure, and practicality. Aquarius suggests originality. And each one creates a prejudice or blind spot that distorts that stream, partially isolating us from our total environment. To understand. To see with unerring clarity. That is the primary goal of the third house. There is a physical world around us. And within the neurons and synapses of the brain we create a second world modeled on the first. That second world is the one we truly inhabit.

To perceive clearly, the two worlds must be aligned. How can we straighten out the distortions? **Only by comparing notes with other perceivers**. Other people. They may be just as warped, but their warps are different. We must express ourselves to them as clearly as we can, sharing all the indefensible biases and crazy opinions we carry within us. And then we must truly absorb what they have to say, however incomprehensible or offensive or threatening it may seem within the framework of our own inner world.

Those who have mastered that delicate art are masters of the third-house terrain. Their navigation has been a success. More than most of us, they see truth. The real truth. The truth that is never in us, but always among us.

Those whose passage through the third house has been a failure must live in a universe in which dreams, nightmares, and reality are forever shifting into one another. Their decisions may be based on facts. Or on fears. Or on propaganda. They never know which. And their lives reflect that uncertainty. They chatter. They flit from task to task, from opinion to opinion, from fact to meaningless, pointless, unconnected fact. And in the end they have done little more than run around blindly in circles.

THE FOURTH HOUSE (THE NADIR)

Traditional Name:
House of Home

Corresponding Sign:
Cancer ♋

Associated Planet:
Moon ☽

Terrain: **Unconscious, emotional, intuitive underpinnings of personality. The "Hero" and the "Shadow." Domestic life; the home.**

Successfully Navigated:
Thorough understanding of one's own motivations, needs, and fears. Establishment of roots in form of home, family, and attunement to inner self.

Unsuccessfully Navigated:
Lack of basic psychological self-knowledge, leading to neurotic, unsatisfying, and obsessive behaviors. Self absorption and self-analysis to the point of withdrawal from the world; shyness.

The nadir. The lowest point a planet can reach. When the sun is there, clocks read approximately midnight. A time of darkness. Mystery. Perhaps of fear. Vague shapes loom in the blackness. We strain to make them out. Friend? Foe? Or just furniture? Our eyes are useless. We strain to "see" with our ears, our extended fingers, our intuition – or is that just imagination? At midnight it is hard to discern the difference: our hopes and terrors take form as palpably as physical objects.

The fourth house is the most subjective of the twelve. The arena it represents is a secret one. No one outside ourselves can see it. And when we enter into its misty, uncertain terrain, we disappear from view. All our attention, all our energy, is withdrawn from the world, turned inward on itself. The house of feelings? Yes, but the word is too pale, too shallow. The house of the unconscious mind? Yes again. But the material locked here **must be made conscious** if we are to feel complete and whole.

To grasp the significance of the nadir, we must thoroughly absorb one key point: **the contents of the fourth house are utterly isolated from the outer world.** They exist only in the mind. "Reality," in the sense that we normally use the word, is irrelevant to them. They grow and develop with a logic all their own. Have a secret fantasy? When you are daydreaming in the office, are you quietly piloting a starship? Are you feeding the hungry? Opening in Las Vegas? You are encountering the **Hero** – one of the two poles of the nadir.

The Hero. A set of grandiose, imaginary self-images, shaped by the signs and planets in the fourth house. Although they are always embarrassingly unrealistic, those images serve a very real function in the ecology of the mind. They inspire us. They help us understand what we really want. Want to open in Vegas? Maybe your fourth house is telling you that you need a little more applause at home. Or maybe it is time to dust off that old guitar. Always, the Hero – in the form of our recurrent fantasies – tells us what we need in order to create **balance between our true nature and the mask we wear in the world**.

Balancing the Hero, we find the opposite pole of the fourth house: the **Shadow**. Here we store all the horrible, unflattering, terrifying images we have of ourselves. Nightmares are encounters with the Shadow. But so are chronic illogical worries: an obsessive fear of cancer, of psychotic killers, of madness.

Like the Hero, the Shadow is trying to convey a message to us, but decoding it is rarely easy. Always afraid of those psychotic killers? Maybe you have got some stored-up anger of your own. Maybe you are afraid to release it. The Shadow tells us what we fear. But it does far more: **The Shadow draws a picture of the fear we are afraid to feel**. Decode it, face it, and once again we establish balance between the inner self and the personality we present to those around us.

Absorbing the Hero and the Shadow takes time. It also requires peace, and freedom from too much external stimulation. Although its primary significance is emotional and intuitive, the old astrologers emphasized the withdrawn qualities of the fourth house and called it the House of the Home. And they were correct as far as they went. The fourth house does describe our attitudes toward the haven we create from the noise of the world. That haven must be created if we are to touch the nadir.

But home making is the means, not the end. Simply to go into hiding in the home is as much an unsuccessful navigation of this house as is taking the Hero and Shadow on face value, making no effort to decipher their messages. Either way, the inner life and the outer life become dissociated from each other. And then both feel as thin and phony as a four-year-old's first lie.

THE FIFTH HOUSE

Traditional Name:
House of Children

Corresponding Sign:
Leo ♌

Associated Planet:
Sun ☉

Terrain: **Pleasure. Playfulness. Creative self-expression. Falling in love.**

Successfully Navigated:
Joyous anticipation of each day. The development of a creative outlet through which tangible evidence of one's internal processes may be expressed. Capacity to establish initial rapport with interesting strangers.

Unsuccessfully Navigated:
Abusive, self-destructive, uncontrollable relationships with particular pleasures. Creative blockages. Inability to relax and play.

Joy – how deeply we need it! Its absence is as fatal as a ten year fast or a month without oxygen. Without that sparkle, we wither. We lose interest in life. We become as cold and mechanical as an airless world orbiting a dead star.

But how can that joy be fed? How can we sustain it? Much of the time, life does not offer much help. Our bodies hurt. Our bills pile up. Silly dramas sour our relationships. And power-hungry heads of state surround us, plotting nuclear war as if it were some kind of new video game.

In the face of all that hellishness, there is only one force between us and despair. That force is pleasure. At some undeniable, immediate level, pleasure is what keeps us in the world. And pleasure is the point of the fifth house.

Traditional descriptions of this house read like a hedonist's shopping list: parties, debauchery, love affairs, horse-racing, gambling, games, luxuries. Those certainly are pleasures. And they can certainly give us joy, provided we navigate their terrain with a certain amount of grace. But imagine how good Michelangelo felt when he first stood back and admired his Sistine Chapel. Or how the Buddha felt when his mind was finally silenced beneath the bodhi tree. Those are pleasures too, but of a subtler sort. They arise out of a person's vision. Out of his individuality.

The fifth house is the house of pleasure. But to navigate it successfully, we must remember that not all pleasures are of the flesh. Creativity is a joy. Meditation is a joy. "Falling in love" with a grizzled sea captain ninety years old is a joy. All those activities – creating art, sitting peacefully, making a new human connection – are part of the fifth-house terrain.

An unsuccessful passage through the fifth house invariably involves getting hung up on a single pleasure, forgetting that there are so many others. Pull a big drunk *every* New Year's Eve and your life is no worse for it. It might even be richer, if your inclinations are along those lines. Get drunk *every* night and the situation is quite different. Your life collapses before your eyes.

And you are not even having, any fun.

Signs and planets shaping our fifth house give a prescription for the maintenance of joy. They symbolize a specific **range of pleasures**, some centered on body, some centered on intellect, some focused at the level of pure spirit. Learn to enjoy **all** of them. Develop the skills and habits they require. Guard against asking too much of any single one. Do all that, and even when you die they won't be able to wipe away your smile. Those little birdsfoot joy lines will be as much a part of your face as your nose and eyes.

Fail, and even the good things that come to you are of no use.

You stare at them, uncomprehending, waiting for the catch. Or you leap on them, crushing them in your effort to make them more than they are. Either way, you are left with nothing. Only the pain of life. The joy has slipped through your fingers, slick as a fish.

THE SIXTH HOUSE

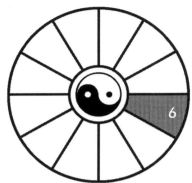

Traditional Name:
House of Servants

Corresponding Sign:
Virgo ♍

Associated Planet:
Mercury ☿

Terrain: **Responsibilities. Skill and competence. Devotion and self-sacrifice.**

Successfully Navigated:
Fulfillment through the development of a personally meaningful skill that is of value to others.

Unsuccessfully Navigated:
Endless busyness at tasks that have no personal meaning; drudgery, wage slavery. Humiliatingly subordinate roles in key relationships.

A friend phones us, distraught. She's got a job interview two hundred miles away. She needs to get on the road within the hour. And her car will not start. We drive over and take a look under the hood. Corroded terminal posts on that old battery. Pull out the pliers and the Boy Scout knife. Pry off the cables. Scrape down those posts. In three minutes her engine is purring.

How do we feel? Happy. Proud. We can't stop grinning. Have we gained anything for ourselves? Not really. At least not in any obvious way. From a purely selfish point of view, all we have done is waste a half-hour of our time. But that is not how we experience it. What we have accomplished is a successful navigation of the sixth house. **We have demonstrated a personal skill in such a way that it helped another person**. And whenever we do that, we feel a characteristic satisfaction.

In medieval astrology, the sixth house is the House of Servants. Anything you want to know about problems you may face with your stable boys and scullery maids, you can get the answer here. Clearly, the twentieth century has demanded some fundamental rethinking about this house. No longer does the House of Servants tell us about **our** servants. Now, **we ourselves are the servant**. But not in any degrading or menial sense. In this house we recognize an elemental human need: **the desire to exercise competence and to be recognized for it**. Fixing a car. Playing a violin. Doing an effective astrological interpretation. The form the competence takes can vary widely. But if we fail to discover that special skill within ourselves, or if we fail to develop it to its limits, there is an emptiness in our lives. Something basic is missing.

How do we find that skill? The answer lies in the sixth house. Signs and planets activated there indicate which part of our personality is best suited to discovering it. They also give us some hints about how that skill will look once we have polished it, educated it, and made it available to the world.

Should our navigation of the sixth house be unsuccessful, the need for meaningful responsibilities remains. But now we have nothing to give. No skill. No special competence. And we begin to work for work's sake, slaving away at a patchwork of labors that are **irrelevant to** us. We become the wage slave or the drudge, praying for the weekend.

Soon we find ourselves living in a world populated with bosses. We lack inner direction in our labors. Outer direction quickly takes up the slack. Soon our confidence in our own decision-making abilities collapses.

More is corrupted than our professional life. As our respect for our own competence dwindles, our friendships, our loves, our family relationships, all are tainted. We lose faith in ourselves. Everywhere we go we seem to be begging that someone make us an assignment. And they do. And we fulfill it, only to seethe with resentment at the endless blither of insignificant hassles to which our life has been reduced.

THE SEVENTH HOUSE (THE DESCENDANT)

Traditional Name:
House of Marriage

Corresponding Sign:
Libra ♎

Associated Planet:
Venus ♀

Terrain: **Intimate relationships. Identification with others.**

Successfully Navigated:
Relationships characterized by:
1. **Equality between the partners**
2. **Open-endedness; i.e. the relationship can be expected to survive changes in circumstance**
3. **Specialness; unique rapport; "magic"**

Unsuccessfully Navigated:
A pattern of chronic submissiveness or directiveness in intimate relationships. Inability to form a stable emotional bond. Fear of intimacy. Extreme dependency or extreme fear of dependency.

The movie is twenty minutes old. Already you wish that you had saved your money. The characters are shallow. Implausible. Their values, their motives. even their personalities seem like dramas you had laid to rest by your fourteenth birthday.

An hour later, you are still in the theater. The film has not improved. But suddenly you realize that there is a tear forming in the corner of your eye. What is happening? At one level, you feel embarrassment: how unsophisticated you would look if anyone knew a movie this dumb had brought you to the verge of tears. At another level, all that has happened is that you have entered the terrain of the seventh house. You have put aside all your judgments, your rigidity, your pride. You have gotten far enough past those blocks actually to **feel** the pathos of the film characters. Despite all your resistance, you have **identified** with those people. **And identification is what enables us successfully to navigate the seventh house**.

Identification. Putting yourself in the other person's shoes. It is the cornerstone of all dramatic art: movies, novels, plays, even songs. And it is also the basis of any intimate relationship. If the mind fails to set up that elemental I-equal-you equation, no story will ever move us and no human being will ever touch us.

But setting up that equation can be tough. Other people are not us. They are different. Alien. Like the characters in our movie, their motives and their values clash with our own. To identify with them – to love them, in other words – we must **temporarily set aside our own point of view**. We must set aside our personality. We must look at life through their eyes. A perilous process. If we cannot manage it, we make no lasting intimate contacts. We may be married. We may have friends. But our isolation is perfect. And in moments of truth, we admit it: our universe is populated only with strangers.

If we do succeed in setting aside the limitations of our own personality, another peril faces us: perhaps we cannot get it back again. We may become lost in the relationship, so swayed by the power of the other person's world view that we lose track of our own identity. We become a shadow cast by another person. And we cling to that relationship as if our identity depended on it, full of desperation and resentment.

A successful passage through the terrain of the seventh house requires one quality above all others: an ability to feel a sense of **equality** with your partner. Nobody is in the driver's seat all the time. No one is the boss. There is dependency, but it is a two-way street. **Equality means interdependency.** There is also a sense of open-endedness in the relationship. Old-fashioned marriage ceremonies get at this idea with the phrase, "till death do us part." We need not go that far to successfully navigate the seventh house. But we must **make a commitment** to the other person. The relationship cannot be based on convenience. There must be a feeling that even if circumstances were to change radically, the bond itself would not be affected. Why? Because **the relationship is not founded on circumstance**. It is rooted in the essence of each person's nature.

Finally, and most critically, there must be a sense of special rapport between the partners. There must be **magic**. Call it romance. Call it psychological symmetry. Say that it is karma or destiny or God's will. The words do not matter. But without those mystical fireworks the walls of ego and fear can never be blasted away sufficiently for us even to enter the House of Marriage, let alone navigate its corridors.

Even with all three requirements fulfilled, that navigation is still tricky. But planets and signs lying in the seventh house guide us. They describe the **type of person** with whom we are most likely to have success in that phase of our lives. And they also indicate **the dimensions of our own character** that must evolve if we are to know what to do with that person once the encounter has taken place.

THE EIGHTH HOUSE

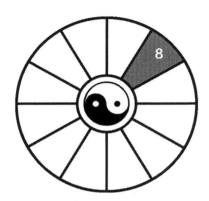

Traditional Name:
House of Death

Corresponding Sign:
Scorpio ♏

Associated Planets:
Mars ♂ & Pluto ♀

Terrain: Instinctive behavioral determinants universally present in human consciousness:

1. The instinctive desire to form a sexual life bond: the mating instinct.
2. Instinctive awareness of one's own physical mortality: the way we cope with death.
3. Instinctive sense of invisible, transcendent dimensions of reality: life after death, the "occult."

Successfully Navigated:
Healthy, flowing, spontaneous sexuality. Acceptance of death and an integration of its reality into daily life. Sense of the immortality of one's consciousness.

Unsuccessfully Navigated:
Blocked sexual functioning or obsessive sexuality. Inordinate fear of death: denial of death. Rigid denial of "religious," "occult," or "mystical" feelings.

Sex, death, and the occult. Quite a stew. Why are these three seemingly disparate terrains linked together in a single house? What common denominators exist among them?

In each one we confront one of the basic givens of human life.

In each we confront a set of needs and issues that are felt universally, and that release intense and disruptive emotional energies into consciousness. In each we meet an instinct.

Our best friend announces she is leaving to take a job in Patagonia. What do we feel? Sadness certainly. But also supportiveness and a poignant sense of the preciousness of the relationship. Our mate or lover makes the same announcement. How do we feel now? Overwhelmed. Ripped apart. Enraged. Rejected.

The difference between the two situations is the difference between the seventh house and the eighth. Although the seventh house is critical in understanding our relationship needs, the eighth is where we encounter the gut feelings that are unique to a sexual bond. And those feelings can sweep over us like a flood, shattering the normal equilibrium of our character. Once evoked, they are virtually unstoppable. We have pulled the cork in the dam separating ego from instinct.

The same can be said for encounters with death. Once again ego encounters feelings that are both **incomprehensible and uncontrollable**. Once again, it is overwhelmed. Our brother dies unexpectedly. Our doctor tells us we have an incurable disease. Our child is killed by a drunk driver. In each case **personality dissolves**. It is submerged in an instinctive response.

Bring up the subject of death in any nonacademic setting and you are soon confronting another instinct. You are soon discussing life after death. According to most surveys, the majority of us believe that consciousness continues in some form beyond the grave. Ice Age Neanderthals buried their dead with food and weapons for the next world. And ever since, in every culture, ritual and religion have revolved around the notion that only our bodies die.

Worrying about the validity of that notion is beyond the scope of this book. What is important for us to know is that a belief in **life after death is a universal content** of the **human mind.** Wherever we look, in whatever time or place, we find it. That is not to say that everyone everywhere accepts the idea not everyone chooses to survive, yet we speak confidently of a survival instinct. It is the same with life after death and most other "occult" phenomena. A belief in them seems to arise **organically and spontaneously** in the human mind.

See a ghost. Remember a previous life. Observe the sudden wave of serenity crossing the face of a friend one minute before her heart stops. Walk past a lonely graveyard on a windswept night. Any of those experiences fills the mind with emotion. Any one of them represents an encounter with something **outside the normal limits of personality**. Each is an encounter with instinct.

Haunted, explosive terrain. How can we navigate it successfully? A successful passage through the eighth house depends on **accepting the reality of feelings arising beyond personality**.

Or we might say accepting illogical feelings. Feelings that may violate our accustomed description of the world. Feelings that undercut our self-image and **threaten us with loss of control**. That is not to say we must invariably act on those feelings. Only that we acknowledge them, be willing to experience them. **By acknowledging those instinctive feelings, we absorb a set of perceptions unavailable to us through intellect alone**. We learn to flow with an "occult power" that normally lies latent in the structure of the mind.

Like the fourth house, the eighth is a window through which ego peers into the larger framework of consciousness. But there are differences between them. The fourth house is very personal. In the eighth, if we are brave and open and trusting, we have the chance to go beyond the personal realm. A chance to absorb into ourselves something universal.

How? Flow with the sexual force. Feel the magic of the bonding process at all levels: physical, emotional, personal, spiritual. Accept death. Integrate it. Absorb it. Learn from it instead of hiding from it. What does death teach you? Look at your job, your relationships, your values. How will you view them when you are 110? Grope within yourself for something immortal. Try to feel your "soul." Let go of logic. Suspend judgment on the validity of your perceptions. Is there something ancient and unquenchable in you?

Do all that and you have successfully navigated the eighth house. Signs and planets there give advice and warnings. But the passage is yours to make.

Fail, and those same instincts snag you. They make you moody and bitter, full of heaviness. You may have a beautiful mate or a million lovers. Still, you are unsatisfied. You may have a strong, healthy body. Still, you are haunted by the certainty that something unspeakably horrible is about to happen to it. You may accomplish miracles of creativity and self-discipline. And still you see them as empty and pointless, mocked into insignificance by the inevitability of your death.

THE NINTH HOUSE

Traditional Name:
House of Long Journeys Over Water

Corresponding Sign:
Sagittarius ♐

Associated Planet:
Jupiter ♃

Terrain: Confrontation with the tendency of life to become mechanical and routine. Formation of personal system of ethics or philosophy; establishment of personal world view. Encounters with the unpredictable and the exotic.

Successfully Navigated:
Ability to break up routines and create new patterns of behavior. Clear, individual sense of life's evolving meaning and purpose. Capacity to absorb shocking, unexpected perceptions.

Unsuccessfully Navigated:
Routinization of experience; boredom. Rigidity of thought; dogmatism. Opportunistic, narrow-minded, or unprincipled behavior; nihilism.

When you emerged from your mother's womb, you differed little from Cro-Magnon children who emerged into a world of mastadons and saber-tooth tigers. Culturally you were a blank slate. But that did not last long. By the time you were a few years old, you were taking airplanes for granted, fiddling with the dials on sophisticated electronic equipment, and wondering what you were going to be when you grew up. In other words, you had become a member in good standing of twentieth-century industrial civilization. You had been taught a way of looking at life. A set of values. A stance in the world. You had been given a **model of the universe**, one that would color your philosophies, fantasies, and life choices for the rest of your days.

Let's imagine that after thoroughly absorbing that model you join the Peace Corps. You are relocated to the Amazon basin. You are living among native people whom most of us would be quick to call primitive. At first their ways shock you. Lack of hygiene. Rigid sex roles. Grubs for breakfast. Evil spirits. Everything is so bewilderingly alien. You feel as American as a hotdog on a plastic tablecloth. Gradually that changes. You come to know these people. You form friendships. You look into their eyes and see intelligence, sensitivity, compassion. Humanness. You begin to grasp their behavior, their culture. Slowly, you absorb **their model** of the universe.

The instant that happens, you are changed forever. Something clicks in you. Suddenly you have two ways of looking at the world. Stereo consciousness. You can think like an American. And you can think like an Amazonian. Both work. One reality. Two models. You have grasped something essential about life and culture and the nature of perception. And you have grasped the key to the terrain of the ninth house: **all our views of reality are conditioned by an unspoken model of the world – and that model is always arbitrary and limiting.**

An unsuccessful navigation of the ninth house invariably involves mistaking a model of reality for reality itself. Maybe we are eighteen years old. We put a picture of life together. When we turn thirty we are ready for a more fluid, more sophisticated picture. But perhaps our mind has become too rigid to change. We are too addicted to the old model. We forget that it is nothing more than a picture we carry in our head.

From that point on, if we continue to adapt unsuccessfully, we live in a world we have outgrown – the mental world we created when we were eighteen. And it is too simple for us. **The old model**

no longer engages or challenges our intelligence.

What was once a creative adaptation now becomes a mechanical routine. And yet we cling to it, becoming efficient automatons gradually boring ourselves to death with tired tales and sermons we invented years ago.

Successful ninth house navigation? It is an art that must constantly be renewed. To put it simply, we must learn to take chances. We must takes leaps of faith. Intellectually. Emotionally. Physically. **We must intentionally move to break up our routines of behavior and thought.** We must make room in our lives for the inexplicable. Room for the miraculous.

Planets and signs influencing the ninth house give us the precise formula for accomplishing this task. Perhaps it involves schooling. Maybe we need to travel. Or it could be that our routines need to be frightened out of us. Learn to fly. Climb a sheer granite face. Quit your job and go live in an ashram. Whatever form it takes, ninth-house experience stretches the fabric of one's being. Navigate its terrain gracefully and your daily life lies right on the cutting edge of your growth. Fail, and you feel like a physicist banished to "Sesame Street." Trapped, bored, and tired.

THE TENTH HOUSE
(THE MIDHEAVEN)

Traditional Name:
House of Career

Corresponding Sign:
Capricorn ♑

Associated Planet:
Saturn ♄

Terrain: **Career. Reputation; position in society. Destiny.**

Successfully Navigated:
Self-expressive, personally satisfying status in the community. Sense of fulfilling one's destiny.

Unsuccessfully Navigated:
Entrapment in a meaningless, alienating social role. Obsession with power, status, and appearances.

The midheaven. As we saw earlier, this is the highest point a planet can reach in the sky. When it hits the midheaven. there is only one way left to go: down. A planet on the midheaven is as obvious as it ever can be. Trees, buildings, groundlight –

If it is ever going to break through those obstacles and become visible, it is now.

Symbolically, the midheaven represents **that which is most obvious about us**. It is as if someone were observing us from a great distance. What does he see? Height. The color of our hair. Maleness or femaleness. The midheaven works just like that. Except now the distance is social. not physical. It represents how we look from a **social distance**. To put it simply, the midheaven describes **how we**

look to people who do not know us.

What do they see? They see what we **symbolize** to them. They see us, not as people, but as embodiments of various **functions** in society. Depersonalized. Two-dimensional. Representative of a class. They see our status. "He is an agent for the CIA." "She is an anthropologist." Doctors, lawyers. Indian chiefs.

The House of Career – that is the traditional name for this phase of house symbolism. But to call the tenth house the House of Career is to limit it. Our profession is only one determinant of our status. There are others. "She is a feminist" – that is a tenth-house statement too. So are "he is a Republican" and "she is an anti-nuclear activist." None of those stances is likely to earn a person a nickel. But they do **establish our identity in the public sphere.** And that is what tenth house terrain is all about.

That terrain is forced upon us. Whether we like it or not, we must cope with it. We are social beings. For most of us, it comes down to survival: how will we pay the rent unless we serve some function in society? And as soon as we do that, we have plugged into a network of myths and pressures that do much to determine the course of our lives.

To navigate tenth-house terrain successfully, we must find our **destiny.** We must, in other words, find a social role that is in harmony with our inner nature. We must figure out a way to get paid for being ourselves.

A tall order. But planets and signs in the tenth house guide us. They serve a dual purpose: on one level they serve as **descriptions of our destiny**. And on another, they represent **aspects of our own nature that must first be developed if we are to find our destiny.** They point out the goal. And the path to the goal.

Navigating the midheaven is never easy. Typically, it is the last of the houses to develop. Before it can blossom, we must first know ourselves very well. We must have sorted out our destiny from all that "doctor, lawyer, Indian chief" programming we received while growing up. If we succeed, we are at home in the world. Our work, our status, our public identity all reflect what is going on inside us. We bring the full force of our being to bear upon our public role. And that gives us power and creativity and freedom there. It gives us natural authority. We become one of the people who shape the myths and destiny of our culture.

And if our tenth-house navigation is unsuccessful, does that mean we are dressed in rags and subsisting on thin soup? No. Not at all. We may become wealthy. We may be glamorous.

We may have influence. But these facts do not reflect who we are. They only describe a part we have been given to play. And as long as we play that part, **we feel illegitimate and insecure.** We feel like an impostor. And in a sense, that is exactly what we are. That insecurity may drive us to cling even more desperately to our power and position. We sense how tenuous our hold on them really is, and seek to become more and more entrenched. We see rivals everywhere. Enemies. Competition. Tricksters. We sense that if we disappeared, a hundred others could fill the void in a second. And it is the truth. We didn't create the role. We were just cast in it.

That is never the case if our tenth-house navigation has been successful. No one else could play our part. That part, whatever it may be, is rooted in our individuality. It is an expression of who we are, inseparable from our own unique inner processes. Knowing that, we feel absolutely secure in our public identity. No one can steal it from us because no one else could do it. It is ours. And when we die, it dies with us.

THE ELEVENTH HOUSE

Traditional Name:
House of Friends

Corresponding Sign:
Aquarius ♒

Associated Planets:
Uranus ♅ & **Saturn** ♄

Terrain: The future; plans, goals, life themes. Identification with groups, organizations, movements, associations, one's crowd.

Successfully Navigated:
Concrete, specific sense of direction in life. Realistic yet inspiring goals, rooted in self-knowledge. Network of relationships that enhance and support the realization of personal goals.

Unsuccessfully Navigated:
Vagueness of purpose; drifting. Inability to make a commitment at any level. Unrealistic, quixotic, whimsical goals. Friends and associates who only contribute to one's confusion and drifting.

Direction. That is the essence of eleventh-house terrain. Where are you going? What are you becoming? What are the hopes and dreams and aspirations that give meaning to your daily life? The arena is unique; we cannot enter it. It always lies just beyond our grasp. Shifting, uncertain, conjectural, it is the **future.** It beckons us, guides us. But whenever we approach it flees like a startled fawn.

We live in the **now.** Anyone who forgets it soon makes a lot of bad decisions. And anyone who wants to make a successful passage through the eleventh house must remember it.

In the eleventh house, we do not enter the future. That is an impossibility. We remain firmly rooted in the now. Instead, we experience **an awareness of the future as it bears upon the present.** No man knows his fate, no woman can see tomorrow. This house has nothing to do with clairvoyance. In it we merely **become aware of our development over time.** And of the need for plans and decisions.

This is the critical point: the future is only a fantasy. Of itself, it can have no relevance to us. But an **awareness** of the future exists for all of us in the present tense. And coping with that awareness is essential to the development of our individuality. Whether or not we like it, all of us are headed somewhere. To navigate the eleventh house successfully, that future must be chosen consciously and intentionally. We must make a commitment to become a certain kind of person, to have certain experiences, to attain particular goals. We must adopt a **life strategy.** And we must adhere to it as long as it still feels relevant to where we are in the present.

If we fail, we drift. And if we drift, we become desperate. Even in the present tense, we are stymied. Without goals, there can be no meaningful action. But life **is** action. So we act, and our actions are tentative, sporadic, uncertain. Full of false starts and empty gestures. Soon we invent goals just to fill the void. But the goals have no roots. They are whimsical. Unrealistic. Quixotic. And because of that, they have no relevance to the now we are actually experiencing. They do not help us. So we feed them. Puff them up. Make them more elaborate, more grandiose. Before long, **we are living in the future**, obsessed and identified with a tomorrow we never reach. And our eleventh house navigation has been a failure.

Why is the eleventh house known as the House of Friends? What do friends have to do with our personal goals?

First we must define the word. **Friend** in this case has little to do with real intimacy. For that kind of insight we look to the seventh house, not to the eleventh. What we see here is far more superficial. We see only an ocean of familiar faces. Our associates. Our peer group. Our crowd. How do we choose those people? We choose them **because they reflect our goals.** If we aspire to being an artist, we seek out the company of artists. If we want to write, we are drawn to writers. If we want to become braver, we seek adventurers and daredevils. To find life's meaning, we associate with mystics and yogis and students of philosophy. By embodying the future we want for ourselves, those people help stabilize our own intentions. For us, **they symbolize the future.** And by interacting with them, our own aim is made more real to us.

First comes the goal. Then come the friends. That is the natural order if our eleventh house navigation is to be successful. But perhaps it is unsuccessful. Then, lacking any sense of direction, we seek friends at random. Friends "happen to us." We find ourselves involved in a network of associates and peers who contribute nothing to our life strategy. They simply take up our time.

Signs and planets in the eleventh house tell us where we are going and who can help us get there. But nowhere in astrology is it more critical to remember that the symbols are flexible. Eleventh-house configurations do not create our future for us; they merely describe our alternatives. We can respond positively and creatively. Or we can respond in a lazy, unimaginative way. Whatever energies exist in this phase of the birthchart, all we know is that by the end of life they will have come to dominate the character, for better or worse. To tame those energies and persuade them to serve our highest purposes is not easy. And to do it alone is more difficult still. But very few of us need do it alone. Support is available. Signs and planets in the House of Friends tell us where to look. They suggest what types of people and what kinds of associations or movements benefit us most. And they also tell us **where our own energies are most needed and will be most appreciated.** We not only take from our "friends." We can give too.

Establish goals. Find people who support them. Then live in the present moment. That is the secret of successful eleventh house navigation.

THE TWELFTH HOUSE

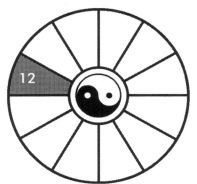

Traditional Name:
House of Troubles

Corresponding Sign:
Pisces ♓

Associated Planets:
Neptune ♆ & Jupiter ♃

Terrain: **Unstructured, unfocused consciousness; consciousness itself. Events and experiences that disrupt our identification with personality. Ego death.**

Successfully Navigated:
Self-transcendence; freedom from worry about the ups and downs of life. Spiritual and psychic experiences; meditation. Sense of the "presence of God" or of higher levels of consciousness.

Unsuccessfully Navigated:
Blurry, confused, uncertain self-image. Escapism; abusive, self-destructive relationships with alcohol, food, sleep, sex, television, and other "drugs." Hypersensitivity, mental imbalance, schizophrenia. Chronic "bad luck."

You stand before the judge. He grants you your bankruptcy. Your business is ruined. All those years of work, down the drain. And then he grants you a divorce. Your marriage is dead too. Finished. You have nothing left. You walk out of the courtroom, into the afternoon sun. By all appearances, a broken man, a shattered woman. A washout, with no place in this world. Are you crying? Do you head for the nearest bar? Bitterness, rage, self-destructiveness – all those reactions are available to you. But let's imagine you choose another response. Let's imagine that you leave that courtroom whistling Dixie, feeling light as a puff of cloud on a summer afternoon.

Is it madness? Is it denial or repression? Perhaps. But perhaps not. A year ago, you were in a living hell. Now it has passed. Now you are free. No more futile battle to save a doomed business. No more endless arguing and bartering with a husband or wife you truly lost long ago. That miserable chapter of your life has drawn to a close. The "nothing" you have now is far better than the "something" you have lost. And so you feel liberated.

You find a park bench. You sit down, warmed by the sun. You close your eyes, let everything melt away. You let go of your worries, your circumstances, even your identity. For a few moments, **you simply experience your consciousness,** unencumbered by labels and responsibilities. Your mind is empty. And from some deep, irrational place in the core of your being, you feel a fountain of peace. In an hour you may be perspiring in the waiting room of the Mafioso Brothers employment agency. But in that moment, you have entered the terrain of the twelfth house and your navigation is flawless.

The twelfth house. To the medievals, it was the House of Troubles. They saw it as a symbol of misfortune, associated with sickness, poverty, and imprisonment. Outwardly, it often brings setbacks like those, even if our navigation is good. **But we need not respond to trouble with self-pity.** We can use it. We can turn inward. We can let go.

Whenever trouble strikes, each of us has a built-in escape route. It is true that we are in the world and must take responsibility for ourselves. But whenever we want to, we can leave for a little while. We can move our attention away from the dramas of personality. We can focus it on a peaceful place deep within us, a place that is always there, waiting. Every successful twelfth house navigation involves activating those mental circuits. We can call that escape route meditation. We can call it prayer or contemplation. If religious language bothers us, we can call it self-hypnosis. And the peace we find we can call God or "our center" or just relaxation. There is no house in which words are less significant.

Escape is the theme in unsuccessful navigations of this house, too. But now the escape takes a different form. Instead of seeking peace, we seek numbness. Instead of leaping through this window beyond personality, we stay right here, rigidly identified with our problems but doing nothing about them. **Instead of retreating temporarily into our depths, we seek to obliterate consciousness altogether**. We simply try to turn it off. Traditional texts associate the twelfth house with the dangers of drink. Modern texts add the abuse of drugs. And certainly they are right. The alcoholic and the drug abuser are both failed twelfth-house navigators. Both have partly obliterated consciousness.

But chemical interventions in awareness are only one hazard in this uncertain terrain. The person who peers blankly into the television set for hours *every* night is numbing himself too. So is the person who must constantly eat or the one who "can think of nothing but sex." **Any intense, repetitious, compulsive behavior can potentially feed an unsuccessful twelfth-house passage**. And that *very* obsessiveness prevents any more positive response to the troubles that pulled the trigger in the first place. We are too numbed to move. We feel crazy. Disconnected. Apathetic. In extreme cases, we may even be diagnosed as schizophrenic. And always, we complain of our chronic "bad luck."

Signs and planets in the twelfth house are like time bombs. The fuse may be long. It may be short. But there is no extinguishing it. Sooner or later, the issues of the twelfth house undercut us. They trip us up. **They face us with an impossible situation.** Once that situation breaks, we can head for the bar and order a double. Or we can withdraw for a while into our depths, feeling that endless reservoir of creativity and life and resilience within us. And feeling that, we can gracefully **let go of a set of dying circumstances**, knowing that when the dust settles, we can begin again.

Such letting go is never easy. Those dying circumstances are dear to us. We are attached to them. They are the foundation of our identity in the world. But our identity in the world is a transitory phenomenon. **Only consciousness itself is eternal.** Nothing else matters. Grasp that, and the House of Troubles is troubled no longer. It is the House of Wisdom. And your passage through it is a passage of unbreakable, enduring inner harmony.

❧ Part Three: ❧
Sentences

"Do you speak English?" If the *query* came from a Peruvian Indian, your answer would be an immediate yes. If William Shakespeare asked you the same question, you might hesitate before responding. Fluency in a language is acquired by degrees, and one person's fluency is another one's stammering. It is the same with astrological language. We can learn the basic vocabulary quickly – you have nearly done that now yourself and then spend the rest of our lives gradually developing eloquence.

Eloquence is our goal in the next few chapters. We know the words. Now we must form the sentences, remembering always that the process, like that of learning to express ourselves fully in our native language, is ongoing. There is always room for improvement, for more subtlety, for more evocative phrasing.

You have the words. Those we learn by drill and memorization. Now it is time to shift our mental gears, to start putting words together in a more playful, self-expressive way. In the next chapter we start building phrases. In the following one we introduce laws of syntax and grammar, as well as adding some more technical vocabulary. Then we learn to construct paragraphs. Absorb the following guidelines, and by the end of the book your astrological English will be past the "Peruvian Indian" stage. And maybe, if you practice hard and don't let yourself get discouraged, one day you will sound like Shakespeare.

Interpretation I:
Planets in Signs & Houses

Everybody has a Venus. Everybody is influenced by Virgo. All of us face the dramas of the sixth house. Those features mark us as human. But they do not describe us individually. To do that we must take astrology a step further.

Venus. Virgo. The sixth house. What are they? Only abstractions, nothing more. But what happens when we put them together like the man in our sample chart? What about Venus in Virgo? And what if the combination of the two expresses itself through the sixth house? That's when the magic begins.

Signs, planets and houses are the bare bones of an ancient psychological theory. A theory that still applies to all of us. But when we **combine** a specific planet with a specific sign and house, we stop talking about theory and start talking about people. To say someone has a Venus is like saying that he has an eye. Who cares? But to say that his Venus lies in Virgo is like adding that his eye is as cold and penetrating as an ice pick. And to say that it lies in the sixth house is like adding that the man who has the eye is staring right at you with a shotgun in his hands.

A sign-planet-house combination is the most elemental astrological statement **applicable to an individual**. It forms a basic "bit" in the human psyche. Concrete. Particular. Unique. And just ten of those bits, plus the ascendant and some connective tissue, give us the birthchart: a statement so articulate, so specialized that it can never be repeated.

Planets in Signs

The key to understanding the interactions of planets and signs lies in remembering the differences between them. Each serves a distinct purpose. Lose sight of that and your interpretations will be as fuzzy as a ball of yarn in a box of kittens.

A planet asks the question **what?** A sign takes that **what** and develops it with a **how** and a **why.**

What is Venus? Like all planets, it is a psychological function. In this case, we spotlight our capacity to **create relationships.** In anything we say about Venus, that issue has center stage. It is the **what.**

Venus has little built-in personality of its own. One person is a loner. Another is the life of the party. In either case, relationship formation is the function and the focus is on Venus. The way that Venus actually operates in the character the **how** and the **why** – is determined by the sign in which the planet lies, not by the planet itself

With Venus in Virgo, a Virgoan set of needs and hungers underlies the pattern of intimate relating. What is Virgo? The Perfectionist. The Servant. The Martyr. The Analyst.

With Venus **conditioned by Virgo,** our subject is an idealist, at least in matters of the heart. Virgo guarantees that. He has a mental image of the perfect marriage or friendship. He works toward it unflaggingly, sacrificing much of himself, perhaps too much of himself, for the sake of realizing it. But let his partner crawl down from her pedestal to go drink a beer and there will be hell to pay. Virgo wants perfection. Anything less is a personal affront. A betrayal.

The **why** of Venus in Virgo is simple to say, hard to live: it is the aim of creating a **perfected relationship,** one that functions in absolute accord with a set of ideals – ideals that are felt intuitively by the person who has the configuration.

The **how** involves all the arrows in the Virgoan quiver. A meticulous attention to the details of the way the relationship is operating. A scrupulous honesty in appraising those details. An unflinching commitment to responsible behavior. Humility. A sense of the difference between talking about growth and real change.

Venus-in-Virgo's **how** has a seamy side as well. The process can short-circuit. The ideal relationship can exist only between two perfected individuals. Two people who have worked out all their issues. A pair of Buddhas. A man or woman with this configuration may become unreasonably demanding, never satisfied, always critical. He or she may fall in love with some internalized fantasy woman or dream man – and drive away all their potential flesh-and-blood partners as unworthy. They may mythologize a real partner to the point that his or her real nature becomes blurred. And then typically their mate's reality asserts itself in some undeniable way – and the Virgoan Venus cries treason. They may feel so unworthy themselves that a mammoth insecurity motivates all their relationships. They may fail to make legitimate demands. They may fall into an obsessive pattern of "earning the mate's love" through an endless progression of menial tasks. They may enter into degrading or self-destructive relationships.

None of these negative behaviors can ever be reliably **predicted** on the basis of having Venus in Virgo, although many texts claim that is the case. That is just fortune-telling. If you keep one eye on reality while you are reading, you will see that those narrow interpretations are very often wrong.

All these negatives are just risks. Occupational hazards. They are distortions of the fundamental Venus-in-Virgo function, which is the realization of an ideal pattern of relationship. Any good astrological interpretation includes a description of those pitfalls. But only as a warning. Even when we know for a fact that someone with that configuration is living with an alcoholic baboon whom she takes to be the Messiah, we must never describe those circumstances as her "fate." She is not stuck there. Whenever she chooses, she can make a happier, more sensitive response. Like all of us, she can grow. Always, when looking at a planet in a sign, think in terms of what, **why,** and **how.** Stick to that, and you will never sink to being a fortune-teller.

What About Houses?

Planets are the **what.** Signs are the **how and why.** Houses complete the system by asking one more question, perhaps the most practical one of all: **where?**

Every battle needs a battlefield. And regardless of the natures of the armies, that battlefield itself is going to leave its stamp on the tone of the conflict. Are the armies clashing in thick jungle? Freezing mountains? Trackless desert? No way to know how the war looks without knowing that.

It is the same with planets and signs. When Mars enters Pisces, sparks may fly. But those sparks look one way in the house of career, another way in the house of the home.

Each house is a distinct battlefield. Each one represents a department of life **within which a person may make choices.** But each one is also a fixed reality with a certain pattern of givens. A specific terrain. We may climb the mountains. Or we may choose to stick to the valleys. But no amount of wishing is going to turn that territory into flatlands.

Where? The question is trickier than it seems. We all live in two universes. One is the **objective world.** Call it the cosmos. Call it the material plane. Call it reality. Whatever we call that dimension of life, it is full of givens and limitations. It represents a world beyond the boundaries of personality, a world with which personality must learn to cope. **And it is the domain of the houses.** Marriage. Career.

The powers and limits of language. Money.

But houses have a second domain. It is the subjective side of life. Call it the unconscious. Call it the astral plane. Call it God. Call it imagination. No matter what label we use, that dimension of life – represented by houses four, eight, and twelve – can be entered and explored. It is a where. House symbolism again.

Fortune-tellers frequently miss that. Their interpretations of the inward houses are often superficial. They attempt to translate inner facts into outer terms and come up only with vague euphemisms.

Always remember that **a house is only a territory our awareness can enter and within which it can express itself.** Some of those territories are visible. Some are invisible. They still answer the question **where.**

Back to our Englishman, the man in our sample birthchart. We have already seen how his Venus is affected by Virgo. But what about its placement in the sixth house?

The sixth house is one of the more outward, concrete ones. With Venus lying there, its theater of expression is open to the public. All of us have front-row seats.

The sixth house. The House of Servants. The phase of house symbolism in which we encounter responsibilities and duties. A house of work. Of skills and techniques. Of competence. Of the support we offer those around us.

Unsuccessfully navigated, the sixth-house terrain is one of drudgery. Duties and responsibilities overwhelm us. We allow ourselves to become trapped and enslaved, subordinated to the will of another person.

Completing the "bit," the sixth house adds the critical **where** dimension to the issues created by Virgo's interaction with Venus. It defines the arena in which the sign and planet play out their dialogue.

Interpretively, we are at an advantage here. Many parallels exist between the sixth house and Virgo. Once again, signs and houses are twelvefold cycles of symbolism, and the particular phases of one correspond to the same phases in the other. Sixth house issues parallel the issues of the sixth sign – and the sixth sign happens to be Virgo.

Are signs and houses the same? No. As always, the sign supplies mind-stuff-motivation, attitude, tone – while the house tells us where to look for the events that that mind-stuff produces. Virgo, for example, represents the **need** to express one's self through some particular competence or skill, while the sixth house defines a **concrete arena of work and responsibility.** Because of the overlap between the two, our work in interpreting Venus lying in both Virgo and the sixth house is easier. We have fewer balls to juggle.

Regardless of what sign or house it occupies, Venus always faces us with the question of intimate human relationships. That is its **what.** But the relationships to which Venus refers are not always romantic ones. Venus is just as much a symbol of friendships and partnerships – and of the relationships between colors, shapes, and sounds. It is as much a symbol of our aesthetic reactions as it is of our ability to form bonds of affection and understanding.

With Venus in his sixth house, the Englishman whose life we are beginning to decode probably does most of his professional work in partnerships. His relationship-forming **what** expresses itself in the **where** of his daily livelihood. Throughout his life he finds himself confronted by the need to **sustain harmonious personal relationships if he is to cope successfully with the realities of his chosen work.**

Does he like it? Is he successful? Maybe yes. Maybe no. Houses show circumstances, not how we feel about them. By disposition, our subject may be a loner. No matter. With Venus shaping his sixth house, the progress of his daily work is inextricably tied to his progress in learning how to accept another person as an equal partner.

What pitfalls does he face there? Virgo has already answered some of that for us: pickiness, runaway perfectionism, over-idealization, unrealistic demands and expectations. The sixth house just adds one more piece to the puzzle: if we see those destructive Virgo Venus behaviors at all, we will certainly see them corrupting his working partnerships as well as his emotional ones.

The simple friendship outside the domain of work may be less susceptible to those Virgo problems – but that simple friendship also plays a relatively insignificant role in our subject's development. It is just not very important to him. Most of his life-shaping bonds *come* to him in the sixth-house arena. **His co-workers are his soul mates:** that is one of the fixed features of his life. That is part of his life's **terrain,** as defined by the sixth house. He can respond to it creatively or with anger and resentment. But he can never change it. No lasting love without shared work, no lasting work without the support of friends and lovers: that is the message of our Englishman's Venus.

Who are these partners who play such a pivotal role in our subject's life? Once again, Venus answers: **his partners are Venusian types.** Artists. Counselors. Graceful, sensitive people. Glamorous ones. And what kind of work does he do with them? Again, Venus answers. The work he seeks must involve the expression and development of his Venusian function. Perhaps he works in human relations. Perhaps he is a psychologist. Maybe he is an "artist" – a poet, a musician, a hairstylist, an interior decorator. We cannot tell his fortune; that is up to him.

Venus offers many options. But astrology narrows down the areas in which those options must be sought. Professionally, his fortune lies with the planet Venus. In the world of work, that psychological function is his guiding star. Should he ignore it, he meets only aimlessness and closed doors.

That is one "bit." A typical one. Every birthchart has ten of them. Unravel them all, then weave them together, and you have mastered the wizardry of interpretation. Let's analyze what we have done in order to come up with some generalized procedures we can apply in all cases. There are many "bits," but they all work the same way. If we keep our whats, whys, and **wheres** straight, no combination of symbols should baffle us for long.

Tactics

So you have a planet sitting in a sign and a house. What does it mean? How do you proceed? Most of us draw a blank at first.

Enter the pop astrologers with their cookbook astrology texts. Confused? No problem. Here is a paragraph about Venus in Virgo. But Venus is in the sixth house? Again, no problem. Check the paragraph about Venus in the sixth. We are relieved. We start patching together an interpretation. But the more we patch, the more our words sound like a patch quilt of contradictions. The problem is simple. The smallest unit of astrological symbolism **relevant to an individual** is a planet-sign-house combination. Life has three dimensions. Identity. Purpose. Circumstance. Leave one out and your interpretations are about as plausible as the skyline in one of those grade-B monster movies: they are just paper hanging in the background, fooling no one.

So why doesn't someone write a book with readouts on all the planet-sign-house "phrases"? Once again, the answer is easy. There are too many of them: 1,440 of them, to be exact. And the "phrases" influence one another. Two women may have an Arian Mars in the tenth house. But if one of them is a Capricorn and the other is a Gemini, those Mars influences are feeding on very different kinds of fuel. A book that took those factors into account would stretch from here to the moon in the fine-print edition.

We must proceed differently. Intuition helps. Creativity is essential. But anyone who implies that you need extrasensory perception to be a good astrologer is muddying the water. What it takes, perhaps more than anything else, is an orderly mind. The interplay of symbolism in a birthchart is so complex that without a systematic approach, the mind is overwhelmed. Details swamp it. It fails to grasp the **whole.** Master that orderly approach. Practice it awhile. Something magical happens. The symbols organize your thinking in a new way. You begin to make creative connections between signs, planets, and houses – connections you never saw in any book.

Five Steps

An orderly approach. Learn these five steps for interpreting an astrological bit. Stick to them slavishly at first as you teach your mind this new skill. After a while, you won't need to be so formal about it – unless you get stumped.

STEP ONE
Look at the planet. **What** mental function are we considering? What part of the mind are we talking about? Identity formation with the sun? Discipline building with Saturn?

STEP TWO
Look at the sign. It is what motivates the planet. What is that planetary function seeking? What is the **why** that underlies its activity? What is its hidden agenda? Only a sign can tell us that. What we are getting at here is a sense of purpose. Evolutionary direction. If our understanding of a phrase seems scattered and aimless, chances are good we have blown step two.

STEP THREE
Think: **How** can that planet-sign combination achieve its goal? What relevant resources does the sign contribute? What about the planet? You might want to look at the **resources** section in the appropriate section in the signs chapter or the **function** section in the planets chapter. If **you** were the person in question and had those strengths and liabilities, how would **you** achieve happiness?

STEP FOUR
Think: **How** can that planet-sign combination be distorted? What kinds of behaviors are consistent with the meaning of the bit but not consistent with its evolutionary purpose?

Look to the **shadow** section in the signs chapter and the **dysfunction** section in the planets chapter if you need your memory jogged.

Remember: present those distortions as warnings, not as predictions.

STEP FIVE
Look at the house. **Where** are the planet-sign issues being developed? What kind of behavior are they creating? In what part of life will a strong response to the planet and sign manifest as an improvement in one's **circumstances?** Where will a weak response lead most certainly to anxiety and frustration? Houses answer all that.

Trust these five steps. They work. They underlie everything we have seen about Venus in Virgo in the sixth house. And they work just as well with the other 1,439 phrases too. Let them guide you and your interpretations will be accurate and specific. They will be personal and creative. And most important, they won't put anyone in a neat little box. You will be an evolutionary astrologer, not a fortune-teller.

Interpretation II: Aspects, Rulerships & The Moon's Nodes

A woman has a horrendous day at work. At ten in the morning she is washing down aspirin with her fourth cup of instant coffee. By two o'clock she realizes that those aspirins were her lunch. By five, she is choosing between early retirement and random violence. She commutes home. Her husband gives her a cheery hello at the door. Half an hour later, they are twenty minutes into a meaningless Waterloo over nothing. Why? Because she needs to let off steam, and bleeding off work-related tensions into her intimate life is part of her pattern in marriage.

A second woman lives through an equally lamentable day on the job. The same aspirin. The same overdose of caffeine. The same homicidal fantasies. She too commutes home. She too is greeted by her husband. But instead of tearing into him, she collapses in his arms and allows herself to be comforted. In half an hour, they are choosing between Chinese food and Italian, and her work problems are forgotten. Why? Not because she is "better" than the first woman. It is simply that her work circuits and her intimacy circuits are hooked together in a different way.

Tension in one does not automatically produce tension in the other. Those two sides of life are not nearly as linked in her as they are in her more explosive counterpart.

Going further into the lives of both women, we might learn that the first woman's husband knows a great deal about her work. He shares her highs as well as her lows. He stays informed. He advises her. He is in her corner professionally, and most of the time she appreciates it. In the second marriage, there is an unspoken agreement that work is something you leave at the office. Neither husband nor wife has much knowledge of the other's daily work, nor much interest in it. And they are both quite content with that arrangement.

Events in a marriage: since we are dealing with **where,** immediately the astrological focus is on the seventh house. Events on the job: now we are looking at the sixth house or perhaps at the tenth. No way to understand the differences between those women without considering at least two houses in each case. So, clearly the interaction between career and marriage cannot be accounted for through an analysis of any single astrological bit, since those phrases can never involve more than one house at a time. Each "phrase" can have only one **where.**

But that is not the way life works, as we see in the example. Career setbacks often do affect our marriages. Self-esteem does color our philosophy of life. Our level of playfulness and expressiveness is relevant to our sexuality. In the mind nothing happens in a vacuum. All the parts are related. All are interactive. To put it astrologically, **the birthchart is greater than the sum of its phrases.**

Interpreting a chart is more than grasping each of the ten sign-planet-house combinations. We must understand how they impact on each other. We must realize how each phrase limits or enhances the expression of the rest. In reading a birthchart, **we must think in terms of unity.** Piecemeal phrase-by-phrase interpretations get us nowhere.

How do we do it? How do we go beyond bits? Some of it is just common sense. The Englishman in our sample chart has a Libran sun in the sixth house. Much of his ability to be himself (Sun =**what**) revolves around his capacity to create harmonious personal relationships (Libra=**how, why**) in his working life (the sixth house = **where**).

Taking a closer look at this birthchart, we quickly observe several factors that seem to be lined up against that Libran sun, factors that suggest a lot of independence. His Arian ascendant, for example, gives him a rather brash exterior. How do we know that? The ascendant is always a big part of the way we appear to people before they get to know us very well, and Aries flavors it in the Englishman's case with directness, intensity, and perhaps even an intimidating quality. Another factor that seems to be working counter to his sixth-house Libran sun is his Aquarian moon. His emotions (remember, moon =**what**) are propelled by independence, eccentricity, and a desire to establish himself as a person quite distinct from the norm (Aquarius = **how, why**).

Considering these factors, plain common sense tells us that at least some of the time, his sun operates at crossed purposes with his moon and ascendant. He needs to cooperate and yet he resents compromise. Tension. The stuff of growth.

Being alert to patterns of dissonance like these is the essence of effective astrology. In the next chapter we pursue that technique in detail. But for now we need only consider a far more straightforward method of pattern detecting, a method that links phrase to phrase in a clear and unmistakable way.

Aspects

If signs, planets, and houses are the basic words in the astrological language, then **aspects** are the **laws of grammar and syntax** that govern how those words must be hooked together. Aspects represent our first solid step toward the formation of full-blown, coherent astrological sentences.

What are they? Physically, aspects are simply geometrical angles between planets. Every birthchart is a circle. Every circle contains 360 degrees. Along that circle, Mars and Venus might, for example, be separated by 90 degrees. That's an aspect.

Over the centuries astrologers have discovered that certain angles trigger powerful interactions between planets while other angles do not.

Take that 90-degree split between Mars and Venus (*see figure below*). That is one of the critical angles. With that number of degrees separating the two planets, we can never talk about one without understanding the other. They are linked.

A 90° Aspect Between Venus & Mars

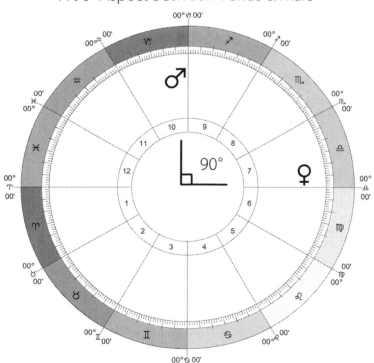

For a man or woman with that configuration, Mars trouble always means Venus trouble too – and strengthening Venus may be a way of helping Mars to operate more smoothly.

Traditional astrologers divide aspects into two categories: good and bad. As always, those words do not promote clear astrological thinking. All aspects are functional; all of them serve a purpose. Some feel better than others, but that is a minor consideration. Often the ones that feel best are the ones that get us into the worst imbroglios. Drop **good and bad** from your thinking – at least from your astrological thinking. Let's look at each of these aspects in terms of **function** rather than in terms of how easy or difficult they might be.

Zero Degrees: The Conjunction

The simplest of all the aspects is the **conjunction.** This occurs when two planets are right on top of each other. Their functions are grafted together. Each one flavors the other, and in their union a kind of "macro-bit" is formed, far more complex than a single sign-planet-house combination.

Fusion – that is the essence of the conjunction. Two "bits" become one.

Let's say that Mars and Mercury are conjunct. Normally aggressiveness (Mars) and intellect (Mercury) each have their own separate territories in the mind. One circuit can be fired up without exciting the other one. Not so when the two planets are in conjunction. When one is ignited, so is the other. The result is a sharp, incisive mind. A forceful one. A mind that thinks in terms of pros and cons, of winners and losers. All the Mercury functioning is colored by the competitiveness of Mars.

And how is Mars affected? Natural aggressiveness tends to be intellectualized. Here is a person who is not likely to figure prominently in barroom brawls – but he or she may have a shameless killer instinct in discussions of politics or religion. Mind and tongue take the place of pounding fists.

All this is certainly tempered and directed by the sign and house in which the conjunction occurs – and by aspects it in turn makes to the rest of the birthchart – but none of that alters the key point: **in a conjunction, two functions, normally separate and distinct, are fused together.** Never can one operate without activating the other.

180 Degrees: The Opposition

The opposition is one of the "bad" aspects in old-time astrology. It is true that this aspect produces enormous tension. But that tension can add profound depth and resiliency to the birthchart. Much depends on how the individual chooses to respond to the issues the opposition presents.

Tension – that is the key to understanding oppositions. Two planets are irreconcilably **polarized.** One turns left, the other automatically turns right – and perversity has nothing to do with it. Functioning naturally, according to their own inner logic, each one must always undercut the other.

Say one planet lies in Taurus. It is opposed by a planet in Scorpio. The **why** behind the Taurean planet is a search for calm and simplicity, while what motivates the planet in Scorpio is precisely the opposite: a hunger for intensity, depth, and transformation.

They do not get along. That is why traditional astrologers say the opposition is "bad." But we need not be bound by such superficial thinking. The tension between the Taurean planet and the Scorpionic one can be invaluable. Each can correct for the excesses and deficiencies of the other. Neither one likes it. But both are better off.

That Taurean planet might like nothing better than to spend every weekend at home. It is quiet. It is safe. Why make trouble? The Scorpio planet sees it differently: let's go meet whatever paperback psychologist is in town this weekend.

If the individual whose birthchart contains that opposition **can hold both halves of the polarity in consciousness simultaneously,** hammering out a compromise between them, his or her life is far richer. She relaxes a lot, and she meets a few interesting psychologists too. That is the point with oppositions – expanding our awareness sufficiently to see both sides of an issue. If we succeed, we gain flexibility, variety, and adaptability.

But what if we fail to make peace with an opposition? What then? Failure with oppositions has dire consequences. The mind oscillates between two halves of a polarity. When one side is dominant, the other is forced out of awareness. We may gain simplicity, but we lose something far more precious: our sanity. At its worst, an opposition can produce Jekyll and Hyde qualities in the character. One half of the polarity claims our attention. We make choices and commitments based on its needs. We bum our bridges behind us. Then the other half emerges, forcing the first bit into the background. A new set of contradictory needs and motivations propels us, undercutting all that we set into motion under the influence of the first bit. And we go back and forth like that, perhaps for years, being our own worst enemy and accomplishing very little.

90 Degrees: The Square

Like the opposition, the **square** is considered to be a malevolent aspect. And, again like the opposition, that "malevolence" appears only if we fail to grasp the developmental issue the aspect represents and to make a positive response to it.

Squares produce **friction,** just as oppositions produce tension. Of the two, the opposition is the more harmonious. Opposing signs always have **something** in common. With Scorpio and Taurus, it is inwardness. With Gemini and Sagittarius, it is curiosity. With Leo and Aquarius, it is an extreme development of personality. Always, opposing signs are linked together somehow. Always, they are different sides of the same coin. Radically different sides perhaps, but at least it is the same coin. Not so with squares.

The friction characteristic of the 90-degree aspect arises out of an absolute, built-in discord. In **a square, the two phrases have no basis for mutual understanding.** There is no common ground, no common language. Only a mile-high wall of incomprehension.

Let's consider a square between a planet in Aries and one in Cancer. The **why** underlying the Arian planet is the development of courage. The **how** always involves intentionally seeking out certain kinds of stress – and the planet and house involved in the phrase identify that stress in precise terms.

The Cancerian phrase is propelled by an entirely different hidden agenda. Its **why** involves a vast deepening of the subjective life, and its **how** is dependent on quieting and stabilizing one's relationship to the outer world – the very world that Aries seeks to stir up.

To Cancer, Arian behavior **makes no sense.** Cancerian behavior is equally cryptic to the Ram. Worse, should one succeed, the other is confounded. Their purposes are crossed. Planets linked by squares vie for control of the personality. Victory for one means destruction for the other.

If the opposition is the aspect of rivals, then **the square is the aspect of natural enemies.**

Strong words. What good can possibly come from carrying such a vendetta between one's ears? Tremendous good, if we let it. Nature is full of natural enemies. Lions and wildebeests. Owls and mice. Foxes and rabbits. Their dramas are brutal, and yet they serve an indispensable purpose: weakness is destroyed. The slow and the sick are caught. The swift and the cunning escape.

Squares serve the same purpose: **the friction produced in a square exerts relentless developmental pressure on each of the planets.** To survive, they must evolve. One slip, one self-indulgence, and they are trampled. Don't look for ways to "resolve" a square. You won't find them. Squares are irresolvable. Even at their best, they are a source of unending restlessness in the character. And ideally, that restlessness is a healing force, leading not to peace, but to growth and accomplishment.

The horror of squares is not their capacity to generate upsetting

Catch-22 situations. That is just the territory that goes along with the aspect. Passing through that territory is never comfortable, but it always makes us stronger, always weeds out any weak responses we might be making to either of the planetary phrases. The horror is that one of the phrases might actually win. It might succeed in crushing the other one, rendering it passive and dysfunctional. Then we are crippled. One of the ten fundamental "psychic circuits" that constitute our humanity is destroyed. Something vital goes out of us. And that part of life, whatever it might be, is from then on a scene of disasters, false starts, and deadeningly repetitive failures.

120 Degrees: The Trine

A "good" aspect – but let's look at that idea more carefully. Aspects are like marriages. Some are based on passion. Some are based on friendship. And in each category, some prosper while others become diseased. The question with aspects is not which type of marriage is "better." Life is far too complex for that kind of simpleminded thinking. The question is more pointed: how can we temper the explosive, "Let's drop the Big One" mentality characteristic of the passionate marriage? And how can we enliven the sleepy, too-easy friendship?

We have already met the passionate aspects: the opposition and the square. Their pitfalls are clear; they pump us full of adrenaline as certainly as the unexpected flash of blue strobes twenty yards from our rear bumper. Now let's face a different kind of marriage. Let's meet the friendly trine and see if we can avoid letting it lull us into lifelong sleep.

The trine. To the fortune-tellers, it is the Rolls-Royce of aspects. They associate it only with positive traits, viewing it as a force that strengthens and deepens any planets it might touch. The more trines, the more luck – that is the traditional view. Don't believe it. Thinking that trines are automatically good is like believing that any marriage in which the partners never fight must automatically be a great one.

Trines can sour the marriage between planets just as readily as any square or opposition. And, again like any square or opposition, they can help the planets reach their highest level of expression. Everything depends on how we choose to respond. Trines mean **harmony**. Planets 120 degrees apart are in agreement with each other. Their natures may be very different. Their goals may be unrelated. But they are **natural allies**. Freely, without forethought or effort, they join forces. Whether that alliance helps us or hinders us is another question.

Let's imagine we have a Sagittarian moon. There is an emotional hunger (moon) for Sagittarian experiences – experiences that break up the normal routines of life and project us into exotic, stimulating environments.

Imagine that moon is trined by an Arian Mars – all the aggressive, impulsive mental circuits (Mars) are driven by an Arian desire for adventure, for triumph, for the peak experience.

Through the trine, Mars and the moon are linked in a pattern of mutual support and enhancement. No crossed purposes here. They are in agreement. Both of them are eager for excitement, and what pleases one is likely to please the other one, too. With Mars trine that Sagittarian moon, we might trek across Nepal or dive among the reefs of the Red Sea. But we might also try to swim the English Channel in January with our hands tied behind our backs.

Internal harmony – that is at once the great strength and the fatal weakness of trines. Planets tied together by this aspect experience no conflict with each other. But conflict is not necessarily evil. Sometimes it breeds balance and good judgment. A trine may be a very efficient psychological mechanism, allowing two phrases to team up and accomplish more together than they could alone. The **whats** may be as different as Mars and the moon, but the **hows and whys** are always harmonious. Is that harmony good? Maybe yes. Maybe no. Because of that internal accord, the phrases support each other in a web of common needs, but **the trine gives planets no perspective** on themselves. They may be as useless to each other as two habitual drunks deciding whether to buy another six pack.

The passionate aspects – squares and oppositions – work like passionate marriages. There may be hell to pay as the planets make impossible demands and defend incomprehensible positions. But that very tension insures growth, change, and clarification. Not so with trines. These are like friendly marriages in which a spirit of mutuality and compromise reigns, and very little tension is ever brought to the surface. The partners may be happy. But perhaps that happiness is as far as it goes. They may learn nothing, experience nothing new, change nothing in themselves. And under pressure, that "happy" marriage may fall apart far sooner than its battle-scarred counterpart.

The trick with trines is to see them as representing areas of **life with almost unlimited potential for growth.** An alliance has been formed in the mind. Two planets are ready to pull together toward a common goal with no energy wasted on friction between them. And yet that lack of friction has allowed them to fall asleep. We must awaken them. We must imagine what powers lie latent in that trine and then **trigger the release of those powers as an act of will and self-discipline.** If we succeed in sparking a trine into action and development, it can carry us further than any square or opposition, and do so with far less effort. But if we fail, the trine squanders our vitality. We behave like spoiled children, unmotivated, lazy, and self-satisfied, always looking for the easy path, and smiling our way down a trail of waste and self-destruction.

60 Degrees: The Sextile

Another "good" aspect, the sextile is usually understood to work like a watered-down trine. In actual fact, its action is quite distinct. Like the other aspects, the sextile represents a particular form of marriage between planetary phrases, one with its own special logic and its own unique hazards. Like the trine, it inclines toward friendship. But the similarities go no further. Comparing the trine to the sextile is like comparing a waltz to a roadhouse boogie. Both are dances, but the overlap ends there.

Sextiles produce **excitation.** They are intense, colorful, dynamic. Both planets are stimulated and enlivened. Both are vitalized. When two planets are joined by a sextile, it is as if they were a pair of teenagers falling in love for the first time. There is magic. There is humor. There is high energy. But there is little restfulness or stability. Like the teenagers' first romance, the sextile can help bring two planets to maturity. Like love, it accelerates evolution, clarifying a person's essence. But the medicine is heady. It can also produce giddiness and unreality. Enthusiasm can flare up, only to subside before much can come of it.

Say that a sextile exists between a planet in Leo and a planet in Gemini. The **why** underlying the action of the first planet is self-expression; that of the second is the gathering of information. The Leo phrase transmits. Gemini receives and asks for more. That delights Leo, which gladly transmits something else. The process accelerates and both planets are **stimulated into action.** That's a sextile.

Sometimes the excitation is more subtle. A planet in Cancer may form a sextile with one in Taurus. The Crab is seeking a development of subjectivity and imagination. The Bull pursues calm and serenity. Those are their **whys,** and they are quite distinct. But their **hows** are much the same: both try to stabilize and simplify their outward lives, eliminating the upsetting and the unpredictable. Once again we see the excitation characteristic of the sextile: the Crab crawls inside his shell, delighting Taurus. Meanwhile, the Bull has been busily establishing security and order in the world. And that warms Cancer's heart.

Like trines, sextiles can suffer from short-sightedness. Cancer and Taurus may bore themselves to death. Gemini can tire of Leo's performance – and then the Lion may feel betrayed. **Sextiles, like trines, generate no perspective on themselves**. Like friendly marriages, their Achilles' heel is their slowness to recognize fundamental interactive weaknesses. And without that recognition there can be no strategy for defense and no possibility of growth. Sextiles add another risk: excitation, like teenage romance, is often fleeting. Steadiness and sustainment – those are elusive qualities for the sextile. Immense energies flow between the bits joined by this aspect. But those energies can flare up without aim or purpose only to subside again, colorful, dramatic, and useless.

Minor Aspects

These five – the conjunction, the opposition, the square, the trine, and the sextile – are the major aspects. They symbolize five fundamental ways in which planets can interact: **fusion, tension, friction, harmony, and excitation.** Understand them and you are well on your way toward interpreting a birthchart.

Some charts have many aspects. Some have relatively few. On a typical birthchart, there are perhaps twenty such relationships. Each one is significant. Each one contributes to our understanding of the chart as a whole.

Even twenty aspects are a lot to remember. Trying to deal with all of them at once can overwhelm us. They are all important – but we also have to be realistic about how much data our brains can correlate at one time. In the next chapter we talk about ways to pick out the most significant aspects on a particular birthchart. That's where our primary attention should be focused. Once the critical planetary "marriages" are figured out, then we can turn to the lesser ones.

The five major aspects are accompanied by a retinue of **minor aspects.** Septiles and biseptiles. Quincunxes. Sesquiquadrates. Noviles. Each is another **type of relationship** between bits. If we include them in our thinking, we quickly escalate from an average of twenty aspects per chart to one of sixty or seventy. We come to a point where **every planet is linked to every other planet,** and to the ascendant and midheaven as well. And at that moment, smoke begins to come out of our ears.

The minor aspects are real. They work. They have significance. But they are called "minor" for a reason. They are not nearly as meaningful as the major aspects. And even if we stick to the majors we have our hands full. My advice for anyone learning astrology is to forget the minors, at least until you have had a few years of experience. You can do effective work without them. And with them, you may only confuse yourself. If you are interested in pursuing the minor aspects, look in the appendix at the back of this book. You will find references to texts that deal with them.

Orbs

A square exists when two planets are separated by 90 degrees. But what if the separation between them is 91 degrees? Is that still a square?

Yes, it is. There is a certain slushiness in all the aspects. Planets need not make precise geometric angles between themselves for the

Understanding Orbs

If using an 8° orb, any planet between 7° and 23°♒ makes a square aspect to Mars at 15°♏.

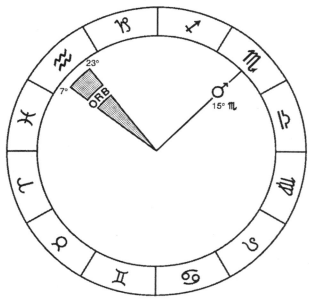

fireworks to begin. If they are within a few degrees, that is sufficient. That tolerance is called the aspect's **orb.**

No orb can be defined rigidly. To attempt to nail them down is like trying to determine the exact day on which your kitten became a cat. It doesn't work.

Precise aspects are by far the most powerful. But one that is out by 2° or 3° is still extremely energetic. Five degrees: too strong to ignore. Six or 7°, still effective, but definitely waning. Eight or 9°: it is there, but so eroded that we can safely direct our attention elsewhere. If the aspect involves the sun or the moon, then stretch the orb by a degree or two. Those two are really the keys to the individuality. Anything influencing them needs to be scrutinized with extra care.

How to Recognize Aspects

The key to recognizing aspects quickly is a thorough familiarity with the wheel of signs. Draw a circle. Draw in the twelve signs around it in their proper order. Tape it to your mirror. Even without any more effort than that, you will have mastered aspects within a month or two. You just have to get used to which sign goes where on the circle.

You must, in other words, **learn which aspect each sign makes to all the others.** From there, getting down to planets and degrees is simple.

The easiest aspect to pick out is the conjunction. Aries is conjunct Aries. Taurus is conjunct Taurus, and so on. No problem there.

The opposition is almost as easy. at least when you have the wheel of signs in front of you. You can see that Aries is opposite Libra. Taurus is opposite Scorpio, and on around the circle.

With trines, the trick is to remember which signs are in which **element.** All fire signs are trine to each other. The same goes for all earth signs, all air signs, and all water signs.

Squares are based on **modes.** Pick any sign. Three other signs are in the same mode – cardinal, fixed or mutable. Of those three, one is the opposing sign. The other two are the squares.

Like trines, sextiles are linked to elements, but they take a little more thought. Earth is sextile water and vice versa. Air and fire are connected in the same way. Of the three signs in the sextile element, one is the opposite. The other two are the true sextiles.

If remembering elements and modes does not come naturally to you, there is an even easier way to pick out aspects: just count off signs.

Pick a sign. Call it number one. Counting both clockwise and counterclockwise from it, sign number two is no aspect, sign number three is the sextile, number four is the square, number five is the trine, and number six is the opposition.

Signs are each 30 degrees wide. But orbs are only 6 or 8 degrees, so we have to take all this a step further if we want to talk about aspects between individual planets.

Say Mars lies in 15 degrees of Scorpio. We want to know what aspects it makes. The conjunction would also be in Scorpio, but not just anywhere in the sign. It would have to be within 8 degrees of the planet we are investigating – in other words, between 7 degrees of Scorpio and 23 degrees of Scorpio. Any planet in that stretch of sky forms a conjunction with Mars. Any planet in the first 7 or the last 7 degrees of the sign does not form a conjunction with Mars.

From now on, 7 degrees to 23 degrees becomes our magic formula.

Let's see how the formula applies to other aspects.

Taurus opposes Scorpio. A planet lying between 7° Taurus and 23° Taurus opposes Mars. One in 2° Taurus or 27° Taurus does not – the orb is too wide.

We reason like that through each of the signs that makes an aspect to Scorpio. When we are finished, we know exactly how Mars is wired into the rest of the birthchart.

There is one more complicating factor. When a planet is near the very end of a sign or near the beginning, we need to be careful. Aspects can occur between the "wrong" signs.

Say Jupiter lies in 26° Aries. What is the orb of the conjunction? Backward, it extends to 18° Aries. That's clear enough. Going forward through the zodiac, we would stretch the orb to 34° Aries. But there is no such degree. At 30°, Aries ends and Taurus begins. So 34° Aries is really 4° Taurus – and a planet in early Taurus is conjunct that late Aries Jupiter.

We would apply identical reasoning to all of Jupiter's other aspects. **In figuring aspects, it is the angles themselves that count.** Signs are just a convenient way of thinking about them.

When an aspect crosses into the "wrong" sign, it is weakened. A square is still a square. But some of the edge is taken off. A helpful practice is to be a degree or two stricter about orbs under those circumstances. That weeds out all but the aspects it is truly unsafe to ignore.

Once recognized, aspects are recorded on the birthchart. There are different methods. Some astrologers draw color-coded lines between the planets on the chart. Most simply use a computer program to generate an **aspect grid** like the one reproduced on the following page showing the major aspects in the birthchart of the Englishman we have been studying. The aspect grid appears below the chart.

Reading an aspect grid is easy. But first we need to learn some glyphs.

Conjunction:	☌
Sextile:	✶
Square:	☐
Trine:	△
Opposition:	☍

Look at the grid below the chart on the following page. Is there an aspect between Mercury (☿) and Saturn (♄)? Find the Mercury column. See where it crosses the Saturn row. At the place where they intersect, you find the symbol for the opposition. It works the same way for all the other planets on the grid.

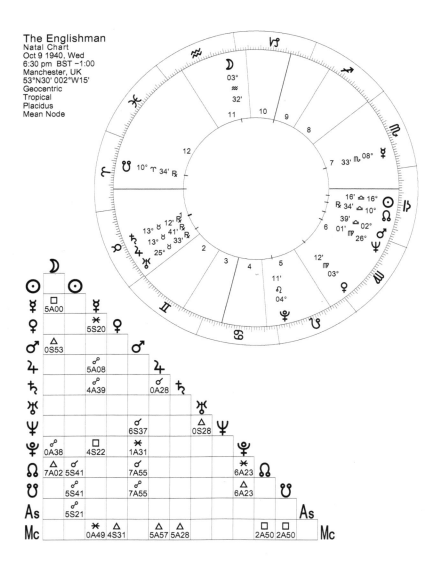

The Englishman
Natal Chart
Oct 9 1940, Wed
6:30 pm BST −1:00
Manchester, UK
53°N30' 002°W15'
Geocentric
Tropical
Placidus
Mean Node

A planet that makes many aspects is an important one. It is as
if it occupies a strategic position on the birthchart, having influence
over many other planets. But that is a subject for the next chapter.
For now, we need only look at a far simpler way for a planet to gain
importance.

Planetary Rulerships

Planets and signs are entirely different kinds of mental machinery. As we have seen, planets represent the ten basic functions into which the mind is divided: ego formation, feelings and imagination, aggressiveness, and so on. Signs are psychological processes with distinct goals and methods for attaining them: the development of courage or the development of an ability to break up routines, for example.

Each psychological process, with its particular aim and methodology, can condition any of the ten functions, flavoring it with tone and purpose. Any planet, in other words, can lie in any sign.

Certain sign-planet combinations are more harmonious than others. Fiery Mars loves being in Aries, the sign of the Warrior. And it has trouble relating to gentle, courteous Libra.

Each sign-planet configuration has meaning. Each can produce behaviors of positive value. And each can be corrupted. No configuration is inherently good or bad. That is not the point. What we are observing is only that **certain planets facilitate the expression of certain signs** more easily than others.

Each planet has a special relationship with a sign or two. Due to a similarity in their natures, when that planet lies in that sign, little friction is generated. We are presented with a very clear expression of both. Medieval astrology has given us a name for that special bond: a planet that has a particular affinity for a sign is said to be the **ruler** of that sign.

Rulership. The word is unfortunate. It is really not a question of dominance or submission. That is just medieval thinking. It would be more accurate to say that the planet and the sign "like each other." But modern astrology has retained the medieval expression.

Complementing rulerships, there is a parallel notion describing a particularly difficult sign-planet interaction. When a planet lies in a sign whose **how and why** are especially alien to it, that planet is said to be in its **fall.** There, both planet and sign must bend a great deal to achieve any common ground for their joint expression.

Planetary falls are linked to the most tense of all aspects, the opposition. **The sign of a planet's fall is always opposed to the sign of its rulership.** If we know one, we know the other.

The sun is the ruler of Leo. Ego formation is largely dependent on the reactions of those around us. Applause or hisses – either helps us form a self-image far more effectively than indifference. For that reason, the sun is strong in Leo, the sign of performance and public expression. Aquarius, the opposite sign, is its fall: the main thrust of the Water-Bearer's development lies in getting past the need for social approval, and that kind of indifference goes against the sun's grain.

The moon rules Cancer – feelings deepen in the sign of subjectivity, introspection, and imagination. And it has its fall in Capricorn, where emphasis on self-discipline and the attainment of goals makes emotional self-expression so secondary. Mercury rules two notably mental signs: Gemini and Virgo. It likes the curiosity and intelligence of the Twins, and it has a great affinity for the Virgin's ability to bring order into complex or chaotic environments. Opposite Gemini we find Sagittarius, Mercury's fall – the Archer's instinctive tendency to leap beyond facts into conclusive answers upsets Mercury. Pisces is hard on Mercury too: the Fishes Simply refuse to live in a logical universe, and that refusal makes them incomprehensible to the planet of reason.

Venus rules Libra and Taurus. As the symbol of our ability to form relationships, it is drawn to the Scales, the sign in which love and partnership play such a critical role. And as the symbol of our ability to calm down, it is attracted to the unflappable Bull.

Mars, the traditional god of war, has little love for peaceful Venus – and, unsurprisingly, the two signs Mars rules are the Venusian falls: turbulent, intense Scorpio and ferocious Aries. Similarly, when Mars finds itself in a Venusian sign, its own expression is inhibited. Taurus and Libra are the signs where Mars itself falls.

Expansive Jupiter loves the exuberance of Sagittarius and the broadness and faith of Pisces. Those signs are its rulerships.

The observant, journalistic quality of Gemini is difficult for the giant planet; its predilection is to leap first and look later. Virgo's carefulness hurts Jupiter for the same reason. Those are Jupiter's falls.

Saturn prospers in the austere, disciplined environment created by Capricorn, and it suffers in the sentimental waters of Cancer, where it has its fall. Aquarius and Saturn do well together too; Saturn appreciates the icy mental clarity of the Water Bearer, and its self-sufficiency. The garrulousness and frivolity of Leo, the Water-bearer's opposite, upset the ringed planet – Leo is Saturn's other fall. We have now accounted for all twelve signs. Each has a planetary ruler. Each is a planet's fall. Through the eighteenth century, that was all there was to planetary rulerships. But then we began discovering new planets, and suddenly everything became more complicated.

These newcomers presented astrology with some ticklish questions. Do they rule signs the way the classical planets do? If they do, which signs get assigned new rulers – and which of the old planets get thrown out of office? Or do we have to think in terms of shared rulerships for some of the signs?

None of these questions has been fully answered. Astrologers are divided about how to handle the invisible planets. Some think they function as "co-rulers" of certain signs, sharing authority with the sign's traditional ruler. Others think that the discovery of Uranus, Neptune, and Pluto has done away with three of the traditional rulerships. Many who follow that school of thought believe that more will be discovered and that ultimately each sign will have a single ruler. Perhaps they are right.

I myself lean toward the shared-rulership notion. There is a certain obvious, face-value validity to it. The old rulerships make sense. They work. No need to do away with them. And yet each of the three invisible planets also has an obvious, face-value connection with a particular sign. No need to deny that either.

Uranus is the planet of individuation. It is rebellious, free-spirited, iconoclastic. It has a clear linkage with the process we call Aquarius – and an equally clear distaste for crowd-pleasing Leo, the sign opposite Aquarius and apparently the Uranian fall.

Mystical Neptune and mystical Pisces have an evident affinity for each other. That is clearly a rulership. Opposite Pisces lies Virgo – and the Virgin's meticulous, hardheaded realism plainly clashes with Neptune's otherworldliness.

Pluto presents us with greater problems. Most astrologers take it to be the co-ruler of Scorpio. The sign's fearsome intensity, personal magnetism, and iron will are patently Plutonian. Aries has also been suggested for similar reasons, as has Virgo, largely for its focus on service. I cautiously endorse the Scorpio rulership, giving practical, peaceful Taurus as Pluto's fall.

Shared rulerships do introduce some complexities, as we will

Planetary Rulerships

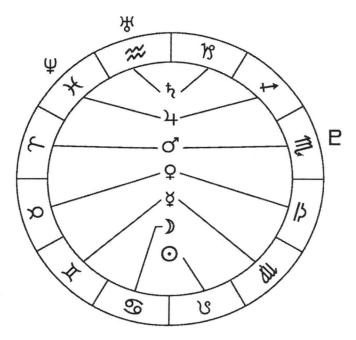

see in the next chapter. But that approach seems most in harmony with the facts. If Jupiter and Neptune both "like" Pisces, there is no need to make it an either-or situation. They can both be strong in that sign and take nothing away from each other in the process. And that is what rulership is all about in the first place – not authority, but harmony.

How do rulerships help us with the task of interpretation? Primarily, they help us gauge the relative strengths of all the phrases. Even when a planet is in its fall, it is still significant. We must still understand it. But a planet in its own sign is in a particularly influential position. That mental circuit – that **what** – plays a central role in the individual's psychology. A Geminian Mercury, for example, suggests a high degree of verbal quickness. A Libran Venus gives personal charm and attractiveness. Due to their strengths relative to the other planetary functions, these qualities tend to become dominant features of the individual's personality – for better or worse.

If that Geminian Mercury or Libran Venus happens to make many aspects to the rest of the chart, that probably clinches its position as top dog among the planets. Perhaps only the sun and moon are more significant.

Such knowledge helps us keep perspective on the birthchart. So often the chart contains ambivalent, even contradictory themes. Knowing which bits are most influential enables us to know which side of the inner argument is going to be acted out behaviorally and which side is likely to be forced to express itself in less-obvious ways.

But that is a subject for chapter 10. For now, let's concentrate on a simpler and grander way to gain perspective on a birthchart – the perspective of history. Let's meet a pair of symbols that tie the chart into the time before the birth and the time after the death.

The Moon's Nodes

NORTH NODE: ☊   SOUTH NODE: ☋

A birthchart is like a baby. First there is nothing. Then, suddenly, the child is there. We may have known the birth was coming. But our knowledge is abstract and general. When we are confronted with the actual reality – a boy, seven pounds two, with brown hair – there is an inexplicable shock. Once we know some astrology, the shocks get even deeper. In addition to the usual birth announcement, we are confronted with some starkly specific information about who that baby really is and what he has come into the world to experience: he is a ninth house Aquarian, with the seventh degree of Cancer rising and a seventh house Capricorn moon. At one moment, there is only a bulge in a woman's belly. At the next, there is a full-blown human story.

That is the way a birth feels. Sudden. Miraculous. What is really happening is very different. No one emerges into the world unmarked by the stamp of history. **Even a newborn infant has a past.** A chain of causes and effects traces back from each of us, finally disappearing into the Big Bang that fired up this universe some twenty billion years ago. Fail to grasp that chain and we miss a great deal. It is as if we have formed a relationship in which there is an inviolable agreement to discuss only the present. Intimacy is possible, but so much richness and understanding is lost.

How can astrology get past that limitation? A birthchart is a **birth** chart. It comes into existence only when an infant takes his first breath. The answer comes with two of astrology's most mysterious and controversial symbols: the north and south nodes of the moon. Physically, the nodes are complex things, moving points that have to do with the relationship of the moon's orbit to the celestial sphere. For our purposes now, we do not need to understand them in scientific terms. It is their symbolic meaning that we must grasp. **The nodes of the moon relate the birthchart to history**. The south node symbolizes the past and its effects on us. The north node symbolizes the future toward which we are being drawn. Unsurprisingly, the two points are always opposed. Enormous tension exists between what we have been and what we must become.

To what kind of past does the south node refer? We must pick one of two models, or consider the nodes from both perspectives, suspending any final judgments.

The first model is genetic. Through our heredity, each of us inherits a legacy from the past. We may get our mother's nose and our father's disposition – and if we knew our great-great-great-grandmother, we might be shocked at her resemblance to us. The same past that lived on within her lives on within us also, transmitted through the genes. In this model, **the south node symbolizes the impact of our ancestors on** us. At birth, a hereditary theme is crystallized within us. And from that moment on, embossed on our chromosomes, we carry a coded program of strengths and weaknesses. No scientist would argue with any of that – except perhaps to question whether the principles of genetics have anything to do with the moon's southern node.

The second model is more difficult to confirm or deny. It is based on the idea of reincarnation. In this model, each of us is viewed as an immortal principle of consciousness, living lifetime after lifetime, gradually evolving toward higher levels of awareness. In each life, we gain new insights – but also often acquire bad habits. These insights and habits are the stamp of the past, brought forward afresh into each new birth. Together they establish a set of predispositions in us, predispositions that underlie the choices we make in the present. Hindus call those predispositions our karma. The word is handy and we will use it here.

In the reincarnation model, **the south node of the moon symbolizes our** karma. And in practice its action is identical to the way the node works in the genetic model. It represents "past lives" either way. You may be the living image of your grandmother's grandmother's grandmother who lived in Norway in the eighteenth century. Or maybe you yourself lived in Norway in the eighteenth century. No matter. That woman lives on within you regardless of which model you prefer.

Is reincarnation a valid concept? Answering that is not the astrologer's business. Each individual must put together his or her own system of beliefs. Maybe we have many lives. Maybe we have just one. Either way, the past shapes the present and in the south node of the moon we can unravel the veil that obscures its influence.

The moon's southern node occupies a sign and a house, and can therefore be studied. It makes aspects (though in working with it we must use orbs of only 3 or 4 degrees). In other words, it operates precisely the same way as a planet. We read it like any other bit. The south node shows a kind of behavior that is **instinctive and automatic.** Its house indicates a field of activity into which the person is unquestioningly drawn **by the natural, effortless flow of his life.** The sign of the south node adds the **how and why;** it speaks of a **mindset** and a **pattern of motivations** that arise spontaneously in him and which may go forever unchallenged.

Just as no human being has a monolithically "good" or "evil" past, there is nothing monolithically good or evil about the south node. Like all other symbols, it embraces both lofty potentials and degrading distortions. Our interpretations must include both poles. The critical point is to remember that the south node represents the past. It is finished. The person's work there is done. Even if the knowledge and behavior it symbolizes are far from perfected, the individual must move on. In that part of life, he or she has done all that can be done. The future lies elsewhere.

Moving on from the south node is never easy. Usually we cannot even see it clearly. A man is ushered in to meet his new doctor, who happens to be a woman. His first words to her are "Nurse, where is my doctor?" He means no harm. **But his perceptions are shaped by an unconscious bias.** He assumes that only men are qualified to be physicians. That is precisely how the south node operates – it sets up an array of arbitrary "givens" in the life. Escaping them requires an act of will. But simply becoming aware of them in the first place is the real trick. If we fail to recognize the unconscious biases our south node generates, we slavishly act out these old behaviors over and over again, getting nowhere. We may achieve success in the world often that happens, since the south node symbolizes something we are good at. But the feeling is wrong. We feel as if we are only treading water. Life seems mechanical and pointless. A deep hunger within us goes unsatisfied. At some fundamental level, we are simply bored.

The antidote? It is the moon's north node. **The north node symbolizes the cutting edge of our growth.** In some ways, it is the most important point in astrology. Always 180 degrees from the south node, it represents the point that puts the most unrelenting tension on the past. As we allow ourselves to experience it, we open up to an utterly alien and exotic reality.

We are stretched to the breaking point. Our mental circuits frazzle, torn between fascination and fear. They are attracted, excited. Yet, red lights are flashing. Something deep within us tries to reject the experience. Something within us yelps, "Does not compute!"

Take a south node in Capricorn and the eleventh house. Whether it is karma or heredity, that person is instinctively, automatically a "go-getter." The driving self-discipline of the Sea-Goat expresses itself in the house of goals and plans. He or she comes into life and very quickly sets up a life strategy. Anything that violates it is immediately eliminated or suppressed.

Opposite that south node lies the person's evolutionary future. The north node is in Cancer and the fifth house. Here we find **experiences that challenge all his or her basic assumptions about life**. They are frightening. In facing them, the person feels awkward, at a loss. What are they? Through Cancer, we see a flooding of the mind with emotions of vulnerability and tenderness. And through the fifth house, we see a focusing of activity on creativity, love, self-expression; life in the present tense, opposite the south node biases in every way.

Suspended between past and future, the man or woman with

that nodal structure must make a choice. To grow, he or she needs the north node. But getting to it involves a lot of stretching, probably some asking for help, and certainly some embarrassment. And always the other option dangles in the air, tempting the person to take the easier road: play out those south node dramas still another time. Stay where it is safe. If he chooses that road he will look like a master, and die feeling like a fool.

Interpretation III
Putting It All Together

Ten planets, each molded into a "bit" by a sign and a house. Five aspects weaving those bits together in five different ways. Throw in rulerships, retrogradation, the moon's nodes. Add a concentration of planets above the horizon, or in the east.

Getting dizzy? That's not surprising. Astrology is complicated. Sometimes, looking at a birthchart, you might begin to feel like a juggler with one too many balls in the air. But rest assured: there are procedures to follow, maps designed to help us navigate through the often bewildering territory of the birthchart. If we stick to them, we will not get lost.

When a neophyte sees a birthchart for the first time, he or she often wonders how anyone could squeeze any meaning at all from those squiggly lines and strange hieroglyphics. The symbols reveal nothing. Later, armed with a basic knowledge of the words in astrology's vocabulary, that same neophyte faces precisely the opposite problem: the birthchart bombards him. Getting a birthchart to speak to us is never a problem. Astrology's symbols are bursting with meaning, and they sit there before us wide open as a child's face on Christmas morning. **The fundamental difficulty in astrological**

interpretation is that the birthchart generates too much information. All the information is valid. All of it is potentially useful. But sometimes it is like being forced to attend medical school when all we wanted to know was whether someone's runny nose had improved.

Order. Clarity. Perspective. These three must he maintained if we are to master the art of astrological interpretation. Without them, we have only chaos. All the guidelines we present in this chapter serve that end: each helps us to keep control over the flow of information from the birthchart. Each is like a hand on the faucet.

Sometimes we need to turn that faucet down until the flow is reduced to a trickle. Otherwise the chart might drown us in a flood of inconsequential insights. **Isolating essential themes** – that is the key to successful interpretation. Only when we have grasped the essential message of a particular birthchart can we go on to consider the fine-tuning. Reducing the birthchart to its bare bones is the first step. Treat the chart like a talkative friend. Ask it leading questions. And when it begins to run away with you, abandon your scruples about interrupting. It has the information; you must supply the control.

Picking out the critical themes in a birthchart is not always an easy matter. Sometimes they are far from obvious. But there is one simple rule of thumb that can never mislead us. It is the first of our **six basic guidelines**, and if we stick to it, we avoid the information overload that has sent many an astrologer reaching for the aspirin and left many a client scratching his head in perplexity.

GUIDELINE NUMBER ONE:
Ignore everything until you have thoroughly grasped the sun, moon, and ascendant.

This simple rule is the most valuable piece of practical advice available to anyone learning to interpret birthcharts. I strongly suggest you never deviate from it.

Sun, moon, and ascendant stand head and shoulders above the other influences. They are the **primal triad.** Regardless of what signs and houses they occupy and what aspects they make, they are the kingpins of the birthchart. Nothing that is not well supported by them is likely to figure prominently in the personality.

Think of the primal triad as forming the skeleton of the character. Venus and Jupiter may add flesh and color. But it is the sun, moon, and ascendant that determine the fundamentals of size and stature. If, for example, an individual's primal triad suggests prudence and timidity, even a red-hot placement of Mars is not going to turn him into a tiger. Conversely if a person's sun, moon, and ascendant all lie in fire signs, even a peaceful Piscean sixth-house Mars is not going to make him mellow.

In both cases Mars still has meaning. But we need to understand that meaning in the context of the birthchart as a whole. And the surest way to accomplish that is to forget about Mars until we have thoroughly absorbed the meaning of the three life shapers.

Each element in the primal triad serves a distinct purpose. Let's review them.

The sun establishes identity. As we saw in chapter 6, it symbolizes the self, giving us a sense of being a distinct person, with a particular nature and a particular set of unconscious biases that shape our values and motivations. The sun, in short, symbolizes ego.

The action of the moon underlies that of the sun. Moon represents the subjective elements – our feelings and our fears, our emotional needs and our affections. It symbolizes the instinctive dimension of mind. Moon is the mood of the psyche, the mood "averaged" over a lifetime. Since it is so deep and so far beyond reason we can call the moon the soul.

The ascendant is the wrapping placed over the interactions of the sun and moon. It symbolizes two closely interrelated psychological principles: first, that each of us must necessarily create a simplified version of ourselves to use as a vehicle in our daily lives. And second, that such a vehicle had better be an effective one, allowing a streamlined but still comfortable expression of our total self. In other words, we both hide behind the ascendant and express ourselves through it. For those reasons, it is helpful to think of the ascendant as the mask.

These three establish a structural model of the human mind that is both broad enough to be useful and simple enough to be grasped quickly and easily. Adding the other planets makes the model far more precise – but it may also confuse us, and in the early stages of looking at a birthchart, confusion is to be avoided at all costs. We must keep one hand on the faucet.

Sun, moon, and ascendant: identity, the soul behind that identity, and the mask it wears in the world. Simple. Clear. Effective.

People who are serious about astrology use the primal triad in much the same way as cocktail-party astrologers use sun signs. Not "I am a Leo," but, "My sun is in Leo, my moon is in Capricorn, and I have Sagittarius rising." And it is the difference between saying, "I am from New York," and, "I am an Irish Zen Buddhist vegetarian from Columbus Avenue in the upper Seventies." Both statements tell us something. But the second one conveys vastly more information.

There are twelve sun signs. That kind of astrology divides the world into a dozen "types." And it works and it is useful sometimes – even a twofold typology like introversion and extroversion has some value. But when we expand our horizons to include the moon and ascendant as well as the sun, our typology becomes far more individualized. Instead of a dozen categories, we have 1,728 – and many more when we include the house positions of the moon and sun as well as their place in the signs. We move from the general to the particular, from vagueness to precision.

How do we do it? What are the procedures? The first point is to remember that the sun and moon in their signs and houses are like any other planetary phrases. We apply the same steps in analyzing them as we would with Mercury or Venus. If you are fuzzy about those rules, go back and review them. They are near the end of chapter 8. The following five steps assume that knowledge.

Five Steps – Analysis of the Primal Triad

❖ STEP ONE

Look at the sun. It's what is the formation of identity. Consider the sign it occupies. **Why** is that person alive? What is his evolutionary goal? **How** can he most effectively realize it? What risks does he face? Now add the sun's house. **Where** is he confronted with the clearest expression of those solar ego-forming issues? Where is the major battlefield of his life?

❖ STEP TWO

Look at the moon. It's **what** is the formation of the individual's subjective, emotional nature. What sign shapes it? What kinds of experience are most essential to his happiness? **How** can he attain them? When moodiness and irrationality overtake him, how are they expressed? Add the moon's house. **Where** does he face the most turbulent emotional issues in his life? Where must he learn to make practical choices in the most intuitive and "transrational" way? Where must he learn to trust his "soul."

❖ STEP THREE

Consider the ascendant. This is not a phrase in the normal sense, since no planet is involved, but our procedures are quite similar. How does this person appear to the world? What is his mask? What kind of social personality is most suited to providing him with a comfortable, everyday sense of identity? How is that mask different from what we see in the sun and moon? How is it similar? What strengths and problems do those contrasts produce?

❖ STEP FOUR

Consider the aspects among the elements of the primal triad. How are sun, moon, and ascendant linked? You may find several such aspects. You may find none. If you do find an aspect, try to grasp how those primary elements of the personality are tied together. What strengths does the aspect suggest? What are its risks?

❖ STEP FIVE

This is the most difficult step, and the most important. Get a feel for the individual's primal triad. If you could make only one statement about it, what would it be? Who is this person? Is there a predominance of water signs and inward houses? Is the texture of the triad mostly extroverted? Is it playful? Is it serious? Arrogant? Shy? Grasp that, and you have established a **context** for the rest of the astrological analysis. Fail, and your interpretation is fragmentary and disconnected.

A Helpful Trick

The critical problem in astrological interpretation is that the birthchart so overwhelms us with information that we can easily lose our balance. Sticking to the sun, moon, and ascendant at first is the surest way of keeping control over the situation. That's why guideline number one is the prime directive in birthchart analysis, and why step five plays such an elemental role in making it operational – it attempts to reduce the triad to its bare bones.

There is a helpful trick that can assist us in further simplifying and crystallizing our insights into the primal triad. Applicable to any birthchart, it provides an instant thumbnail sketch of the personality, based on the sun, moon, and ascendant. The trick depends on the archetypes we introduced for each of the signs back in chapter 5. You'll find each of them in the following table.

Table of Archetypes

Aries	Taurus	Gemini
The Warrior	The Earth Spirit	The Witness
The Pioneer	The Musician	The Teacher
The Daredevil	The Silent One	The Storyteller
The Survivor		The Journalist

Cancer	Leo	Virgo
The Mother	The King/Queen	The Servant
The Healer	The Performer	The Martyr
The Invisible Man/ Woman	The Clown	The Perfectionist
	The Child	The Analyst

Libra	Scorpio	Sagittarius
The Lover	The Detective	The Gypsy
The Artist	The Sorcerer	The Student
The Peacemaker	The Hypnotist	The Philosopher

Capricorn	Aquarius	Pisces
The Hermit	The Genius	The Mystic
The Father	The Revolutionary	The Dreamer
The Prime Minister	The Truth Sayer	The Poet
	The Exile	The Face Dancer
	The Scientist	

These archetypes are basic human images – the warrior, the poet, the clown – which capture some of the flavor of each sign. For each sign, I have provided several such images. Once you have a grasp on the signs, you can add your own inventions to the following list. To use this table, first find the person's sun sign. That sign's archetypes tell us who he **is**. Next look at the moon. The archetypes for that sign describe his **soul**. And finally, the archetypes for his ascendant symbolize the **mask** behind which he hides and through which he expresses himself. The man in our sample birthchart has his sun in Libra, his moon in Aquarius, and Aries rising. In the following chapter we analyze his chart in detail. But let's apply our trick to his primal triad right now.

We could say that he is the **artist,** with the **soul** of the **genius,** wearing the **mask of the warrior.** Or that he **is** the **lover,** with the soul of the **exile,** wearing the **daredevil's** mask.

The archetypes can be mixed and matched in any way you please. Each sign has several. Anyone of them will highlight a certain aspect of the individual's primal triad. Settling on a single formulation is helpful, but it is also largely an intuitive process. Try a few. Which one "feels" best?

The value of the formula is that it reduces the sun, moon, and ascendant blend to a single, manageable sentence. An evocative sentence. A simple one. It is just one more hand on the faucet, holding the information flow down to a manageable level.

Absorb that sentence. In later stages of analysis, remember it. It will help you keep perspective. And when you are about to make a pronouncement about a planetary phrase, ask yourself this: does what I am about to say make any sense for an artist with the soul of a genius who is wearing the mask of a daredevil?

Our second guideline serves a purpose quite similar to the first: it assists us in keeping perspective on the birthchart. It provides us with a procedure for drawing some general conclusions before we blow any of the chart's minor features out of proportion. The difference is that now we are ready to include all the planets in our consideration.

Hemisphere emphasis: that is the focus of our second guideline. Are most of the planets in the east or the west? Are they predominantly above the horizon or below it? Or are they scattered more evenly throughout the circle?

> # GUIDELINE NUMBER TWO:
> Temporarily forget the individual meanings of the planets. Simply observe whether a majority of them lie in anyone of the four hemispheres of the birthchart.

If you are fuzzy about the meanings of the hemispheres, you might want to go back to chapter 7 for a detailed review. Let's briefly recapitulate here, to refresh ourselves.

The **horizon** divides the chart into an upper hemisphere, representing **objectivity,** and a lower one, representing **subjectivity**. When a majority of planets lies above the horizon, the focus of the person's life is in the objective realm: he or she grows through the crafting of a series of **events** through which the evolving individuality is **publicly and visibly** expressed. Such a configuration does not always signify sociability and extroversion. But it certainly implies that in the long run, the person cannot happily retreat from the world. That is his arena. If he withdraws from it, growth is impossible. And without growth, happiness is impossible.

A majority of planets below the horizon has the opposite connotation: such a person's life is focused far more in the subjective realm. He or she may be playful as a drunken monkey or ambitious as Napoleon. But all growth lies in the depths, in the world of thoughts and reactions. Just as the upper hemisphere person must craft **events**, his lower-hemisphere counterpart must seek **realizations**. That is where his happiness lies.

The two hemispheres created by the vertical axis of the birthchart – the **meridian** – establish a different polarity altogether. The east symbolizes **freedom and individual choice** while the west represents **fate or destiny**. (Remember – east is left and west is right!)

Once again, an eastern – or western – hemisphere emphasis does not tell us much about the **personality** of the individual. A fiery, willful person may have all his or her planets in the west, while a lazy, indecisive type may have a great concentration in the east. The point is not personality; **hemisphere emphasis describes the shape** of the life, not the tones and textures that make up the fabric of the person's nature. It reveals the rules of the game, not the personality of the player.

How do we put hemisphere emphasis to practical use? In my own work, often I never mention it to the person for whom I am doing the interpretation. But hemisphere emphasis always underlies my choice of words as I describe the birthchart as a whole. The eastern-hemisphere person hears a lot about individual responsibility. He or she is presented a model of life as a blank slate, to be filled in as we please. Drifting and idleness are coded as heinous transgression against the natural order, filled with perilous existential consequences.

Why? Because that is the world in which that individual actually lives. Regardless of his nature, this eastern hemisphere emphasis assures us that for him, the conscious use of personal freedom is the **single most critical element** in determining his level of fulfillment.

A man or woman with most of the planets on the western side of the meridian hears a different story. Now there is a pointed emphasis on the value of flexibility and the capacity to recognize the larger patterns in which our lives are caught up. Such a person is a pawn in a far grander game than he or she is ever likely to grasp. That is the way of **destiny**. Laziness and indecision are not implied – only a need to heed the omens life offers, omens for which an eastern-hemisphere person could wait until doomsday.

What about the divisions created by the horizon?

The language to use with upper-hemisphere people is the language of accomplishment, challenge, and adventure. They must leave some kind of mark in the world, some deed that will outlive them. For a lower-hemisphere individual, the model of life we must present is far more subjective. Now everything orbits around **consciousness itself**. All events, all relationships, all outward successes and failures are coded in terms of their **impact on the structure of the mind**. The events themselves are seen only as means to that end, sometimes necessary, other times quite dispensable.

The point to remember with hemisphere concentrations is that they **establish the framework of the life**. The rules of the game. And, unlike the laws of the world, these rules cannot be broken. A person with the sun and moon in Aries may love to hear that he is free to do exactly as he likes – but if that sun and moon lie in the seventh house and the other eight planets all lie nearby, that kind of simple freedom is just not available to him. **The actual pattern of his experience does not allow it**. He can swim to the left. He can swim to the right. But whether or not he likes it, there is a river carrying him downstream. And in recognizing that river, whatever freedom he has is enhanced.

Do all the planets need to be above the horizon for there to be an upper-hemisphere emphasis? That is certainly the classic situation, but an upper-hemisphere focus can still exist even if three or four planets lie below the horizon. Here is an effective rule of thumb. Say the sun and moon are each worth three points. All other planets are worth one. If nine or more points fall in any of the four hemispheres, you have hemispheric emphasis.

When there is no hemispheric emphasis, the individual's life rules are more complex. Our best policy then is to ignore the whole question and concentrate on other interpretive techniques.

From now on, our voyage through the birthchart is stormier. We must begin to consider the meanings of individual planets. This exposes us to the full force of the astrological mind map. It opens up the faucet. Whether the ensuing rush of information clarifies our vision or simply leaves us confused is mostly a result of how well we have prepared. If we have stuck to our first two guidelines, chances are good that we are ready to bob along with the flood.

Each planet introduces its own special issues and questions, fine-tuning the mechanisms first established by the primal triad and any hemispheric emphasis. But not all planets in a given birthchart are equal in strength. All have significance but some dominate the person's life while others hide out in the background, awaiting exactly the right trigger to spur them into action.

Our next step is to isolate these dominant planetary influences. We call these planets **focalizers**, because they represent key focalizations of mental energy in the individual's character. In seeking them out, our goal is the same as always: we are striving to maintain perspective on the chart. But now our task is harder. Sun, moon, and ascendant are always critical points. That never varies. But any planet can be a focalizer. There may well be more than one. We must now begin to make assessments that are unique to each birthchart.

> ## GUIDELINE NUMBER THREE:
> After absorbing the meaning of the primal triad and understanding the birthchart's hemispheric emphasis, establish the identities of the planetary focalizers. Once identified, understand what role they play in the chart.

Many different factors can spotlight a particular planet, making it stand out above the others. Many other factors can weaken a planet, rendering its influence obscure. Medieval astrologers referred to these two situations as **dignities** and **debilities**. The words are still useful, provided we do not equate them with "good" and "bad."

A planet that is particularly "well dignified" is a focalizer, but how can we recognize it? Picking out focalizers is not always a straightforward operation. In practice, even a very strong focalizer probably has a debility or two. We must balance different factors and make our own judgments.

Our first step is to survey the ways in which a planet can establish itself as a force to be reckoned with on the birthchart. How can it qualify as a focalizer?

The Ruler of the Ascendant

Every birthchart has at least one focalizer, and picking it out is easy. It is the **ruler of the ascendant,** and no matter how debilitated it might be by other factors it is still a powerhouse. The ruler of the ascendant. If Gemini is rising, then it is Mercury. If Libra is rising, it is Venus. Sagittarius? It's Jupiter. You can review rulerships in the previous chapter if you are unclear about them. For convenience, a table of rulerships is included here.

Three signs have dual rulerships. That introduces some ambiguity. Astrologers differ on this. My own advice is to say that both planets become focalizers. If Pisces is rising, for example, then Jupiter and Neptune rule the ascending sign. Both take on dignity.

Simply knowing that a planet is a focalizer tells us very little. We must go further. We must understand how that dignity affects its function in the birthchart.

Exactly what does the ruler of the ascendant **do?** To answer that, we need to remember the purpose of the ascendant itself. It is the mask, the social personality behind which we hide and through which we express the rest of the birthchart. From an evolutionary viewpoint, the ascendant advises us about how best **to organize a social personality** for ourselves, one that works well for us, giving us a sense of poise and grace, a sense of "centeredness."

The ruler of the ascendant takes that centering process a step further. Think of it as the ascendant's ambassador, transported to another part of the birthchart, but still serving the same end. Wherever it lies, its activity plays a pivotal role **in establishing the individual's sense of personal distinction and identity**. It helps him define himself.

Analyzing the ruler of the ascendant is usually a straightforward procedure. We begin by approaching it as we would any other bit. Understand its operation in terms of sign and house. Recognize any aspects it forms to other planets, especially to the primal triad. Then take the interpretation one step further: **emphasize that the functions you have just described are intimately bound up in the formation of the person's self image.** A strong response to them suggests positive feelings about the self and a successful adaptation to everyday life. A weak response implies just the opposite: role conflict, awkwardness, feelings of clumsiness and illegitimacy, and, very typically, social withdrawal.

Should the ascendant have two rulers, proceed the same way. Consider each of the bits in the light of this extra dimension of significance. And only if a square or opposition exists between them is it appropriate to view their relationship as in any way competitive.

Planets in Their Rulerships

Mercury loves to be in Gemini. Saturn enjoys its passage through Capricorn. Neptune shines when it passes through Pisces. No matter which sign is rising or which houses those planets occupy, when they lie in their own signs, they are dignified. They become focalizers.

Once again, recognizing dignity is only the first step. It establishes perspective: we know that we must pay special attention to that planet. Whatever it does is going to be important. Our next step is to determine that planet's **meaning.** And to do that, we approach it like any other bit. No new tricks or techniques are involved: rulership simply alerts us to the fact that we are dealing with a focalizer. Planets in their falls (see chapter 9 if you need a refresher) are debilitated. It is still possible for them to be focalizers – they may still rule the ascendant, for example. But their action is inhibited – distorted by the contrary nature of the sign in which they lie. Our approach is the same as always: we take note of the debility, and then proceed to unravel the phrase in the normal way. Distorted or not, the planet still has meaning. Strong or weak, our job is to discover that meaning. We must only avoid the mistake of taking too seriously the influence of a planet that is thoroughly debilitated.

Planets prefer certain houses over others, just as they prefer certain signs. Mercury likes Gemini, which is the third sign. For similar reasons, it also likes the third house. The same logic applies to all the other planets – each rules the house that corresponds to its sign rulership. Placement in its own natural house strengthens a planet, increasing its dignity. Such planets may also serve as focalizers.

Planets Conjunct the Sun

Any planet forming a conjunction with the sun is a focalizer. Sun-sign astrologers make a lot of mistakes, but they do recognize a fundamental astrological truth: that the sun is the nucleus of the personality. It symbolizes our essence, the inner core of motives and biases that shape our lives. When a planet conjuncts the sun, its own nature is grafted onto that far more influential solar principle. We must study it carefully if we are to understand the individual.

If Saturn conjuncts the sun, strength and self-control permeate the character. Solitude and disciplined effort play prominent parts in the person's life. But he or she also faces the pitfalls of the ringed planet – bouts with melancholy are possible, as is the sort of loneliness that comes from too much control of others and too little expression of personal feelings.

All that impact can be seen even if the rest of the birthchart has a much lighter tone, such is the power of a solar conjunction to mold a life. A planet in that position becomes an honorary member of the primal triad, and must be treated with nearly the same deference. Underestimating its influence is a fatal error.

The Stellium

A **stellium** occurs when three or more planets all occupy the same sign or house. Considering that there are only ten planets and that they must distribute themselves among twelve houses and signs, such a pattern represents an unmistakable concentration of mental energy.

Even if the planets are individually weak, their presence in the stellium grants them membership in an alliance that exerts monumental influence over the tone of the birthchart. **The stellium itself becomes the focalizer**, and the needs of that sign or the events of that house become dominant features in the individual's experience.

Often the sun is involved in a stellium with Venus or Mercury. That happens because those two planets never wander very far from the sun (you can review the reasons for that in chapter 6). That astronomical fact warps the probabilities in the direction of sun-centered stellia. Those are the strongest kind. But others exist too. In the following chapter, we investigate one involving Jupiter, Saturn, and Uranus, all in Taurus and the first house.

Whatever planets are involved, analyzing a stellium is tricky business. The **whats** of the individual planets may be quite incompatible. Our procedure is to unravel each phrase separately, then weave together a pattern of compromises among them. In so doing, we must keep in mind the overriding influence of the sign or house in which the stellium occurs. Its shadow is cast starkly over the entire birthchart.

Angular Planets

The four **angles** of the birthchart – the ascendant, the descendant, the midheaven, and the nadir – are power points. Any planet that forms a conjunction with one of them is immediately catapulted into a position of tremendous prominence. It becomes a focalizer of inordinate power, rivaling the sun, moon, and ascendant in influence.

Underestimating the authority of an angular planet is one of the surest ways to lose perspective on an interpretation.

Actual conjunction with an angle is the greatest dignity. But the presence of a planet in any of the houses that follow those angles is also significant. The first house, the fourth house, the seventh house, and the tenth house: these are the **angular houses,** and any planet lying in one of them is elevated in status. It too becomes a focalizer.

The most sensitive of the four angles is the ascendant. A planet forming a conjunction with it, or placed in the first house, must be dealt with definitively. Treat it as you would the ruler of the ascendant. The logic is identical, except that another dimension is now added: that planet itself becomes an integral part of the individual's mask, deepening and often substantially modifying the message of the rising sign. Like the ascendant, it shapes his appearance and personal style.

Despite their overwhelming prominence, angular planets are still parts of phrases. We still approach them according to the same rules. Their importance comes from the fact that the angular houses are such critical life shapers: the identity, the deepest drives, the most intimate relationships, the destiny. Any planet involved in molding such sensitive issues is instantly placed on center stage. We immediately recognize it as a focalizer.

Singletons

A **singleton** is a planet that lies alone in anyone of the four hemispheres of the birthchart. One of the moon's nodes might be in the same hemisphere, but no other planet shares that half of the sky.

Such a position places a heavy load on the planet. The focus of that hemisphere – objectivity, subjectivity, freedom, or fate lies exclusively on it. And the mind compensates for the imbalance by augmenting the influence of the phrase. The personality of that planet now pervades the birthchart far more thoroughly than we might expect based only on its sign, house, and aspects.

A singleton Venus, for example, can produce artistic interests and an affable nature, even when those patterns are not clearly suggested in the rest of the chart. Similarly, a singleton Jupiter might create buoyancy; a singleton Saturn, self-discipline and austerity, and so on.

Singletons are not common. But when they do exist, they certainly serve as critical focalizers. Ignoring one is another sure way to lose perspective.

Stationary Planets

Planets are **stationary** when they are standing still in the sky, about to turn retrograde or direct. (If you would like a review of the astronomy involved in that phenomenon, turn back to chapter 7.) Such a planet has increased authority in the birthchart. It too can serve as a focalizer, although not with quite the same electricity as we see in the conditions discussed previously.

View a planet making a station like this: if it has some dignity from other sources, the fact that it is stationary clinches its role as a key focalizer. If the planet's placement is otherwise indifferent, making too much of it would probably distort the accuracy of your interpretation.

Strong Aspects

Any planet that makes a great number of aspects is a focalizer. Why? Simply because it has a finger in everyone's pie. Wherever we go, we find that we must refer back to it in order to understand the operation of the other phrases. It squares Mars, it trines the sun, it opposes Uranus, it sextiles Jupiter, and so on. Woven so tightly into the fabric of the birthchart, its influence permeates almost everything the individual does. Understanding the individual without having a solid grasp of the strengths and risks of that heavily-aspected planet is impossible.

Aspects to the sun, moon, or ascendant are particularly critical. Any planet aspecting the sun and moon, even if it makes no other aspects at all, is a focalizer. It may look like a minor influence, but don't be fooled: it is as if it plays poker with the president every Thursday night and does the first lady's hair on Saturday. Take it seriously. It is influential.

When can we say that a planet is heavily aspected? There are no solid rules here. So many variables are involved. One aspect to a focalizer is worth three or four to debilitated planets. One very precise aspect is far more critical in its influence than several that are out by 6 or 8 degrees. In a birthchart containing relatively few aspects in all, a planet making a couple of important ones is in a very strategic position. A planet making those exact same aspects in a chart that is aspect-intensive is not nearly so important. If there is any rule of thumb here, it is this: **compare each planet to all the others in the same birthchart.** Which one is wired into the chart most inextricably? That one is certainly your focalizer.

Keeping Perspective on Focalizers

Singletons. Stellia. Rulerships. Stations. Heavy aspects. By the time we get into the territory of guideline number three, we have our hands full. The faucet is wide open, and staying afloat is no simple matter.

Maintaining order is everything. Once past the safety of the primal triad, there is an overwhelming temptation to start interpreting willy-nilly, without any kind of strategy or any understanding of which bits are the critical ones. That road leads to disaster.

Relax. Take your time. Sit with the birthchart for a few minutes. Which planet rules the ascendant? That's a focalizer for sure. Is there a singleton? Probably not. How about a stellium? They are always easy to see, at least. Is there an angular planet? Again, that is readily established: just look. What about a planet making a lot of aspects? Check the aspect grid – does one planet keep popping up? Is it linked to the sun, moon, or ascendant?

Go through the checklist. Sometimes almost every planet is vying for control of the chart. Other times, they all seem to be hiding out in obscure corners. Birthcharts are like that.

Most often, two or three planets stand out from the rest. Maybe you find an angular Mars ruling that Scorpio ascendant. Maybe Uranus conjuncts the nadir, making a square to the sun and a sextile to the moon. Perhaps Neptune is conjunct the midheaven in Pisces.

Practice a little while. You will get a feel for it.

The old-fashioned astrologers sometimes used a point system for establishing relative dignities and debilities. Three points for ruling the ascendant, minus two for being in the fall plus one for making a station, and so on. In the end, Mars might have twenty-two points to Jupiter's nineteen – and from that moment on, Mars was Lord High Muckamuck of the birthchart and poor Jupiter made the coffee.

That approach does not reflect reality.

The point with focalizers is not to determine which planet gets to wipe out all the others. That is not how the mind works. Each planet has its own separate territory. Its influence there is sovereign and cannot be challenged. Each human mind. in other words, has a place for all ten planetary functions.

What focalizers help us do is to **organize our approach to the planets.** They tell us which phrases are most vividly present in an individual's character, and which ones play secondary roles. **All we seek in determining focalizers is a sense of priorities.** Of these eight phrases, which ones are cornerstones? With which ones is the person most strongly identified? Which present the most critical developmental pressures?

The question focalizers answer best is a purely practical one: Which planets should we talk about first? Priorities, that's all.

The Moon's Nodes

The moon's nodes can never be focalizers in the strict sense of the term. They are not planets: their action is different. They strike chords on a plane all their own.

If you feel like you need a refresher course on the nodes, look at the end of the preceding chapter. Briefly, the moon's south node is a symbol of the time before the birth and its impact on a person's subsequent development. It can be viewed as a symbol of one's **karma** – one's residual personality left over from previous physical incarnations – or as a clue to the formative pressures brought on us by our hereditary or genetic background. Either way, the south node refers to "past lives."

The north node always symbolizes our evolutionary future. Whether we are thinking in terms of reincarnation or heredity, it represents where we are going. Virgin territory, utterly alien to us, the moon's north node presents us with seemingly incomprehensible challenges. If we rise to them we feel stress – and fulfillment. If we choose to ignore them, an insidious sense of boredom and predictability seeps into our lives, leaving us as aimless as a ten-year-old boy trapped in a suit.

What is so important about the nodes? Perspective again. The moon's nodes indicate which of the qualities established by other astrological factors rest firmly on the foundation of past experience – and which ones are founded on thin air, depending totally on conscious effort for their development. That knowledge is the basis for our fourth developmental guideline.

GUIDELINE NUMBER FOUR:
Determine how the north and south nodes of the moon impact on the other features of the birthchart.

Always look first to the south node. It lies in a sign and a house. Perhaps it makes some aspects, though remember to be strict about your orbs – 2 or 3 degrees is plenty. Unravel its meaning as you would any other phrase, remembering that it's **what** is the lingering influence of events that took place before the birth.

Now compare the message of the south node with your impression of the birth chart as a whole. You have been working with the primal triad. You have noted any hemispheric emphasis. You have picked out some critical focalizers. What is their general tone? How well does it harmonize with what you have discovered in the south node?

What we are getting at is this: **In comparing the south node of the moon to the birthchart as a whole, we determine what particular tensions exist between all that the person "has done before" and what he or she is attempting to accomplish with the present chart.**

That knowledge is of vital importance. It tells us which of the planetary issues are most likely to be blind spots – areas in which the individual may have to beat his head against the wall just to "see the obvious." But there is a bright side to the coin too: the south node may also point out planetary functions spotlighted for quick development. Why? Simply because **that knowledge already exists in the person**. He or she was born with it.

Think of it like this: a banjo player slips on a banana peel and suffers amnesia. Six months later, a thousand miles away, she happens to pick up a banjo. In a few weeks it sounds as if someone must have smuggled her that banjo while she was still in her mother's womb. Face that banjo player with a computer console or a disassembled auto transmission, and it is a different story: she is as inept as the rest of us. That is how the south node works: certain of our endeavors are supported by past experiences, mostly forgotten. Other endeavors, perhaps ultimately more important to us, are not.

The influence of the moon's north node is more subtle. The past is immutable. It is what it is. The south node reflects that: it is a fixed entity, influencing us in fairly predictable ways. Not so the north node. Here everything is uncertain.

If the south node tells us what we were, then **the north node tells us what we must become.** Not what we **will** become. Not destiny. Not fate. Only direction. Only a suggestion, nothing more. With the moon's north node, the ball is in our court. We can hit it back or we can let it lie. Those features of the birthchart that most closely resemble the north node represent enormous challenges. In a sense, they are castles built on sand. Nothing in our inherited disposition, be it karmic or genetic, disposes us to comprehend them. And yet they fascinate us. We are pulled by some inexorable curiosity within ourselves to explore those exotic terrains. In so doing, we typically execute some glorious pratfalls, but we also fill our minds with a sense of growth and change, an image of life as an endless miracle to be savored and absorbed.

You are an actress on Broadway. It is a rainy Tuesday night. You have a headache. The curtain rises on your 112th performance of a certain play. With the skill that comes from endless repetition, you play your part flawlessly. You receive a standing ovation, then go home to bed. That is life on the south node – routine, certain, and often impressive.

You are a child with your first bicycle. You fall. You climb back on again. Again you fall. After two or three hours, you manage to totter along, eyes wide as half-dollars, right past your admiring parents. And in that moment you feel like God on the day the world began. That's how the north node feels: dangerous, fresh, triumphant.

Fortune-tellers have little interest in the moon's north node. They want to know what "traits" a person has. And the north node provides little information on that subject. Evolutionary astrologers view it quite differently. Growth and change are the lifeblood of their philosophy. To them, the north node, with its emphasis on potentials and possibilities, is the most important symbol on the birthchart. Everything else – signs, planets, houses – are the means. The north node is the end.

GUIDELINE NUMBER FIVE:
Isolate patterns and themes in the birthchart.
Recognize planetary alliances. Observe clusters
of meaning. Note thematic tensions.

People study astrology for years and years. They are diligent. They learn the words and phrases. They feel the power of the system, appreciate its beauty. And yet when they are asked to interpret a birthchart they freeze up. All those words and phrases fail them. Sentences refuse to form. Why? Disorganization, mostly. They have not learned to keep a hand on the faucet. You can beat that problem if you stick to the first four guidelines we have developed here. They give you the order and the perspective that is so essential for effective interpretation.

But if you want truly to master this ancient language, you must go a step further. You must begin to grasp the birthchart as a whole. You must learn to experience it as you would a person, not as a patchwork of ideas, but as **a feeling**, something you sense with your heart and your intuition as well as your intellect.

Guideline number five aims us in that direction. Of all the rules we have introduced, it is the most indispensable. But it is number five for a reason: without a thorough mastery of the first four, it is as useless as a swimsuit in Antarctica.

Patterns. Themes. Clusters of meaning. No way we can even begin to recognize them until we have at least partially unraveled the messages of the ascendant and the ten planets. That would be like setting out to debate arms control in Swahili without knowing any vocabulary. It cannot be done.

Our first steps with a birthchart must largely be intellectual ones. We follow procedures. We plug into our memory banks regarding each one of the symbols – or we look them up again for a quick refresher. We analyze. We balance conflicting testimonies. We methodically dissect the gears and pulleys, the dynamos and pushrods that make one individual mind tick.

Then, if we let it, something magical begins to happen. The birthchart comes to life. It speaks to us. What does it say? Anything. In the course of human history, something like eighty billion people have passed through this territory. Each one of them had a birthchart and each chart was different. The only limits on the language of a birthchart are the limits of one's own imagination. The less rigid those limits are, the more skilled you will prove to be in the art of interpretation.

Perhaps you notice that in applying the first four guidelines to a particular chart, you use the word **independence** quite a lot. An Arian sun. The moon in Sagittarius. Capricorn rising. A stellium including the ruler of the ascendant in Aquarius. Uranus conjunct Mars on the nadir.

Each of those configurations has its own distinct significance. **But independence is their common denominator.** You have detected an alliance composed of many separate factors. And in the tricky terrain of astrological interpretation, you have struck pay dirt: you have found a **theme.**

Every now and then, you encounter a birthchart that is as simple as that. There is one clear theme, and the meanings of all the bits cluster around it. That kind of uniformity is quite unusual. Minds are rarely homogenized.

Maybe Neptune stands out like a sore thumb: it lies in Cancer just above the descendant, in the seventh house. It is angular. It squares the sun. A focalizer for sure. But what does it tell us? The birthchart's owner is a dreamy, romantic type, full of affection, and maybe needing to work through some exaggerated dependency and some possessiveness.

Wait a minute. A few moments ago she was the warrior with the soul of a gypsy wearing the mask of the hermit. Now all of a sudden she is a clinging vine?

No. The theme we picked up through the primal triad and those other focalizers is the dominant one. All that has happened is that we have detected a discordant note. Overemphasizing it would constitute a grave loss of perspective. Had the rest of her chart supported that Neptunian theme – lots of Libran and Piscean patterns, for example – then we could read it in a straightforward way. As it is, we must be more cautious.

Neptune is not simply overwhelmed by the other influences – of that we can be certain. Nothing astrological ever "goes away." But sometimes it must find its place in a hostile environment.

How should we proceed? There are no more maps at this point. We are on our own. But each of us is holding a pair of aces: a certain degree of common sense, and the fact that we have been living intimately with at least one human mind: our own.

When faced with **thematic tension** in a birthchart, it is time to play those aces.

Stretch your imagination. Identify with that woman. Put yourself in her shoes. How do you imagine she feels? What would you do if the tables were turned?

Maybe she does her best to bury the Neptune. Maybe she hides it behind her all-too-convincing veneer of self-sufficiency. She could get away with that if she wanted. Her primal triad gives her that power.

But, if she has gone down that road, we can be sure that Neptune has broken through the wall from time to time. She has probably allowed herself to fall in love more than once – and been appalled at the unsuspected and uncharacteristic **clinginess and unrealism** the experience brought out in her.

Here is where the fortune-teller would get bogged down. He or she would put a lot of energy into describing scenarios like that, probably coding them as insights into the woman's past, or, even worse, as predictions for her future. Such statements might well prove to be chillingly precise. But they certainly would not be helpful.

The evolutionary astrologer would approach such thematic tension in an entirely different way. He or she might describe that destructive pattern of Neptunian behavior, but only as an example of one path available to the woman, and clearly not as the happiest one.

What alternatives does the woman have? Again, use your common sense. Forget astrology. Forget the birthchart. The symbols have done their job. They have conveyed a set of impressions, a particular human drama, to you. Absorb it. Open your intellect to it. Open your heart, too. If that woman were your friend and she came to you crying and angry over that kind of problem, what advice would you give her? And make it human advice, not astrology.

Perhaps you would tell her that she puts people off with her hermit's mask. Perhaps you would tell her that she frightens them with her warrior's ways and her gypsy's soul. Maybe you would say that she really is strong and tough and self-sufficient but that she has a tender side too. Perhaps you'd say you think that her tender side scares the pants off her and that she has been running away from it for years, and that if she doesn't stop and face it she will be running for the rest of her life. And that every now and then she will trip over that tender part of herself that scares her so badly, hurting herself and anyone who gets close to her. Maybe you would tell her that the only person in the world who can break the pattern is she herself, and that it is her choice. She can grow – or she can play those behavioral tapes until she turns blue.

Hard words, but helpful ones. They are the sort of words friends say to each other when the chips are down. And they are the language of evolutionary astrology, a language that recognizes thematic tension as a part of life, but not an immutable one. We can change. We can become more conscious of our own processes. We can alter them for the better. We can, in short, tell our own fortunes.

GUIDELINE NUMBER SIX:

When you have taken the first five guidelines as far as they can go, drop them. Recognize that astrology has done its job. It has helped you to crystallize the essence of a set of life issues. Now use your own heart and mind to find ways to resolve them.

All our guidelines relate to the problem of maintaining perspective. This last one is the greatest of them, and in many ways the most difficult to observe. At first the astrological symbols are so foreign to us that our initial instinct is to drop them. That doesn't last long. As we learn the language and form the sentences, a metamorphosis takes place. The symbolism seduces us, absorbs our attention. We become lost in the intricacies of the phrases, hypnotized by their power to expand our awareness.

That is one of the occupational hazards of studying astrology. One unpleasant symptom of the disorder is that our conversation is peppered with references to "Mercury problems" or to "Bill and his damned Leo moon" – references that often serve only to baffle and annoy our friends.

A far more destructive symptom is that we also fail as astrologers. Our interpretations become mechanical. It is as if we have built a great spaceship. We have boosted it up into the outer atmosphere. And now, having arrived at these icy heights, we forget to look out the window.

The Englishman

Who is the man in our sample birthchart? Let's keep that a secret for a while longer. Glamorous fictions surround any public figure. Our Englishman is no exception. Perhaps by studying his chart without preconceptions we will arrive at a truer understanding of the man.

Take another look now at his complete birthchart in the appendix. You have seen it before, in previous chapters. By now, all those numbers and glyphs have probably taken on a lot more meaning for you than they had then. But if the chart still seems overwhelming, don't be discouraged. Let's dissect it slowly, using the guidelines we established in the preceding chapter.

Our first step is to strip out everything but the primal triad of sun, moon, and ascendant. That throws away a great mass of solid information, but it also enables us to control the flow of impressions.

The drawing that follows shows his birthchart, streamlined down to the primal triad. There is no need always to redraw the chart as we have done here – but that is exactly what you should do mentally. Simplify it like that and you guarantee yourself a good start. Attempt to get into the interpretation in any other way, and it is like being born as a grownup. You get confused.

What do we see? Sun in Libra in the sixth house. Moon in Aquarius in the eleventh. Aries rising. Two air signs, one fire: a

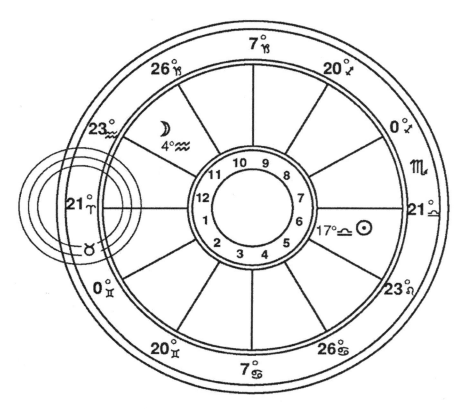

mental, conceptual kind of person, but with the driving edge that only fire can supply.

Let's apply the simple formula we introduced in the preceding chapter. Based only on his primal triad, who is he? His sun tells us that he is the **artist** (or the Lover or the Peacemaker). His Aquarian moon adds the deeper dimension: he has the soul of the **genius** (or of the Exile or the Truth Sayer). And his ascendant lets us know how he presents himself to the world: he wears the mask of the **warrior** (or of the Pioneer or the Daredevil).

If anything we say from now on violates the impression created in us by that formula, we know beyond the shadow of a doubt that we are losing grip on the birthchart.

The artist with the soul of the genius wearing the mask of the warrior. What does it mean? Don't think astrologically. Think in plain English. What kind of person are we talking about? The artist: one who creates beauty. One who must create **harmonious relationships** between colors, shapes, and sounds. And between people, too – remember that Libra's archetypes include the Lover and the Peacemaker. Our subject's **individuality** (sun) is sustained by those kinds of relationship-forming (Libra) activities. Without them, he withers.

The soul of the genius: instinctively, he seeks to **separate himself from the conventional and the predictable**. He is motivated by a profound emotional (moon) need to think the unthinkable and do the unexpected. Restraints, especially those imposed by authority figures, are unacceptable to him. He cannot bear to be told what to do.

The mask of the warrior: intense, confrontational, passionate, perhaps abrasive – that is his "style." That is what people see when they meet him at a cocktail party. On the surface, he is forceful and assertive, and those are traits that he himself exaggerates in order to establish a distinct personality: remember that the ascendant is not merely a mask – it is the vehicle through which we express ourselves. If we do not play it out, we are a walking identity crisis.

The artist. The genius. The warrior. Quite a stew. Already there are internal tensions. The peacefulness of the Libran sun is pitted against the rebelliousness of the Aquarian moon and the confrontational nature of the Arian ascendant. And it gets even more complicated when we consider the houses.

The Englishman's sun is in the sixth house. Traditionally, that is the House of Servants. The terrain involves mastering skills and techniques that are of value to other people. Sharing them, too. If his navigation of the sixth house is unsuccessful then he falls into patterns of subservience, drudgery, and low self-esteem.

How can he avoid that? What skills and techniques can he develop that give him something meaningful to offer?

Libra holds the answer: the skills of the artist, the relationship builder, the peacemaker. Those are the inner paths of development he must pursue, and then express outwardly as a craft or vocation. He must **find work through which he can display his Libran qualities**. In so doing, he creates a synthesis of his sun's house and sign.

The moon lies in the eleventh house. The House of Friends. The terrain shifts into a far grander perspective now. Plans. Dreams. Life strategies, and all the allies we draw to ourselves to support them.

Toward what future is our hero drawn? Where is he going? Into the moon, into Aquarius – that much is certain. We observe him "softening" with age, becoming more domestic. More lunar, in other words. But we also see him identifying increasingly with his Aquarian qualities – he gradually becomes more and more of an outsider, a rebel. He moves increasingly under the archetype of the Exile.

Who helps him with that process? Who are his "friends?" Once again, the Aquarian moon speaks to us: he is drawn to identify with other outsiders, other rebels, other "geniuses." But their belligerence must be modified by the moon for them to be attractive to him. They must be imaginative, dreamy, affectionate people as well as fellow exiles. Only then does he recognize them as allies.

Let's stop and assess what we have learned so far. We could get lost in interpretive details and that would be a disaster. In this work, perspective is everything.

Our general impression is one of a complex and ambivalent individual. The sun suggests that in essence he is a gentle human being, with peace-loving, artistic qualities (Libra), and a strong desire to be useful and supportive of others (the sixth house). It also implies that he might have some problems with indecision and commitment phobia (Libra dysfunction), perhaps aggravated by a weak self-image (sixth house dysfunction).

That is his solar core, and it is simple enough of itself. Complications arise when we realize on what kind of psychological landscape that sun is shining. To the world, he seems brash and confident. That is the legacy of the Arian ascendant. And it is in league with his Aquarian moon – that is where he gets his unquenchable passion for mutiny and freedom. Put it all together and we see what might become a classic chip-on-the-shoulder mentality: a ferocious, challenging exterior obscuring a far less certain interior.

Fortunes cannot be told reliably by astrology. From the moment they are born, people are free. But it is a fair bet that in his early years at least, our Englishman acted out that tension in his primal triad by creating a boisterous, defiant facade, reserving the expression of his gentler, less-confident side for a few highly controlled situations.

The fact that his sun is nearly unaspected further strengthens our notion that his Libran qualities might not automatically play an obvious part in his everyday personality. Burying those qualities, as destructive as that may be, is probably his first response to the problems they present.

Is he stuck there? Only if he chooses to be. It is within his freedom to die like that if it pleases him. But he does not have to. He can change. He can achieve a more harmonious integration of his triad. And it is the business of evolutionary astrology to encourage him to do that.

How? Common ground. That is the answer. **He must find some common ground for the expression of all three factors.** By enlisting sun, moon, and ascendant in some task that requires input from all three, he encourages harmony among them and combats the fragmentation of his mind into many separate "selves."

How can we determine the nature of such a task? Logic plays a big part in defining it. So does imagination. We know that the sun, which symbolizes his essence, must be at the heart of it. The task is artistic, or perhaps one that involves harmonizing or pacifying human relationships. It takes the form of some kind of work or pattern of responsibilities. That is the contribution of the sixth house. Libra adds that, in order to accomplish the task, he has to form a partnership with at least one other person – and make sure that he establishes real trust and intimacy there.

Once that task is defined, it must be presented to the public in an Arian and Aquarian way: with color and confidence, with an air of challenge and assurance. With boldness. The task itself must be

Libran – harmonious, peace-loving, beauty-building – but it must be introduced in such a way that it provokes and upsets people, causes them to think fresh thoughts and examine their basic values. In this case, the artist must make enemies, but that reaction must arise as people observe his art, not as a result of any pointless adolescent cockiness on his part. Whenever we see that latter pattern, we are back at square one. The common ground is lost.

Libra likes to be liked. That is fine until it begins to pretend to be something other than what it really is in order to gain that affection. In a pure Libran situation, that danger might express itself as an overly courteous, conflict-suppressing personal style. With our Englishman, it comes out differently. His exterior is brash, and so his need for affection can easily be twisted into a need for any kind of reaction, anything that suggests that the other person has noticed him.

That pattern must be shattered if he is to find the special task that harmonizes his sun, moon, and ascendant. Scandal and outrage are insufficient. They are cheap answers, readily available to him, but answers that accomplish nothing. For the true synthesis to take place, he must do more: he must express his sensitivity, his art, and his vulnerability – his solar qualities – and let them take the heat, rather than just safely expressing all that is already so tough and callous in him that no amount of pressure could affect it.

Doing that is not easy, but he has an ace in the hole. His hemispheric emphasis favors the development of that kind of resiliency.

The next illustration shows the way the birthchart should look to us at second glance. Our first glance shows us the primal triad with everything else stripped away. Our second glance includes the triad, but now all the planets have appeared except that they show up only as black dots.

Which planet is which? At this point we do not know and we do not care. All that interests us is where those planets lie. All that interests us is whether or not there is any hemispheric emphasis.

Immediately we observe a concentration of planets below the

Hemispheric Emphasis

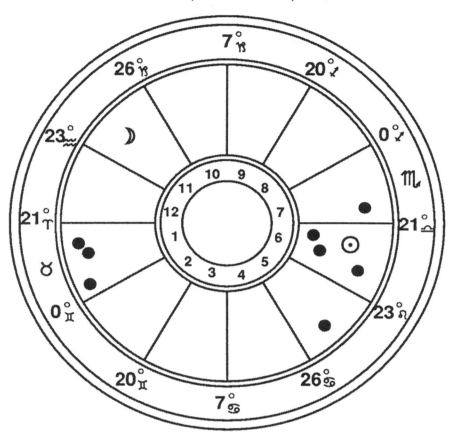

horizon. But Mercury and the moon lie above the line. Do we have a true lower-hemisphere emphasis?

Let's apply the rule. Sun and moon are worth three points. The other planets are each worth one. If we have nine points in a hemisphere, we have an emphasis there.

Below the horizon we have seven planets. Seven dots. No matter what planets they represent, seven dots are seven points. Add three points for the sun, and we have ten, and a clear concentration in the hidden half of the sky.

Our Englishman has a lower-hemisphere emphasis. His world is **subjective.** His focus is on **consciousness itself** rather than on events. This by no means implies that he is shy or that his life is eventless or routine. Only that his orientation is inward, aimed more at attaining **realizations or states of awareness** than at building empires.

Those are the rules by which the game of his life is played. And those rules help him. He must still do his work in the world. No hemispheric emphasis can free him from his sixth house responsibilities. All we have said about his task remains valid. **But what matters most to him is the lingering effect of those experiences on his mind.** Memories, visions, wisdom perhaps – those are his goals. Recognition is secondary.

How is that such an advantage? It frees him. If he is accepted and praised as he releases his hard-edged brand of Libran energy into society, that is fine. If he is pelted by rotten tomatoes, that is fine too. From the lower-hemisphere perspective, life is just a grand-scale video game anyway. It is only consciousness that counts. Not the game, but the memory of it.

The artist with the soul of the genius expressing both through the mask of the warrior – the pattern of our Englishman's destiny is beginning to come to a focus. His strengths, his weaknesses, the traps that life has set before him, the prizes it offers, the allies who will join him on his path – all are coalescing into a set of general impressions. The birthchart is starting to speak to us.

So far, its language is orderly and clear. By eliminating all extraneous factors, we have been able to keep the chart from babbling at us, confusing us with a flood of details. We have kept one hand on the faucet.

We must continue to hold that faucet, but from now on controlling the flow is more difficult. Up to this point, we have relied on simple rules applicable to the initial exploration of any birthchart. Now we need to shift gears, to enter less certain territory.

From now on, the chart makes its own rules. If we follow them we will not get lost. But to follow them we must first discern them. And to do that, we need to turn those black dots into planets. We must expose ourselves to the full complexity of the astrological symbolism, and do that without allowing ourselves to be overwhelmed.

We must pick out the **focalizers.** Our first step is to scan the planetary phrases, looking for ones that stand out from the others.

Two stellia – a most unusual feature – attract our attention right away. Three Taurean planets lie in the first house. And if we count the sun, four more planets lie in the sixth, divided between Libra and Virgo. Both configurations constitute critical focalizations of mental energy.

Outside those two stellia, there are only three other planets. One is the moon, and that is always an important influence. Pluto opposes it quite precisely from Leo and the fifth house. That aspect alone is enough to make Pluto a force to be reckoned with. Mercury is the only remaining planet – and it is angular, lying in the seventh house, and makes more aspects than any other body. Clearly, Mercury is a focalizer too.

Our first scan has proven too effective. Everything is a focalizer, and that leaves us right back at the starting line. We still do not know where to begin.

Have we learned anything? Yes – with all planets playing such prominent roles, we have more evidence that our hero is a very distinctive, very visible kind of person. Once encountered, he would not be easily forgotten. We might say that in the context of his society he himself is **a focalizer.** When a personality is so vivid, it tends to rally other personalities around it, focusing their energies, giving them direction.

Our scan has produced one more insight: those two stellia dominate the birthchart, concentrating the lion's share of his attention onto only two of the twelve terrains available to us work and responsibilities (the sixth house) and the development of free will and individuality (the first house). The seesawing interplay of those two issues is clearly one of the thematic keys to the chart.

But we are still in a bind. Where should we begin? There is no single right answer to that question. Some birthcharts do offer a clear starting point. This one does not. That does not mean that we should just dive in and start interpreting the remaining planets in alphabetical order. If anything, it implies that we need to be more cautious than ever, picking our way deliberately and with constant alertness. A chart like this one is full of booby traps for the unwary. Let's avoid them.

Once again, stand back from the chart. Relax. Take time to gather perspective. Close down the faucet. Ask the birthchart to **convey only that which is most obvious and most essential**.

Those two stellia really stand out. Even if the individual planets composing them were relatively unimportant, the issues their houses represent are scenes of relentless activity. To a large extent they show us **where our subject's life is happening.** We lose perspective to a dangerous degree if we proceed much further without knowing more about that terrain.

Which stellium comes first? Again, that is a difficult question. The first house is paramount among the angular houses. To have a stellium there in that most sensitive of territories is to have a focalization of mind energy rivaling that of the sun, moon, and ascendant.

But the sixth-house stellium is a powerhouse too. It contains the sun. Right away that puts it in the big leagues. And Mars is there too – with Aries rising, Mars rules the ascendant, so that puts a lot of emphasis on that house too. Add Neptune and Venus, and it is a toss-up which stellium is more crucial.

Immediately we know that freedom versus responsibility, selfishness versus loving and giving, independence versus interdependent partnership, and other similar first house – sixth house conundrums are critical life themes for our Englishman.

Which side is dominant? There is no clear answer and **that itself is our answer:** the first house and the sixth house are balanced, existing in a state of dynamic tension. Neither is in imminent danger of being swallowed by the other.

Let's start with the sixth house, if only for a practical reason. In discussing his sun, we have already introduced that terrain. Let's finish the job we have begun, then go on to pursue the first house.

The presence of three more planets in the sun's house initially tells us little beyond what we have already seen in our preliminary survey of the primal triad: that the sixth-house issues of work, duty, and service are critical ones, and that their shadows – drudgery and humiliation – dog our Englishman whenever he loses track of himself. To go further, we must look at each of the phrases separately. Mars, being the ruler of the ascendant, is a natural starting point.

Mars: the god of war. Symbol of aggression, willpower, and courage – and if we weaken in the face of learning those lessons, the symbol of conflict and meaningless hassles. That is the **what**.

The **how and why** are supplied by Libra. His Mars qualities are channeled into art and partnerships, not Mars's favorite occupations – this is the war god's **fall**. What do we learn? **The basic drive that motivates and inspires his aggressiveness is the urge to establish relationships.** Those relationships might be personal. They might be societal. They might be among sounds and shapes and colors. However they are defined, our Englishman must **fight for relationships.** He must fight (Mars) for peace (Libra).

If he chooses a lesser path, then we find him caught up in an overwhelming network of **conflicting personal entanglements**. Friction and tension plague his Libran partnerships. With his Arian ascendant, we might even see violence in that area. He is left feeling jinxed in relationships when the actual source of his difficulties is **his own lack of straightforward, confrontational honesty within those intimate bonds**. And very likely that lack of confrontation in the intimate sphere would lead to even more intensive sword-rattling and belligerence in his everyday social personality, a predilection we have already observed in analyzing his primal triad.

Work-related partnerships are particularly sensitive to these Libran Mars questions, that is the contribution of the sixth house. It defines the **where.**

With Mars functioning as the ruler of the ascendant, establishing a positive, assertive approach to his work and creating effective working partnerships free of silly melodramas, is bound up in the formation of a clearly defined, smoothly operating self-image. Weak responses to Mars corrupt more than Libra and sixth house. They corrupt the ascendant too, undercutting the efficacy of his day-to-day personality.

Being trine the moon, we observe an alliance between his free-spirited, irreverent emotional nature and his Mars function. The Aquarian moon supports his pursuit of clarity and straightforward-ness in his love bonds and working partnerships, while success in those areas helps provide the moon with wider arenas of self-expression. Unfortunately, another option is available: Mars and the moon could team up to produce a sardonic aloofness in which feelings are released in the form of nasty, biting one-liners instead of sincere communication.

Later we see how his Scorpionic Mercury supports that unpleasant possibility.

In presenting these Mars themes to the Englishman, an evolutionary astrologer would discuss them all, but code everything in terms of choice. He can take his pick, and live with the consequences of what choice he makes.

Neptune lies in late Virgo, actually forming a conjunction with our subject's early Libran Mars. It is the next stop in our tour of the sixth house.

Neptune: the planet of raw, unfocused, undefined awareness. The Mystic. And the absentminded "space case." Neptune's **what** is self-transcendence, or, negatively, the collapse of personality.

Motivated by Virgo's urge for perfection, clarity, and precision, poor Neptune is baffled. Once again, we see a planet in its fall – and another particularly challenging sixth-house configuration for our hero.

Confused, glamorous, otherworldly circumstances characterize his working environment. Events there defy logic. In that area, he must learn to trust his intuition and be prepared to accept career developments that no reasonable person would predict. And through it all, he must hold on to his Virgoan vision, that is, his desire to make his work, whatever form it takes, **as nearly perfect as it can be**. It must reflect his ideals.

In holding to that high Virgoan Neptune standard, he also stimulates his Mars, since the two planets are conjunct. His idealism in his work and the often perplexing circumstances he finds there have the effect of precipitating some of the patterns of interpersonal conflict we noted while observing his Mars functions. With the conjunction linking them, the two are a package deal.

The last planet in his sixth-house stellium is Venus, which also lies in Virgo. We analyzed that phrase in detail in chapter 8, but let's briefly recapitulate here.

His relationship-forming drive (the Venusian **what**) is conditioned by Virgo, leading him to have high and exacting standards for his partners, most especially for his life mate. He enters those relationships with a strong sense of responsibility, but he may make unreasonable demands on himself and others, only to become destructively self-critical or harshly reproachful when reality asserts itself. Tolerance and forgiveness are virtues he must cultivate, or else the only relationship he will ever enjoy is the one between himself and the fantasy woman he keeps sequestered safely in his imagination – and that is a terrible fate for a loving Libran.

Once again, his Venus alerts us to the fact that he faces most of these relationship dramas in his working environment – its **where** is also the sixth house. That has become a recurrent theme. His sun initiates the pattern. His Libran Mars picks it up, adding its own explosive issues. And now, with the "goddess of love" in the "house of work," once more we observe the radical emotional intensification of his working partnerships.

It becomes difficult to imagine our Englishman functioning successfully in a marriage in which his wife was not an integral part of his career. In general, he experiences little urge even to befriend a person who is unconnected with his work. That is certainly not the "normal" human situation – but in this particular birthchart, the work indicators and the relationship indicators are unmistakably fused. **If he makes a successful response to his birthchart, he will be known professionally as one member of an intimate creative partnership**. It may be a marriage. It may be strictly business. Either way, its formation is an essential stepping stone on his path to personal fulfillment. And that places even more stress on learning to get his "Libra-ness" out from behind its mask of false bravado and arrogance. He has got to learn how to get along with people. Everything depends on that. Without partnerships, he has nothing. Not even a meaningful job.

The first-house stellium may help him or hinder him in his effort to cope with those sixth-house issues. It gives him great willpower, but it may also lead to selfishness and tyranny. As the house of choice and positive action, the first house gives the three planets lying there considerable freedom of expression. The man can do **what he chooses** to do. At the same time, they can be enlisted in the service of a lower cause: they can add more bricks to the wall of arrogance he has constructed around himself. Whatever choice he makes, it is a firm one; the stellium lies in Taurus, the astrological sign that gives us our modern day expression, "stubborn as a bull."

Even if the three planets were just black dots, we would still see those basic Taurean first-house themes. That is always our first step with a stellium: get a grasp on the sign and house. That gives us the overview. That is how we define the territory. Only then do we proceed to look at specific planets, confident that we will not lose perspective. Once again, it is a question of keeping one hand on the faucet. First the trickle, then the torrent – that is the elemental interpretive tactic.

Jupiter and Saturn form a precise conjunction, dominating the first-house terrain. Later in the house, we find Uranus, forming a tight trine to Neptune. All three are retrograde, and each one flavors the "warrior's mask" – being in the first house, they temper and develop the message of the rising sign.

A Jupiter-Saturn conjunction is a tough nut to crack. The two planets are opposed in meaning; their **whats** are contradictory. And yet, in this birthchart, they are forced into marriage.

Jupiter: the symbol of expansiveness, buoyancy, and optimism. The bright symbol of faith. Saturn: realism, practicality, self-discipline. The dark lord of solitude. How can they interact? It is as if Captain Kangaroo got stuck on an elevator with Darth Vader. They don't even know what to say to each other.

Our first step is to understand them separately. Then we attempt the more formidable task of fusing them.

What kind of mask might we expect on one whose first house was conditioned by Jupiter? What kind of "vibes" would such a person project? He would act like the garrulous, playful "king of the gods." Clowning, open-heartedness, generosity – these would be his trademarks.

And what if Saturn alone occupied the first house? What then? Very much the opposite. Now we would encounter a person who radiated deep seriousness, perhaps even a dark or brooding spirit. Responsibility, realism, an economy of words and actions – these would mark his demeanor.

With these two contradictory influences fused together in our Englishman's mask, he is plainly a very complex fellow.

Our question is this: is one of these influences dominant? Both are focalizers, being in the first house, but does one of them have more dignity? If so, then that is the one that is more likely to be immediately apparent in the man's behavior. Not that the other one would go away – it would just be forced into a subordinate role, popping out into the world of behavior only when triggered by exactly the right stimuli.

Unfortunately that approach does not help us much in this case. The two planets are about equally well supported by the rest of the birthchart. Saturn likes the inwardness and practicality implied by the Taurean **how and why,** and it accepts retrogradation more readily than Jupiter – the ringed planet **likes** to be turned away from the outer world. But Jupiter finds a natural ally in the active, expressive

Arian ascendant, and it makes ready peace with the friendliness of the Libran sun. So it is a standoff. Neither Jupiter nor Saturn is going to back down. Somehow, they must work out a truce.

Certainly, there is deep ambivalence in the man's character. It is as if he shuttles back and forth between the two polarized planetary influences. One moment he is frolicsome and mischievous. The next, he is as serious as the plague. One moment he is supportive, full of compliments and optimism. The next, he is distant, full of hard facts and criticism. One moment he looks like a happy little boy. The next, he looks like a wizard who remembers the Ice Age.

Ambivalence. This is not the first time we have encountered that theme. It has been there right from the beginning in the tension between his sixth house Libran sun and his moon-ascendant alliance. The Jupiter-Saturn conjunction locks into the same pattern. Jupiter adds a note of jollity and impishness to his already misleadingly obstreperous exterior. And Saturn, with its propensity for playing everything close to the vest, further obscures the more tender, self-questioning qualities built into his sun.

Once again, the solution to the disruptive flip-flopping of the two planets lies in finding some **common ground** for their expression. Our hero must devise some expansive, bigger – than life task (Jupiter), then use Saturn's studiousness, perfectionism, and self-discipline to pull it off: Jupiter wants to play; Saturn wants to work. The only hope lies in finding **tasks in which playfulness is raised to a high discipline**. Ina birthchart less oriented toward work, we might seek our common ground in some other department. But with a stellium in the House of Servants, and with work-oriented Taurus supplying the conjunction's **how and why,** the fusion of Jupiter and Saturn is best accomplished in that terrain.

Although the indications here are far more subtle, we again uncover evidence that our Englishman benefits immeasurably from establishing himself in some **creative profession,** that is, in a profession in which play and work are linked. That step appears to be the key that unlocks so many of the basic tensions in the birthchart.

His first-house Uranus lies 12 degrees deeper into Taurus than Jupiter and Saturn. That is beyond the orb of the conjunction, and so this planet needs to be considered independently.

Being considered independently is just fine with Uranus this is the planet of freedom and individuality, the planet that stands between us and the temptation to become just one more predictable member of our tribe. It is the ruler of our subject's moon sign, Aquarius. That deepens his attunement to the influence – and even without that added dignity, Uranus would certainly still be a focalizer. Just lying in the first house is enough to guarantee that.

What does Uranus tell us? Much of its story has already been told. With Uranus shaping the man's projected self-image (first house), many of the effects resemble closely what we see when Aquarius shapes one of the members of the primal triad. The same themes emerge: autonomy, a love of the unexpected or the shocking, an irreverent distaste for public moralizers and social leaders. If the moon were in another sign, we would now need to develop those themes more extensively. As it is, even though the Aquarian moon actually strengthens the Uranian influence, the planet's basic significance has already been established and we can safely move on. The key Uranian contribution is its unambivalent assurance that those Aquarian qualities are immediately apparent in our Englishman's everyday behavior. They are part of his mask. Not only does he have the soul of the exile, he **looks and acts** like he has the soul of the exile.

And those are his stellia. Two themes. Two massive clusters of meaning. Between them and the primal triad, all but two planets are swept under our interpretive blanket. All that remains is to unlock the secrets of Mercury and Pluto, and then observe the effects of the moon's nodes.

Mercury is the logical choice for our next interpretive step.

Here we have a classic focalizer. In most birthcharts, a planet of this power would be discussed right after the primal triad. Only the unusual circumstance of having two distinct stellia encompassing most of the birthchart's phrases prevents that. And even with Mercury appearing so low in our planetary pecking order, we should not be fooled: we have a real dynamo here. Underestimating its impact would be a bad mistake.

What gives Mercury so much authority? First of all, it is angular. While it does not form a conjunction with the descendant, it is certainly placed in the seventh house. Any planet stationed in the all-important House of Marriage is unmistakably marked as a focalizer. That would be true in any birthchart, but in our Englishman's chart, the influence of a planet in that house is even more pressing – with his Libran sun, relationship questions are crucial to his development. As always, the sun symbolizes a person's essence. With our hero's sun conditioned by the sign of the Scales, whenever any planet has something to say about partnership and marriage, his ears perk up.

Mercury's dignities go further. A quick look at the aspect grid reveals the enormously strategic position it occupies. Not only is Mercury angular, but it also makes more aspects to the rest of the chart than any other planet. Our grid lists six of those relationships. Mercury's nearest planetary rival is Mars, and even the war god manages to connect with only four other points.

Angular, and collecting all the tolls at an aspectual crossroads – we had better get a firm grasp on the Englishman's Mercury if we are not to miss one of the critical links in his psychological chain.

Even before we start analyzing the planet in detail, just knowing that it is so prominent tells us a lot: our hero is a **word person**. He likes to talk. With his sun and moon in air signs, we already see a mental-conceptual orientation. With Mercury dignified, those airy ideas have an outlet: his mouth. He is certainly a raconteur. Perhaps he is a writer as well.

We know much more than that. Mercury's **what** is the sending and receiving of information. But his own Mercury is motivated by the **how and why** of Scorpio and it expresses itself into the **where** of the seventh house. Those are the factors that give the planet indi-

vidual meaning.

Scorpio: the Detective, the Sorcerer, the Hypnotist. It loves to probe, to get to the bottom of people's motivations, to pierce through their hypocrisies. It can penetrate like no other sign, but its Achilles' heel is a tendency to lose perspective on what it sees. Sometimes a big kindness is sacrificed on the altar of a tiny truth.

With the Scorpion propelling his Mercury, our subject is clearly a man of devastatingly sharp intelligence. In league with his Arian ascendant and his first-house Uranus and Saturn, he would make a formidable verbal enemy, able to zero in on the places where people are most vulnerable. Not "your mother wears army boots" but "how are you doing with your repressed homosexuality?" Sharp, acidic, and deadly.

And where does his Scorpionic Mercury find its most characteristic expression? In the seventh house: among his partners and his deepest loves, among the people he holds most dear.

Should he make a healthy evolutionary response to his Mercury, we see **relationships distinguished by their absolute honesty.** If he feels it, he says it. And those relationships are **verbally intensive.** He and his partners share their thoughts and ideas, their perceptions of the world, and, most especially their Scorpio-clear X-ray scans of each other.

Learning those interpersonal skills is the password that gets him into a successful navigation of his seventh house. But all relationships involve at least two people. Even if he mastered those Mercury talents, they would do him no good were he married to a dolt. Instinctively, he knows that. Even before he knows what to do with them he finds himself attracted to **lovers and partners in whom the Mercury function is also strong.**

Wit, words, and wisdom – they draw him like a magnet.

What if he chooses not to grow? What if he just lets that Mercury cruise along on automatic pilot while he waits for the world to dish him up his soul mate on a silver platter? He will have a long wait.

That lazy path would be a painful one. Once again, with his Libran sun, so much of his personal fulfillment is dependent on establishing meaningful human relationships. Should he fail there, the center of gravity in his character collapses. He is left with nothing but a brassy shell. And a weak response to his seventh house Mercury could precipitate that collapse.

Insight and intimacy would be replaced by bitter, cutting words. A first-strike mentality would overtake him whenever anyone threatened to get close to his fears and his defenses. All the worst of his Libran Mars would be brought out, allied with the more venomous and combative possibilities inherent in his mask. He would still be drawn to intelligence in other people, but now those relationships would degenerate into verbal fencing matches. His heart would never be touched.

Either way, his Saturn and his Jupiter present that Mercury with some unique challenges. They oppose it. He must make an effort if he wants to get his own hands on his verbal faucet. There is a tendency alternately to talk too much (Jupiter) and too little (Saturn). All that we saw about that first-house conjunction is now linked to his verbal style, for better or worse.

Mercury's sextile to Venus is important too. The two planets excite each other, again for better or worse. The perfectionism of Virgo already expresses itself in the relationship department since the "goddess of love" lies in that sign. It is easy to see how that Scorpio seventh-house Mercury, with its incessant probing into the inner workings of the partner's mind, is teamed up with that hard-driving Venus. Both are endlessly pushing toward the depths, toward the perfect fusion of two hearts and minds.

A less-comfortable aspect exists between our Englishman's moon and his Mercury. There we find a square – and a good opportunity to understand the difference between eleventh house "friends" and the far deeper relationships encountered in the seventh house.

The Aquarian eleventh-house moon draws our subject into a vast crowd of **essentially superficial** relationships. They are not hypocritical or exploitive, just not very deep. He is drawn into movements and group efforts where he associates with "lunar Aquarian types" as we discussed earlier. There, he himself takes on the cast of the Water-Bearer and of the moon: he is the Genius and the Exile, the Truth Sayer with the loving heart and the vivid imagination.

That public personality clashes violently with his private one. His true intimates see an utterly different side to his character, one far more along the lines of his seventh-house Scorpionic Mercury: narrower, more intense, harder, and far more acerbic.

The lunar and Mercurial dimensions of his character wrestle with each other, each correcting the excesses of the other. When he is about to plunge his dagger home in an intimate tiff, the Aquarian moon reminds him of a more expansive, more idealistic side of himself. And when he is about to turn into a piece of idealistic conceptual fluff regarding Perfect Relationships, Mercury brings him face to face with the blood-and-guts reality of two egos trying to share the same bed for a decade. Neither planet likes the other, but the battle benefits both of them.

Pluto, the last of our planetary phrases, is linked to both the moon and Mercury by aspect. It squares Mercury and opposes the moon from its position in Leo and the fifth house.

Pluto: the most abstract of the ten planetary functions. Our ability to tap into a vein in the brain of society. Our capacity to offer something of ourselves to the world, to shape history, to go beyond ourselves. And if it sours in us, then Pluto represents only a place where we seek to force our views on others, a place where we suffer under the unconscious delusion that we speak for God.

Our Englishman's Plutonic mission is easy to unravel: with Pluto in self-expressive Leo and occupying the creative, performance-oriented fifth house, his capacity to leave a mark on history is inextricably bound to his Libran art. The two feed on each other. Libra gives the aesthetic sensitivity. Pluto gives it direction – the **how** and the **why** and the **where.** Not only must he create beauty in order to maintain his own mental solidarity (Libran sun), he must somehow make that beauty socially **and publicly relevant.** His art must change the world.

The horror is that it could all turn to dogmatic preaching, to art enslaved by ideology. And with his Aquarian moon, his Arian ascendant, and his hard-edged first-house stellium, he could play the part of the demagogue in high style, using his role as preacher and moralizer as one more link in the armor concealing his gentle, uncertain heart. And should he fall prey to that temptation, our Englishman would have the starring role in a very public cosmic joke: he would become the preacher and moralizer preaching **against preachers and moralizers,** probably never seeing the absurdity of his position.

Such a blunder may very well have befallen him in the karmic past − or, if you prefer, in the genetic past transmitted to him through his parents. His south node of the moon lies in ferocious Aries and in the risky twelfth house.

Karma or genetics? As we saw when we introduced the moon's nodes in chapter 9, it does not make much difference which model we use. They are interchangeable. I am going to use the reincarnational model here. Please make the appropriate translations if you prefer thinking in terms of chromosomes.

The south node in Aries and in the twelfth house. What does it mean?

In the karmic past, he has been learning lessons associated with those two symbols. It is a curious blend: courage and willpower through Aries and self-transcendence through the twelfth house. The Ram gets its message across to us by facing us with stress. The mountain is placed before us. We either climb it or spend a lifetime trembling in its shadow.

In the twelfth house, the message is often conveyed to us through defeat. We face the impossible: we must still climb the mountain but now it is sheer icy granite and we have no rope and two broken legs. There is no hope; our only course is to let go of our need to climb. We must transcend ourselves, accepting whatever losses that entails with dignity and grace. We must abandon ourselves to the arms of

God. That, or frantically scheme and bargain until the ax comes crashing down.

We do not know what choice our subject made when faced with those impossibilities. But we do know that he faced them and that the legacy of those experiences forms the foundation of his present-day personality.

In a word, our Englishman's karmic self is that of a warrior who lost the war. And those scars – and the lessons they burned into his soul – motivate him in this lifetime.

All the potential for fiery bombast inherent in his mask and in his fifth-house Pluto are supported by that south node. He might well have been born with a chip on his shoulder. He could die with one too, but that is his own choice.

He may have made a profound spiritual leap in his previous life experiences. It is possible that he has thoroughly grasped the notion that success and failure are just more phantasmagoria' here today and gone tomorrow. Certainly, he has learned to mistrust the glory and glamour the world offers.

His patterns in the past have been solitary and independent – that too is characteristic of both Aries and the twelfth house. Loyalty and devotion he knows, but intimacy is completely foreign to his karmic inclinations.

And yet he is a Libra!

This is a most demanding nodal structure: the very basis of sanity and personhood for him in this lifetime – that Libran sun – has no foundation and no precedent in anything he has done before. Simply holding together a rudimentary personality requires that he put down solid roots in thin air.

Even without reference to the moon's nodes, we see a tendency for his sun to get lost behind the noisy veil of his Aries ascendant. All along, that has been a key theme in his birthchart. Now we see just how deep the problem runs, and get a clearer picture of its source. He was born without any sense whatsoever of how to "be a Libra." He has to learn it all.

And, unsurprisingly, his north node – the symbol of the cutting edge of his growth – lies in Libra just 6 degrees from the sun.

A Libran sixth house north node: our reading of it introduces nothing new, only a new perspective on material we have thoroughly absorbed. What we spoke of in terms of psychology, we must now understand in far broader terms. **His soul came into the world to learn the lessons of Libra and of the sixth house.** The fact that his everyday personality needs the same input in order to maintain its stability is dwarfed into insignificance by this far larger question.

But, in practice, that does not really make any difference. Whether we are talking about immortal spirit or day-to-day life, the issues remain identical. Soul and personality get up out of the same bed in the morning, eat the same breakfast, trip over the same misplaced pair of shoes. Their experiences are the same. It is only the meaning of those experiences that changes.

Either way, our Englishman's happiness depends on him creating a loving human partnership, and through that partnership, offering his society something of enduring beauty. Should he fail there, his mind grows numb. He retreats behind an intimidating facade of vain pretense. And his soul, kept in his heart like a dark secret, shrinks in dismay from the emptiness of his days and nights in the world.

Who is our Englishman? His name was John Lennon.

Dreaming the Universe

I love maps. Even when I was a little boy I would spend hours staring at them, navigating imaginary galleons through Polynesian archipelagos, plotting the conquest of Ceylon and Burma.

Age hasn't changed me much, just stripped me of some of my grandiosity. I still love maps. I still plan the routes of journeys I am not likely to take. But now I actually do disappear from time to time, heading out for the woods or sailing into the bays and salt marshes of the North Carolina coast near where I live.

Not long ago, the fever struck again: I purchased a map showing most of the local hiking and canoeing routes. Spreading it out on my kitchen table, I was soon hypnotized. Those trails and rivers fell before me like a conquistador – until I saw something that knocked the wind out of my sails. Woven into the compass rose, the cartographer had written the words, **The Map Is Not the Territory.** And my bubble burst. I could bravely study every square inch of that map in an hour, but to run its waterways and walk its paths I would have to face calluses and cowardice enough to last a lifetime.

Astrology is like that. It is a map. It describes the terrain of the human mind. But the map is not the territory. To really experience what the astrological mind map represents, we need to lace up our boots and start exploring. We must put the birthchart away and confront the mind itself. There is no other way. Staring at the chart gets us nowhere. We must swallow our fear, put the map in our pocket, and walk into the woods, ready to face rainbows and rattlesnakes for which no mapmaker can prepare us.

Like any expedition, the astrological journey requires forethought. Long before we enter the territory, we must learn all we can about maps in general. The symbols must be familiar to us. Only then are we ready to enter the wilderness on our own.

That is what this book is all about. It is a primer in the art of astrological map reading. Through absorbing the vocabulary of signs, houses, and planets, through learning to decipher the counterpoised paragraphs of a birthchart, through finally seeing it all come together in the life of John Lennon, we have learned a new language.

And what is language but a map? Just one more set of symbols pasted over the unknowable.

The next step is yours. There are other books, other approaches. I plan another book soon myself, this time about the predictive techniques – how to talk about the next two years instead of the whole life. But don't be fooled. You can read until the sun cools down and still not learn how to do astrology. To really fathom it, you must open your heart to the birthchart and then open your mouth and talk about what you see. Commitment. Risk. The leap of faith. That is the only way. It's scary.

The first time you sit down with a friend's birthchart you are likely to experience a major power failure in your cerebral cortex. It happens to almost everyone, even if he or she has been thoroughly dedicated to studying the symbolism. Suddenly, there it is: a mass of Babylonian hieroglyphics, a date, the name of a city – and, across the table, the patient, trusting, expectant eyes of a friend. It is the stuff of nightmares.

Don't despair. If you fold up now, muttering an apology about needing to go back and read the book again, you may never break through the wall. You may spend the rest of your life studying the map and never once venture into the territory.

Take your time. Keep one hand on the faucet. Follow the procedures we have outlined. They will not fail you. How long did it take you to get to know that friend? A week? A year?

And how long have you been sitting with his birthchart? Only a few moments. Give it some time. That birthchart is almost as complicated as the friend, just a little less sophisticated in its defenses. Don't be petrified if you haven't achieved electrifying insights in the first five minutes. Understanding a chart, just like understanding a friend, takes a while. You need an unhurried, organized approach. Give the birthchart a chance to speak to you.

Above all, trust the symbols. They do not lie. You may misread them, but if your information about the person's birth is accurate, you can count on the truth of the message the birthchart conveys. The weakest link in the interpretive chain is always your own understanding, not the accuracy of the astrological symbolism.

Even when the chart babbles like a schizophrenic insurance lawyer, trust it. Even when your friend seems to be doing impressions of Mount Rushmore, keep going. Say what you see. Once again, trust the symbols. They will not mislead you.

Is astrology perfect? Emphatically, no. There is much that remains to be discovered. After many centuries of dormancy, the old art-science is reawakening, kindled by breakthroughs in astronomy and psychology. A renaissance in astrological thinking is only now beginning to unfold. By the end of the century, astrologers will be taken as seriously as ministers were a century ago.

But we do not need to wait for astrology to become "respectable." We can use it now. Even with its imperfections, the system works.

Astrology might be perfected someday – but only when our understanding of the human mind is also perfected. And that is up there with "enlightenment" and "finally getting all the housework done," in the world of distant possibilities. We can hope and pray, but we had better not hold our breath.

Use it today. It is helpful today. Tomorrow it will be more

helpful.

In any astrological interpretation, you can expect lapses and uncertainties. Some of them arise from weaknesses in the system itself, but the majority have a more mundane source: your own prejudices, projections, and pet peeves. The more we put our faith in the symbolism – imperfect though it is – the more we minimize the even greater distortions introduced by our own personalities.

And of course we can work directly on rectifying those personal distortions. We can undertake the most awesome astrological task of all: attempting to decipher our own birthchart.

One's own chart: for nearly everyone, that is the starting line. The book in one hand, his birthchart in the other – if ever I design a statue of a beginning astrologer, that will be the motif.

Not that studying one's own birthchart is wrong. Not at all.

Your own birthchart is your laboratory. Even apart from its capacity to assist you in the tricky process of getting your head on straight, it can teach you the meanings of the signs, planets, and houses faster than any course of reading.

The problem is that your own chart is forever the most difficult one to grasp. Not only must you face the intricacies of astrological symbolism, you must also turn your heart and mind loose on a set of defenses they designed for their own protection. And that is a lot like asking the rat to guard the cheese.

Start with your own birthchart. Start with a friend's. Start with Marie Antoinette's. It does not matter. Each path has its difficulties and its advantages. Whatever route you choose, you will return to your own chart again and again, each time seeing it a bit more objectively, with a little more humility and hopefully with a little more honest pride in the steps you have managed to take.

Whatever you do, remember this: the birthchart is the map. Your head is the territory. Sooner or later, you need to stop plotting aspects and start working on that crippling shyness or that Napoleonic complex. Astrology may show you the quickest route through the woods, but to actually get through it, you have to start putting one foot in front of the other.

That is true for anyone who comes to you for an interpretation. And it is true for you too.

The birthchart is a map: so far we have been using the statement metaphorically. But as we learned earlier, the idea is literal truth as well. Birthcharts really are maps. They are like photographs of the sky. Simple, accurate, and straightforward, they tell us where the planets were when we were born, nothing more, nothing less.

And yet these humble sky maps hold the keys to our happiness, the blueprints of our lives, and embarrassing readouts on our darkest secrets. All from a map of the heavens!

As you sharpen your fluency in this ancient earth language, don't forget to go out and stare at those heavens from time to time. Don't forget that birthcharts are sky maps. That iridescent blue dome is the mother of the whole system. The moon you see setting over the lake is the same one that gives you joy and sorrow. The pale yellow star in the east is the same Saturn that pushes you toward the limits of growth.

What you see in the sky, you feel in your mind. Two languages, one reality. We can neglect all conscious reference to the sky and still do effective astrological interpretations. But so much is lost. From that indoor perspective, astrology is just a curious offshoot of psychology, just one more dried-out theory to be memorized.

Given an awareness of astrology's celestial connections, the birthchart can carry us so much deeper.

We all want magic. We all want a sense of mystery and power, of cosmic order in our lives. We want to feel our primeval heritage as children of earth and sky. Astrology can give us that, and give it without demanding that we surrender our reason in return. All we have to do is look.

Pick a clear summer night, black as pitch. Stars gleam down like burning diamonds. Some seem near. Some seem far away. Relax. Open your senses. Where are you?

You are floating in a three-dimensional void, a space of stark shadows and blinding lights we are taught to call the universe.

Lock yourself in a closet. Close your eyes so tight the muscles ache. Breathe in. Breathe out. Watch what happens. Where are you now?

You are floating in a three-dimensional void, a space of stark shadows and blinding lights we are taught to call the mind.

Once again: two languages, one reality. The universe beyond us. The universe inside us. The two are the same, structured according to the same laws, and even feeling much the same to our senses. That primal perception is the foundation of astrology, and the source of its endless fascination.

Mind stuff. Sky stuff. The universe we observe and measure. The universe we dream. It is all the same. Wherever we look, we see mind. Whatever we imagine, we see cosmos.

And who are we? Who is doing the observing? That is the deepest riddle of them all, and answering it is the endless, impossible task that makes us human.

Astrology cannot solve that riddle for us. But perhaps it can carry us a little closer, make us a little wiser. In astrology, we are the border dwellers. We are the ones who live on the shoreline, where waves of consciousness break on the rocks and dunes of the physical world. We exist in both. And both are reflected in us.

In astrology, we are the dreamers, and what we are dreaming is the universe.

APPENDIX A

The Englishman's Birth Chart

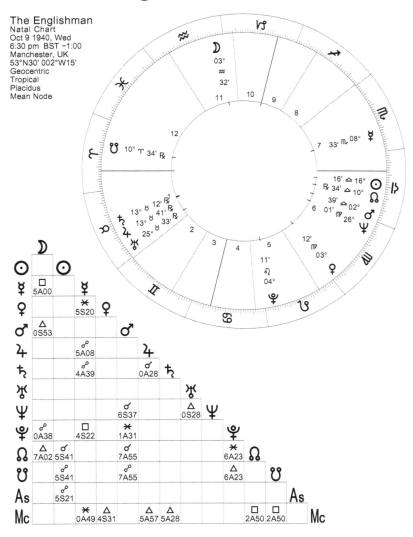

The Englishman
Natal Chart
Oct 9 1940, Wed
6:30 pm BST −1:00
Manchester, UK
53°N30' 002°W15'
Geocentric
Tropical
Placidus
Mean Node

APPENDIX B

Astrological Software

Following is a list of companies that sell astrological software. Check with each company directly for detailed information.

AIR Software
Star Trax Millenium
www.alpee.com

Astrograph
Time Passages
www.astrograph.com

Astrolabe
Solar Fire
www.alabe.com

Cosmic Patterns
Kepler & Sirius
www.patterns.com

Matrix Software
Win*Star
www.astrologysoftware.com

Until you have your own software, you can run free charts online through Astro Dienst at www.astro.com.

APPENDIX C
Sample Birthcharts

One of the best ways to sharpen your interpretive skills is to study the birthcharts of well-known people. Generally, the reason they have become well-known is that they have made a decisive response to the questions their charts ask. As a result, the patterns of their lives illuminate the significance of their astrological configurations far more vividly than that of someone who has spent a half-century in front of the television set.

You will find references to collections of birthcharts on the reading list. You can also find a searchable database of many charts online at http://www.astro.com/astro-databank/Main_Page. I highly recommend these charts as study aids and also as remarkably stimulating passports into long-lost minds and times. Imagine spending an evening with Caligula or Beethoven. With their birthcharts and some knowledge of astrology, this is as close as you are likely to come.

Note: The eight birthcharts included here are set up according to the Placidus System of house division.

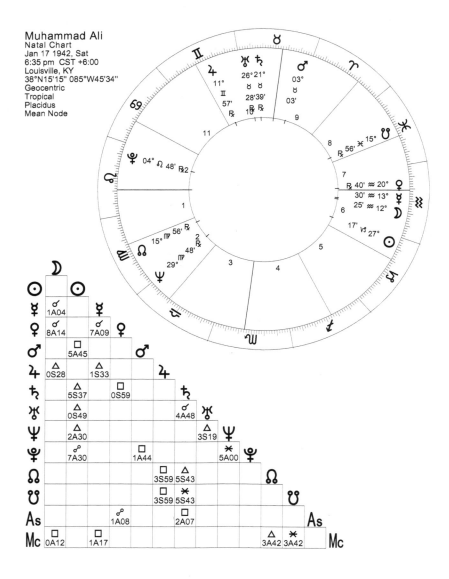

Muhammad Ali
Natal Chart
Jan 17 1942, Sat
6:35 pm CST +6:00
Louisville, KY
38°N15'15" 085°W45'34"
Geocentric
Tropical
Placidus
Mean Node

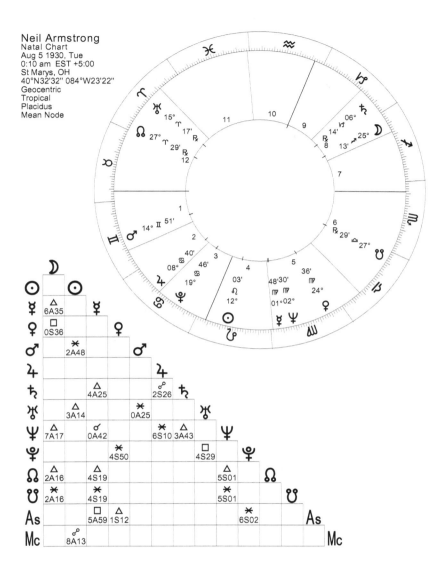

Neil Armstrong
Natal Chart
Aug 5 1930, Tue
0:10 am EST +5:00
St Marys, OH
40°N32'32" 084°W23'22"
Geocentric
Tropical
Placidus
Mean Node

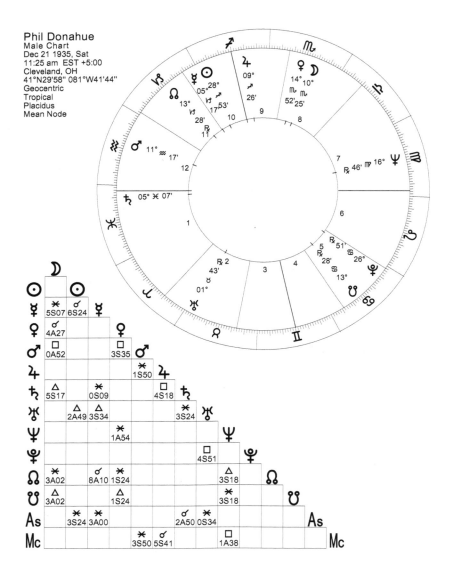

Phil Donahue
Male Chart
Dec 21 1935, Sat
11:25 am EST +5:00
Cleveland, OH
41°N29'58" 081°W41'44"
Geocentric
Tropical
Placidus
Mean Node

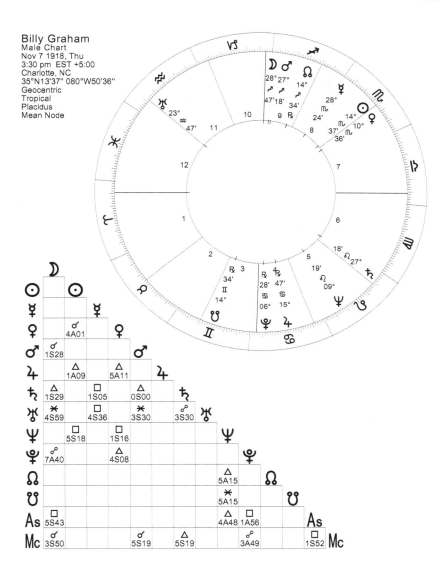

Billy Graham
Male Chart
Nov 7 1918, Thu
3:30 pm EST +5:00
Charlotte, NC
35°N13'37" 080°W50'36"
Geocentric
Tropical
Placidus
Mean Node

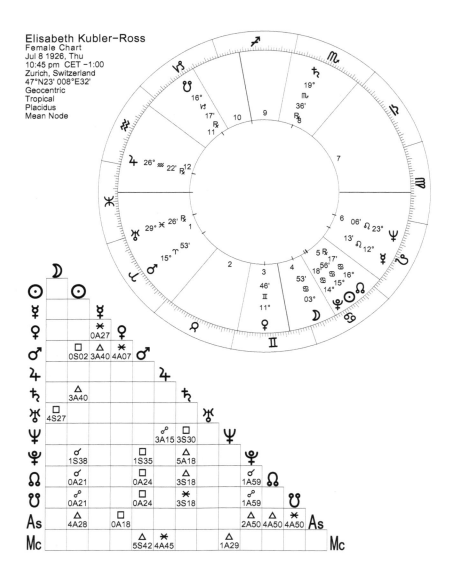

Elisabeth Kubler–Ross
Female Chart
Jul 8 1926, Thu
10:45 pm CET –1:00
Zurich, Switzerland
47°N23' 008°E32'
Geocentric
Tropical
Placidus
Mean Node

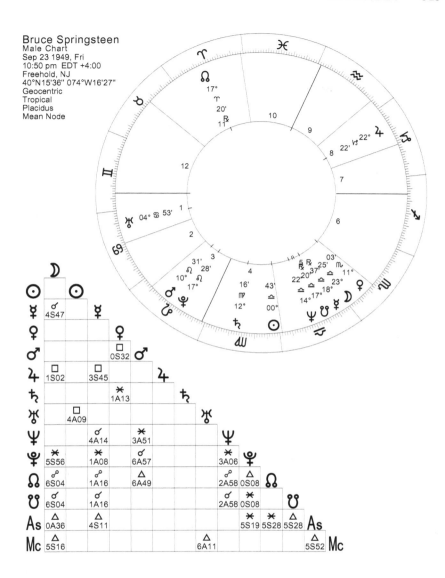

Bruce Springsteen
Male Chart
Sep 23 1949, Fri
10:50 pm EDT +4:00
Freehold, NJ
40°N15'36" 074°W16'27"
Geocentric
Tropical
Placidus
Mean Node

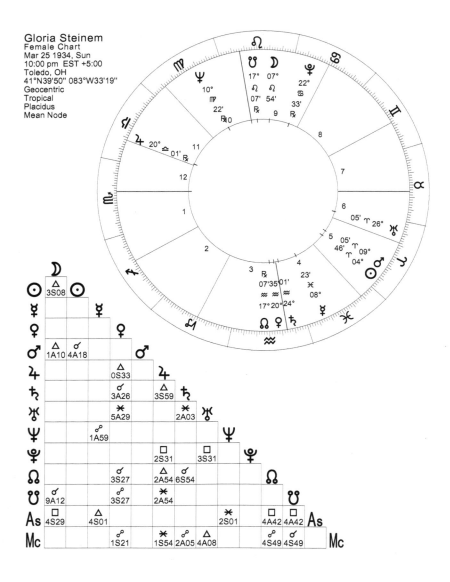

Gloria Steinem
Female Chart
Mar 25 1934, Sun
10:00 pm EST +5:00
Toledo, OH
41°N39'50" 083°W33'19"
Geocentric
Tropical
Placidus
Mean Node

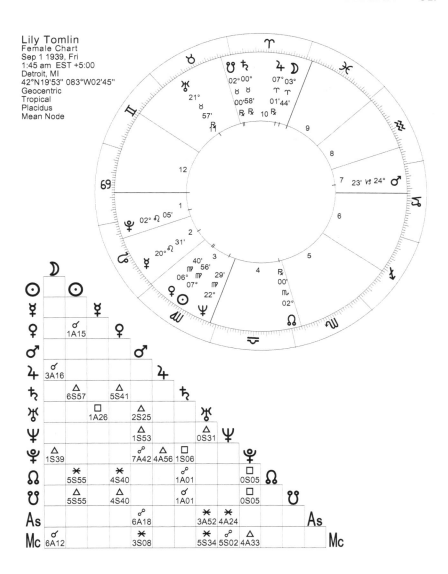

Lily Tomlin
Female Chart
Sep 1 1939, Fri
1:45 am EST +5:00
Detroit, MI
42°N19'53" 083°W02'45"
Geocentric
Tropical
Placidus
Mean Node

APPENDIX D

Suggestions for Further Reading

Tools of the Trade

The American Ephemeris for the 20th Century, 1900 to 2000. (Available in both noon and midnight editions.) ACS Publications, 1980.

The American Ephemeris for the 21st Century, 2000 to 2050. (Available in both noon and midnight editions.) ACS Publications, 1996.

Dalton, Joseph G. *The Spherical Basis of Astrology*. Macoy, 1893.

The Michelsen Book of Tables. (Placidus and Koch cusps.) ACS Publications, 1997.

The American Atlas: U.S. Latitudes and Longitudes, Time Changes, and Time Zones. ACS Publications, 1978.

The International Atlas: Latitudes, Longitudes and Time Changes. ACS Publications, 1985.

Foundational Books

Arroyo, Stephen. *Astrology, Psychology, and the Four Elements*. CRCS Publications, 1975.
Carter, Charles E. O. *The Astrological Aspects*. Fowler, 1930.
_____. *The Principals of Astrology*. Theosophical, 1925.
Freeman, Martin. *How to Interpret a Birthchart*. Aquarian, 1981.
Goodavage, Joseph F. *Write Your Own Horoscope*. World, 1968.

Greene, Liz. *Saturn: A New Look at an Old Devil.* Weiser, 1976.

Jones, Marc Edmund. *How to Learn Astrology.* Doubleday, 1969.

Leo, Alan. *The Art of Synthesis.* Fowler, 1968 (reissue).

Mayer, Michael. *Handbook for the Humanistic Astrologer.* Anchor/Doubleday, 1974.

Penfield, Marc. *An Astrological Who's Who.* Arcane, 1972.

Rodden, Lois M. *Astro Data I: Profiles of Women.* Data News Press, 1996.

_____. *Astro Data II.* Data News Press, 1997. (Formerly *The American Book of Charts.*)

Rudhyar, Dane. *The Astrological Houses.* Doubleday, 1972.

_____. *Astrological Insights into the Spiritual Life.* ASI, 1979.

_____. *The Astrology of Personality.* Doubleday, 1936.

_____. *An Astrological Study of Psychological Complexes and Emotional Problems.* Servire/Wassenaar, 1966.

_____. *An Astrological Triptych.* ASI, 1968.

_____. *The Planetary and Lunar Nodes.* CSA Press, 1971.

_____. *The Practice of Astrology.* Penguin, 1968.

Schulman, Martin. *The Moon's Nodes and Reincarnation.* Weiser, 1975.

Toonder, Jan Gerhard, and John Anthony West. *The Case for Astrology.* Penguin, 1970.

Tyl, Noel. *Special Horoscope Dimensions: Success, Sex, and Illness.* Llewellyn, 1975.

Advanced Books

Addey, John. *Harmonics in Astrology.*

Arroyo, Stephen. *Astrology, Karma, and Transformation.* CRCS Publications, 1978.

_____. *Relationships and Life Cycles.* CRCS, 1979.

Davison, Ronald C. *Synastry.* Aurora Press, 1983. ("Synastry" is the study of relationships from an astrological perspective.)

_____. *The Technique of Prediction.* Fowler, 1971.

Forrest, Stephen and Jodie. *Skymates.* Seven Paws Press, 1992.

Forrest, Stephen. *The Changing Sky*. Seven Paws Press, 1989.

Garrison, Omar V. *Medical Astrology*. University Books, 1971.

Gauquelin, Michel. *Scientific Basis of Astrology*.

Rudhyar, Dane. *An Astrological Mandala*. Random House, 1973.

_____. *The Lunation Cycle*. Shambala, 1971.

Tyl, Noel. *Analysis and Prediction*. Llewellyn, 1974.

_____. *The Expanded Present*. Llewellyn, 1974.

_____. *Integrated Transits*. Llewellyn, 1974.

Books for Perspective

Brown, Norman O. *Love's Body*. Random House, 1966.

Castaneda, Carlos. *Tales of Power*. Pocket Books, 1974.

Collin, Rodney. *The Theory of Celestial Influence*. Weiser, 1984.

Dass, Ram. *The Only Dance There Is*. Doubleday, 1974.

_____. *Grist for the Mill*. Bantam, 1977.

Golas, Thaddeus. *The Lazy Man's Guide to Enlightenment*. Bantam, 1971.

Jung, Carl G. *Man and His Symbols*. Dell, 1964.

de Laszlo, Violet S. *Psyche & Symbol in the Psychology of C. G. Jung*. Doubleday, 1958.

Sugrue, Thomas. *There is a River: The Story of Edgar Cayce*. Holt, Rinehart and Winston, 1942.

Watson, Lyall. *Super Nature: A Natural History of the Supernatural*. Doubleday, 1973.

APPENDIX E

Glossary

Air One of the four elements; air symbolizes alertness, clarity of perception, and intelligence.

Angle Cusp of the first, fourth, seventh, or tenth houses; either end of the horizon or meridian.

Archetype A fundamental image held collectively and universally in human consciousness; the mythic raw material out of which individual identity is synthesized.

Ascendant The eastern horizon or the sign rising there; the first house as a whole.

Aspect One of several critical geometrical angles formed between planets or between planets and angles.

Aspect Grid Schematic graph representing all the aspects of a particular birthchart.

Astrology The art-science of clarifying the fundamental themes of a person's life through reference to a map of the sky drawn for the moment of his or her birth.

Benefic Traditionally, one of the "good" planets: Venus (the "lesser benefic") and Jupiter (the "greater benefic").

Birthchart A map of the heavens as seen at the date and time of a person's birth, from the viewpoint of his or her birth place.

Bit   Any combination of a planet, sign, and house.

Cardinal   One of the three modes of signs. Active, initiatory, and determinative. the cardinal signs are Aries. Cancer, Libra, and Capricorn.

Conjunction   An aspect characterized by a 0° separation between two planets. symbolizing the process of fusion.

Constellation   A group of stars. often bearing the name of a sign, but not to be confused with a sign.

Cusp   The beginning of a house. Actually, a somewhat fuzzy zone extending about a degree and a half on either side of the precise beginning of a house.

Descendant   The western horizon, or the sign on it; the seventh house as a whole.

Debility   Any of several distinct astrological configurations that decrease the emphasis placed on a particular planet. See *Dignity; Fall.*

Dignity   Any of several distinct astrological configurations that give increased emphasis to a particular planet. See *Focalizer; Rulership; Singleton; Debility.*

Direct   Normal motion of a planet forward through the signs. See *Retrograde; Stationary.*

Earth   One of the four elements; earth symbolizes patience, practicality, realism, and stability.

Ecliptic   The apparent path of the sun, moon, and planets against the stars and around the earth; the zodiac.

Equinox   One of two days of the year when night and day are of equal length; the first day of spring (vernal equinox) or the first day of autumn (autumnal equinox).

Element   Fire, earth, air, or water. One of four fundamental psychic processes or orientations of consciousness.

Ephemeris   A book listing the positions of all planets each day at a certain time over a long period.

Fall   A planetary debility characterized by the presence of a planet in the sign opposite the one it rules. See *Rulership*.

Fire   One of the four elements; fire symbolizes the formation of will, of initiative, of dominion.

Fixed   One of the three modes of signs. Stability, strength of purpose, clear identity, stubbornness. The fixed signs are Taurus, Leo, Scorpio, and Aquarius.

Focalizer   In a birthchart, a strongly emphasized or strategically located planet. See *Dignity*.

Glyph   Any one of the written symbols in astrology, used as a kind of shorthand.

Hemisphere   There are four "hemispheres" in any birthchart: the space above the horizon, the space below it, the space east of the meridian, and the space west of it.

Horizon   The horizontal axis of a birthchart connecting the ascendant and the descendant.

House   Any of the twelve divisions of space above or below the local horizon, the basic "arenas" or "terrains" of life that mind enters and experiences.

Karma   Hindu word meaning habits, good and bad, retained in the personality from previous lifetimes. See *Nodes of the Moon*.

Malefic   Traditionally, one of the "bad" planets: Mars (the "lesser malefic") or Saturn (the "greater malefic").

Meridian   The vertical axis of the birthchart; the line connecting the midheaven and the nadir.

Midheaven   The highest zodiacal point above the horizon; the approximate position of the sun at noon; the cusp of the tenth house or the tenth house as a whole.

Minor Aspects   Aspects other than the conjunction, senile, square, trine. and opposition.

Minute of Arc   One sixtieth of a degree. often simply called a "minute."

Mode   One of the three expressions of sign energy: cardinal, fixed, and mutable.

Mutable   One of the three modes of signs. Changeable, responsive, flowing, the mutable signs are Gemini, Virgo, Sagittarius, and Pisces.

Nadir   The zodiacal point farthest below the local horizon; the approximate position of the sun at midnight, the cusp of the fourth house or the fourth house as a whole.

Nodes of the Moon   Opposed points symbolizing the individual's evolutionary past and future. The south node represents either the influence of heredity or of karma, while the north node shows new material to be absorbed.

Opposition An aspect characterized by a 180° separation between two planets, symbolizing the process of polarization or tension.

Orb The limits of tolerance within which an aspect is considered functional. Variable and subjective, but usually taken to be about seven degrees.

Planet Any celestial body that moves through the zodiac in a predictable way. Astrologically, the term includes the sun and moon.

Prime Symbol The sphere of space that surrounds us. A symbol of perfection, wholeness, and eternity. A symbol of consciousness itself, or of God.

Primal Triad The sun, moon, and ascendant taken together as the "skeleton" of the individuality.

Retrograde Planetary condition characterized by an apparent "backward" motion through the sky. See *Direct*.

Rulership A particularly strong affinity between a planet and a sign. allowing a clear expression of both.

Sextile An aspect characterized by a 60° separation between two planets symbolizing the process of excitation.

Sidereal Time An astronomically precise time used in setting up birthcharts.

Sign One of the twelve basic divisions of the zodiac. a phase in the orbital relationship of the earth and the sun; a fundamental psychological process.

Singleton Any planet placed alone in a hemisphere.

Solstice The day of the year when the night is longest (the winter solstice) or shortest (the summer solstice).

Square An aspect characterized by a separation of 90° between two planets symbolizing the process of friction.
Station A planet is said to be "making a station" when it is stationary.

Stationary A planet is stationary when it appears to be standing motionless relative to the zodiac, about to turn retrograde or direct.

Stationary Direct Stationary and about to turn direct.

Stationary Retrograde Stationary and about to turn retrograde.

Stellium Any clustering of three or more planets in a single sign or house.

Table of Houses A book based on complex calculations in spherical trigonometry that shows the location of house cusps at various sidereal times and latitudes.

Trine An aspect characterized by a separation between two planets of 120", symbolizing the process of harmonization.

Water One of the four elements; water symbolizes subjectivity, emotion, depth, and the ability to love.

Zodiac The apparent path of the sun, moon, and planets around the earth; the twelve signs.

Index

About the Author

Steven Forrest is the author of several astrological bestsellers, including *THE INNER SKY, THE CHANGING SKY, THE BOOK OF PLUTO, THE NIGHT SPEAKS*, and the new classic *YESTERDAY'S SKY*, written with support from a grant by the Integrative Medicine Foundation.

Steven's work has been translated into a dozen languages, most recently Chinese and Italian. He travels worldwide to speak and teach his brand of choice-centered "evolutionary" astrology – an astrology which integrates free will, grounded humanistic psychology and ancient metaphysics.

Along with his busy private practice, he maintains active astrological apprenticeship programs in California, Australia, North Carolina, and Switzerland. He is a founding member of the Ethics Committee of the International Society for Astrological Research (ISAR).

The musician Sting calls Steven's work "as intelligent and cogent as it is poetic." DELL HOROSCOPE describes him as "not only a premier astrologer, but also a wise man." Callie Khouri, who wrote the screenplay for the mega-hit film *Thelma and Louise*, praises his "humor, insight, poetry, and astute, articulate observations of human nature." O: THE OPRAH MAGAZINE describes his philosophy this way: "Forrest's approach...stops the blame game in its tracks... we're warriors fulfilling our turbulent evolutionary paths." Actor Robert Downey Jr. says, "I marvel at the accuracy of Steve's readings. He insists that nothing is so grave as to be beyond repair, and correspondingly that there is no rainbow that won't be evaporated by poor judgment in the now. I can't recommend him highly enough." And Rob Brezsny, in his popular "Real Astrology" column, simply calls him "the most brilliant astrologer alive."

After forty years in Chapel Hill, North Carolina, Steve now lives in Borrego Springs, California.

See his website www.forrestastrology.com for more details.

Learn Astrology with Steven Forrest

Interested in learning more about Steven's unique approach to astrology? **For a listing of lectures and workshops that are available in a variety of audio and video formats,** go to: http://www.forrestastrology.com/MP3-Audio-Downloads.

Better yet, join the many successful students who have completed Steven's *Astrological Apprenticeship Program,* where he teaches both the specific techniques of interpretation and the style of presentation that have made him one of the most successful and influential astrologers in the world. Steven takes great joy in passing on the teachings and strategies that have worked for him over the years through his Apprenticeship Program (or "AP").

The AP presents students with a rare opportunity to learn astrology in a supportive environment of like-minded individuals, who together create a feeling of community and connection, leading to bonds that last throughout life. Some come to the program to train professionally, while others come for personal or spiritual enrichment.

Apprenticeship Groups are currently meeting in North Carolina, Southern California (near San Diego,) Northern California (north of San Francisco), Australia, and Europe.

Once enrolled in the program, students gain access to 10 years of Steven's private teachings, recorded in audio format, and in pdf transcripts.

Learn more at www.forrestastrology.com

87067020R00197

Made in the USA
Middletown, DE
01 September 2018